COMPUTERS AND MODERN LANGUAGE STUDIES

ELLIS HORWOOD SERIES IN COMPUTERS AND THEIR APPLICATIONS
Series Editor: Brian Meek, Computer Centre, King's College, University of London

NEW TECHNOLOGIES IN TRAINING
Series Editor: Nick Rushby, Centre for Staff Development in Higher Education, London.

COMPUTERS
AND MODERN
LANGUAGE STUDIES

Editors:

K.C. CAMERON, BA(Hons)., PGCE., D.Univ., L.ès.L.,
Department of French and Italian,
University of Exeter

W.S. DODD, BA., MA.,
Language Centre,
University of Exeter

S.P.Q. RAHTZ, BA., MA.,
Department of Computer Studies,
University of Southampton

ELLIS HORWOOD LIMITED
Publishers · Chichester

Halsted Press: a division of
JOHN WILEY & SONS
New York · Chichester · Brisbane · Toronto

First published in 1986 by
ELLIS HORWOOD LIMITED
Market Cross House, Cooper Street, Chichester, West Sussex,
PO19 1EB, England

The publisher's colophon is reproduced from James Gillison's drawing of the ancient Market Cross, Chichester.

Distributors:

Australia and New Zealand:
Jacaranda Wiley Ltd.,
GPO Box 859, Brisbane, Queensland 4001, Australia

Canada:
JOHN WILEY & SONS CANADA LIMITED
22 Worcester Road, Rexdale, Ontario, Canada

Europe and Africa:
JOHN WILEY & SONS LIMITED
Baffins Lane, Chichester, West Sussex, England

North and South America and the rest of the world:
Halsted Press: a division of
JOHN WILEY & SONS
605 Third Avenue, New York, NY 10158, USA

© 1986 K.C. Cameron, W.S. Dodd and S.P.Q. Rahtz/Ellis Horwood Limited
British Library Cataloguing in Publication Data

LIBRARY OF CONGRESS Card No. 86-9408
British Library Cataloguing in Publication Data
Computers and modern language studies. – (New
techniques in training)
1. Language and languages – Computer-
assisted instruction I. Cameron, Keith II. Dodd, W.S.
III. Rahtz, S.P.Q. IV. Series
407'.8 P53.28

ISBN 0-7458-0057-2 (Ellis Horwood Limited)
ISBN 0-470-20343-9 (Halsted Press)

Typeset on a Monotype Lasercomp at Oxford University Computing Service
Printed in Great Britain by R.J. Acford, Chichester

Table of Contents

Chapter 1 INTEGRATING THE COMPUTER INTO A LANGUAGE COURSE 15
Mrs G. A. Benwell, Coventry (Lanchester) Polytechnic

Chapter 2 THE USE OF THE MICRO IN AN INTEGRATED GERMAN LANGUAGE COURSE AT UNIVERSITY LEVEL 20
Gordon J. A. Burgess, King's College, University of Aberdeen

Chapter 8 COMPUTER ASSISTED READING—WORK IN PROGRESS AT THE UNIVERSITY OF EAST ANGLIA 70

Jeremy Fox, University of East Anglia

Chapter 9 ANALYSIS OF CONJUGATION MISTAKES IN FRENCH VERBS ON A MICROCOMPUTER 78

Monique L'Huillier, Brunel University

Chapter 10 COMPUTER ASSISTED LEARNING OR COMPUTER INHIBITED ACQUISITON? 85

Brian Farrington, University of Aberdeen

Chapter 11 NEW APPROACHES TO COMPUTER AIDED LANGUAGE LEARNING 93

Jonathan Barchan, University of Exeter

Preface

Keith Cameron, University of Exeter

One of the characteristics of the good teacher is the ability to keep abreast of developments in his own discipline and to adapt developments in other disciplines to his own. The task of the Modern Language specialist is great: to keep her or himself informed not only about linguistic changes and tendencies, but also about the trends in all aspects of the civilization of the country whóse language he teaches. In the 1960s, aware of the need to introduce students to the niceties of the spoken language, Modern Language specialists developed the technology of another discipline and produced the language laboratory. More recently, there has been a considerable advance in the construction of computers and they have become widely available within schools and colleges. They are increasingly attracting the attention of linguists. There has been general agreement about the need to find a means of helping learners to remember and use correctly the basic structures of any language. It has also been realized more and more that today's children need language instruction which is in keeping with their normal interests and their own way of learning.

The first attempts to incorporate the computer into the classroom appeared disappointing — meaningless drills, unsatisfactory games etc. In the last few years, however, encouraged by such pioneers as Brian Farrington of Aberdeen and Rex Last of Dundee, much progress has been made. The articles which follow arise from a Conference on 'The Computer and Post 'A'-Level Modern Language Teaching', held at the University of Exeter in September 1985. It was felt that the time was ripe to try to organize a meeting of those interested in Computer Assisted Language Learning (CALL) so as to appraise what had already been done and to learn of innovations and new methods. One of the unfortunate limitations of the materials prepared for use in the language laboratory was that so many of them were compiled with the beginner or the young learner in mind: the Conference was an attempt to ensure that this mistake was not repeated. The published contributions provide a valuable insight into the use of the computer in Universities and Polytechnics throughout the British Isles. Together, they form a compendium of practical experience and allow the potential user of CALL to benefit from the efforts of others, illustrating as they do, ways of adapting the computer to language teaching, highlighting its present limitations and possibilities. For the person who already uses CALL, it is to be hoped that this book will stimulate new ideas of new and different methods worthy of exploitation. It seems certain that the exponents of CALL are having recourse to machines because they realize their usefulness in a pedagogical situation and not because of a desire to use new technology simply because it exists.

This latter point is one to be emphasized. Devising exercises for use on the computer could be an eccentric indulgence unless the way in which such exercises are going to be incorporated into the teaching syllabus is considered. All places of education have problems of time-tabling, and it is not easy to rearrange the time-table to integrate sessions giving access to the computer, and yet it can be done (see chapters 1 and 2). The CALL materials have to be prepared with care so as to maximize their efficiency as learning tools (Chapter 12) and healthy doubt can often be expressed as to their effectiveness (Chapter 10).

In certain disciplines, there is a need for a review of the materials available (Chapter 6), or for suggestions for more stimulating exercises (Chapters 5 and 9), and there is a case for using CALL for more advanced work (Chapters 3 and 10). CALL is proving useful for the improvement of reading skills (Chapters 4 and 8) and the algorithms of the computer lend themselves admirably to the preparation of programs for instruction in Arabic (Chapter 7).

Exciting developments have been made in using the computer to create simulation situations (Chapter 13) and to make advances in the teaching of interpreting as a skill (Chapter 14). It can also be used for supporting information services (Chapter 15), not to mention a score of administrative chores it can alleviate for the teacher.

The reader will sense the excitement Modern Language teachers have for the use of the computer in their work. To make full use, however, of the potential of the computer, whether it be a microcomputer or a mainframe, it is important that we pool our resources and that we work together on joint research projects, thereby saving wasted effort and also, and certainly not least important, money.

In the short term, this book reveals what use, in spite of the limitations of the hardware available, can be made of the computer *now*. And yet, it may be that the real future lies in Artificial Intelligence (AI). The development of expert systems will take time, and will also need cooperation from various research bodies and researchers (Chapters 11 and 16). As one reads through the chapters in this book, one realizes that much has been achieved and that much more will be achieved by selecting ideas which have been tried out by individuals and by amalgamating them. We should not forget either that the computer can be used for ancillary tasks which will help improve our teaching, and for literary analysis.

Enormous strides have been taken in the design of the hardware. If we language specialists are to take advantage of them, then it is essential that the computer scientist and the linguist work together. The conference in Exeter has shown the problem and has revealed a commendable enthusiasm on the part of the teachers, which suggests that Modern Language teaching is a healthy part of the country's academic community.

Acknowledgements

We wish to thank Mrs Juliet Curry for her help in the initial stages of organizing the Conference, the Computer Unit of the University of Exeter for its cooperation and above all the University of Exeter Pallas Project team (Audrey Croucher, Sebastian Rahtz and Mark Waddicor) for their support and participation during the event. We would also like to thank the ethereal JANET (Joint Academic NETwork) for her help in communication, enabling editing to be carried out simultaneously in Exeter and Southampton.

It may be of interest to describe how this book was put together: speakers at the conference were asked to bring the text of their papers on floppy disks or send them via JANET; the majority of disks materialized during the conference, more arrived within a few days and the University of Exeter Computer Unit Data Preparation staff were able to type in the three scripts that came on paper; one paper was sent via JANET from Leeds. Most of the floppy disks were written on BBC micros with *View* or *Wordwise*, but there was one IBM PC disk written by *Wordstar*. All the scripts were initially collated on an IBM PC AT using Microsoft *Word* and marked up with 'runoff'-type formatting commands; the resulting files were combined, transferred to a Prime 9650 mainframe and converted to Prime *RUNOFF* by a *SPITBOL* program (including some automated consistency checks) for working copy to be printed on a Lasergrafix QMS 1200 laserprinter; camera-ready copy was typeset by Sebastian Rahtz on the Monotype Lasercomp at Oxford University Computing Service (after being passed through an appropriate version of the *SPITBOL* program).

Contributors

Professor D. E. Ager, Department of Modern Languages, Aston University, Aston Triangle, Birmingham B4 7ET

Mr Jonathan Barchan, Computer Science, University of Exeter, Exeter

Mrs G. A. Benwell, Department of Language Studies, Coventry (lanchester) Polytechnic, Priory Street, Coventry CV1 5FB

Dr Gordon J. A. Burgess, Department of German, King's College, University of Aberdeen, Aberdeen AB9 2UB

Dr K. C. Cameron, Department of French & Italian, Queen's Building, The University, Exeter EX4 4LE

Mr P. M. Crompton, Department of Languages, Faculty of Humanities, Manchester Polytechnic, Aytoun Street, Manchester

Mr David Crookall, Faculté de Droit, Université de Toulon et du Var, Ave de l'Université, 83130 La GARDE, France

Mr W. S. Dodd, Language Centre, Queen's Building, University of Exeter, Exeter EX4 4LE

Dr Osman Durrani, Department of German, Durham University, Elvet Riverside, Durham DHI 3JT

Mr Brian Farrington, Language Laboratory, Kings College, University of Aberdeen, Aberdeen, Scotland AB9 1FX

Mr Jeremy Fox, School of Modern Languages and European History, University of East Anglia, Norwich NR4 7TJ

Miss Pamela Gummery, Department of Languages, Faculty of Humanities, Manchester Polytechnic, Aytoun Street, Manchester

Mr Jim Halliday, Department of Languages, Heriot-Watt University, Edinburgh EH1

Major J. Harding, 3 Long Row, Moat Lane, Prestwood, Nr Great Missenden, Bucks.

Mr Anthony Hartley, Modern Languages Centre, Bradford University, Bradford BD7 1DP

Miss Monique L'Huillier, Language Centre, Brunel University, Uxbridge, Middlesex UB8 3PH

Mr Sebastian Rahtz, Department of Computer Studies, University, Highfield, Southampton SO9 5NH

Mr Brian Richardson, Department of Italian, The University, Leeds LS2 9JT

Mr D. R. Stewart, Department of Languages, Liverpool Polytechnic, 79 Tithebarn Street, Liverpool L2 2ER

Colonel O. B. Taylor, "Blagdon", Vauxhall Crescent, Ham Hill, Nr Snodland, Kent ME6 5JT

Mr Masoud Yazdani, Department of Computer Science, University of Exeter, Exeter

Integrating the computer into a language course

Mrs G. A. Benwell, Coventry (Lanchester) Polytechnic

1 INTRODUCTION

The key-word and indeed the theme of this paper is "integration". I want to show how Computer Assisted Language Learning can be integrated into a languages course and why this is desirable. I intend to take a very practical approach and describe the course we have devised at the Coventry (Lanchester) Polytechnic for the first year in German in the B.A. course in Modern Languages. By looking at one particular course and examining the role of the microcomputer within it, I hope you will be stimulated to think about how microcomputers might be used, whether in polytechnics, colleges or universities.

Before describing the course itself, a brief history of our use of microcomputers may be useful. Language teachers have always been ready to use modern technology as teaching aids. We readily use not only books, chalk and talk, but also tape recorders and video. In the Department of Language Studies at the Coventry (Lanchester) Polytechnic there are three Tandberg language laboratories which are intensively used. When microcomputers became widely available in the Polytechnic in 1980, it was a natural step forward to investigate how they could be used in the learning of foreign languages. The first microcomputer purchased was a CBM 4032 (PET). From the moment it arrived at the beginning of 1982 it has been in constant use. Student response was most enthusiastic and very positive from the first, and it was soon evident that microcomputers provide an excellent method of carrying out remedial and reinforcing work in language learning.

We have been concerned for some time that post- "A" level students of German often display serious weaknesses in their grasp of German grammar and are insufficiently accurate in written work. The microcomputer provides a tool to improve standards of accuracy. Language laboratories are excellent for improving oral and aural linguistic skills, and now the microcomputer can be used to improve written linguistic skills.

2   HOW DID OUR THINKING DEVELOP?

One micro was obviously inadequate, so we decided to expand the provision of microcomputers within the department. We now have 24 BBC microcomputers in an ECONET system, in addition to the original PET.

The second development in our thinking was the importance of *integrating* CALL into the teaching/learning programme. It did not seem to exploit the potential of CALL fully, if it remained a solitary, individual pursuit on the periphery of the course. We envisaged a course where some students use the computers, while at the same time staff work face to face with other students. A vital idea emerged — these tools of modern technology should free teachers to enable them to concentrate on intensive oral work with small groups of students. Another important principle also emerged — not only to integrate CALL into the course, but also to make sure that all the material used is also integrated — the lecture, the discussion topics, the written assignments, the language laboratory work and the computer programs are all closely related.

In the first year course the students have five curriculum hours of German a week. (They also have another main language, a subsidiary language and a background course, called Introduction to European Studies). When planning the new integrated approach we decided it did not make sense to have odd hours of German scattered through the week. The logical next step was to arrange the time-table so as to give us maximum flexibility. The five hours are now fixed as follows:

a)   One hour on Monday morning — lecture in German.
b)   Four hours on Wednesday morning of varied activities — a German morning.

In creating the German morning we freed staff and students from the confines of the hour-long class and we adopted the team approach. We realised that such a course would have to be carefully structured and carefully and meticulously prepared, so that the students could work freely and flexibly within a firm framework. What does this firm framework consist of?

1.   The year is divided into units, each of three or four weeks. Each unit covers a section of the syllabus and a work book is provided for each unit. The work books are of vital importance, since they contain lecture outlines, texts, information about practical work to be done

in the language laboratories and at the computers, and written assignments.

2.   The second element in the framework is the organisation of rooms for the German morning. All the activities take place on one floor — in a large classroom, in two language laboratories (both of which contain a row of microcomputers along one wall) and in two other smaller rooms equipped with microcomputers. The doors are left open and the students are able to move easily from one activity to another.

3.   The third element in the framework is a very carefully worked out rota system for staff and students, so that every student has specific slots allocated during the morning for oral work and work at the computers.

3   FEATURES OF THE GERMAN MORNING

At 9.00 am. all the students (about 40) meet in the large classroom with two teachers and the German language assistant. For half an hour we all stay together, while written work is returned and commented on. Advice and guidance is given for new written assignments and clear instructions are given for the morning's activities. At 9.30 we divide up. Two teachers remain in the classroom, each one working orally with a group of four or five students. We have noticed that even the shyest students have become more confident and fluent orally. Students have to communicate when they are in such small groups. No-one fades into the background, since there is no background to fade into! At the same time, in the same classroom, other students are doing written work, often working together in groups, using dictionaries provided by the department. The working atmosphere is excellent — a quiet hum of purposeful activity.

After about half an hour there is a changeover and other students come to the teachers for oral work.

While this is going on, the other half of the year group is doing practical work in the laboratories and with the computers. This work is supervised by one member of staff with a technician on hand.

At 10.30 we have a civilized half-hour's coffee break, then from 11.00 to 12.00 there is the same pattern of activities going on, but with different students having their oral work and computer work.

At 12.00 the oral groups finish and all the students are free to work as they please, until 1.00 — either at written work, in the laboratories or at the computers. Two members of staff supervise and this is an excellent opportunity to discuss specific problems with individual students. Sometimes this hour is used for precis writing or for group essay writing.

This close contact between staff and students is made possible because of microcomputers. Microcomputers can work away with infinite patience, helping students to achieve higher standards of written accuracy, to get genders, cases, endings right, and to extend their vocabulary. Teachers then have more time to do intensive oral work with students and to help individuals. This, I think, is a crucial point. Far from being alienating, these machines are actually the means of bringing staff and students closer together.

We have been working in this way for two years now and are convinced that this is the right approach. Attendance is very good. Students work maturely and independently and have commented on the excellent working atmosphere. They are also motivated to work on their own and come back to the laboratories and computers at other times in the week.

The course has been evaluated twice by the Principal Lecturer in Learning Systems Development at the Polytechnic, who has written most favourable reports. In the conclusion of his first report, he remarked:

> "It is quite apparent that the course is highly successful, in terms of the attitudes and opinions which students hold about it. In my experience of similar evaluation exercises during the past 5 years, such a generally positive feeling about a course is unique."

and this year he wrote:

> "The revised course continues to be successful in the eyes of the students, and the overwhelmingly positive response from last year has been generally maintained, and in some cases exceeded. Students are particularly appreciative of the 'Arbeitsheft', the relaxed atmosphere in which they and the staff work together, and the flexibility of the course organisation which allows them to choose what they can do and when."

In conclusion, something should be said about the computer software we use. We do use some dedicated software in the form of a package of German grammar programs, but the main type of software is the authoring package. This provides a framework into which we can put our texts, and authoring packages are ideal for our needs.

The packages used most at first were written by Graham Davies of Ealing College of Higher Education. We have now developed our own authoring packages. R. M. Benwell, of the Department of Applied Physical Sciences, Coventry (Lanchester) Polytechnic, has developed a multi-lingual authoring program, UNITEXT, which is ECONET-compatible, has some word-processing features for editing purposes, and can be printed out. UNITEXT is used by the teacher to prepare text in English, German, French, Italian and Spanish, for use with different kinds of student testing programs. A separate version, RUSTEXT, is available for Russian and English. Three types of student testing program have been developed:

1. UNIFILL/RUSFILL: A text in German (or English, French, Italian, Spanish or Russian) has to be reconstructed on the screen. This could be too much of a memory test, so students are provided with an English translation (included in the work book). The students then reconstruct the German with the help of the English version. Students accept the constraints and find "guided translation" a very useful activity.
2. UNIGAP/RUSGAP can be used for all kinds of gap-filling exercises. It is particularly useful for testing adjectival endings and prepositions in a German text. The gaps to be filled can be parts of words, words, phrases, or even sentences.
3. UNISUB/RUSSUB: In this program students are asked to substitute words or phrases. This is a particularly flexible program and can be used, for example, for changing tenses or for inserting words or phrases into the text. It can be emphazised that the textual material used in the computer programs is all relevant to the subject being studied in a particular unit.

Looking to the future, we can see that our flexible, integrated approach can easily accommodate new developments — AECALL, interactive video and computerized translation. The Department of Language Studies already has an ALPS system (Automated Language Processing Systems) and we shall be using it with students this year.

2

The use of the micro in an integrated German language course at university level

Gordon J. A. Burgess, King's College, University of Aberdeen

1 THE PLACE OF CALL IN THE OVERALL LANGUAGE COURSE STRUCTURE

Late in June 1984 a departmental decision was taken to develop a new language course for our first and second year students of German, making use of shared technological facilities that had recently become available in the university, on the arts campus, in the shape of a 16-terminal BBC ECONET Level 2 classroom. The aim was that this should be a fully integrated course, in which traditional and less traditional components would complement and reinforce each other. As things turned out, pressure of other innovatory language work on the German 1 (first-year) tutors resulted in their using the micro classroom initially only to a limited extent, so the following remarks are based on the year's experience with German 2 (second-year) students.

The 'traditional' programme of German 2 language instruction looked like this:

1. Weekly translation class, with written work regularly handed in ('the weekly prose')
2. Language study class, alternating fortnightly with —
3. Conversation class

The translation class thus took 50% of the formal instruction time, the language study and conversation classes each accounting for 25%. In addition, over the academic year, students were required to

4. pursue 25 sessions of private study in the language laboratory (unsupervised)
5. hand in four pieces of non-translation written language work (précis, short essays in German, etc.).

At the time, in June 1984, we had no CALL programs, no CALL textual or drill material, no departmental computing equipment, and no idea of how to work the ECONET system; and we were faced with the prospect of a course starting in roughly three months' time.

Our approach therefore had to be pragmatic in the extreme: on the one hand, what could we use that was already available, and on the other hand, what was the computer, specifically the microcomputer, adept at doing well, quickly, and without too many problems of limited memory, etc.? In the event, we found that we had to adapt even those programs which were already tried and tested: nothing we bought in or were given from outside actually worked without modification on the ECONET system, quite apart from the differing DFS/ECONET Level 2 file formatting and hierarchies and the fact that the visual presentation of commercial programs was generally fairly unimaginative. Indeed, from our experience, it is a fallacy to believe that it is possible to use fully the CALL materials at present available, without at least some knowledge of programming. At that time, speed was of the essence: although the two of us primarily involved (Jim Mellis and myself) had mainframe experience and experience in programming in BASIC, SNOBOL and FORTRAN, we had to learn BBC BASIC, get to know the capabilities and limitations of the machine, and get CALL programs and material up and running by the beginning of the term.

When we looked at the 'traditional' course elements, it quickly became clear (or so it seemed to us) what the computer would not be suited to. Obviously, the present state of the art did not make the computer a subistitute for a native-speaker conversational assistant, or for language laboratory materials: these emphazised and (one hoped) developed listening and oral skills, whereas the micro seemed to be more suited to training in the visual skills of reading and, to a lesser extent perhaps, writing, and to developing grammatical accuracy through drill-type exercises (AECAL equipment was not available to us then). Brian Farrington's extensive work on LITTRE, using the micro for translation exercises, also suggested that this would not be a suitable path for us immediately. Firstly, at that time, it did not fit easily into the BBC's limited memory; and secondly, it required more time and expertise than we had to prepare translations and mistranslations of texts adequately so as to do justice to the explorative approach at the heart of Mr Farrington's work. We needed initially something in the way of ready-made authoring packages. Taking these considerations into account left us with only one 'traditional' language teaching element, that of the language study class.

Traditionally, the language study class had involved small tutorial groups (8–15 students) examining, in some detail, a text in German for points of linguistic, grammatical, lexical or idiomatic interest, and then working through exercises based on points thrown up by the text. This seemed to offer the greatest potential for CALL work:

1. The textual environment was carefully controlled and specifically limited.
2. Exercises such as gap-filling, substitution, or multiple choice were generally designed so as to require and permit one specific solution which could be checked against the 'parent' text. In addition, certain types of this sort of exercise were already commercially available (Gapkit, Copywrite/Storyboard, Multichoice).
3. Students would be able to work through such exercises at their own pace and rhythm; more importantly though, students would be forced to work through all the exercises for themselves, whereas in class while one student answered the others were relieved of the burden of thinking for themselves.
4. Additional exercises based on lexically, grammatically, or thematically related texts could be created, introducing students to passages of German with which they would otherwise not have been confronted of their own volition, from periodicals such as *Der Spiegel*, *Die Stern* or *Die Zeit*.

One aspect of some concern was that of possible student resistance. Generally speaking, German 2 students were used to regarding a weekly translation class as the lynch pin of their language work and all else as marginal frills. If the language study class were to be completely computerized, then students might regard it either as some sort of glorified playtime or with suspicion, and thus be alienated. In the event, we compromised. Part of the so-called 'translation' class was given over to the textual study that had previously taken place in the language study class, and the language study hour was now devoted to CALL exercises linked to the classroom textual study. The course now looked like this:

1. Translation class with written work, alternating fortnightly with
2. Language study class
3. CALL class based on (2), alternating fortnightly with
4. Conversation class

Each of these classes accounted for 25 per cent of the formal language instruction; in addition, students were still required to undertake private study work in the language laboratory, and to hand in non-translation written language work as before. Thus, although the CALL class now accounted for a quarter of the time allotted to classroom language instruction, it was, we hoped, given respectability, credibility and integrity, as it were, in the students' minds by being closely linked with a class taught in the traditionally prestigious, lynch-pin translation class slot. And, it may be worth stressing, the CALL class was used for the purposes of reinforcement and consolidation of material that had already been taught in another element of the course.

2   THE CALL CLASS

Although attendance was a compulsory part of the course, care was taken from the outset to allow the students as much freedom as possible in what they actually did in the CALL class, both in the types of exercise and in the textual or exercise material they chose to cover. Although the computers (and therefore the students) were arranged in a classroom configuration, the ECONET system allowed each student to access his/her own choice of program and material and work on what was, in effect, a private-study basis. There is something of a paradox here, in that what was essentially private-study work was being undertaken in a classroom context. They had the comfort, however, of working in a supportive classroom atmosphere rather than in the sometimes lonely solitude of private study, and this was felt to be important particularly in the early sessions when, faced with both unfamiliar technology (starting with the on/off switch in some cases, let alone the keyboard) and an unfamiliar mode of interacting with the foreign language, they were able to share their problems with their fellow-students. Additionally, a tutor was always present in an informal role as trouble-shooter, either dealing with technical problems (particularly in the early sessions!) or helping with points of linguistic or grammatical difficulty. It became our experience that students were much readier to discuss language problems in this situation rather than in the formal classroom context; and the role of the tutor changed from that of the teacher ('them' and 'us') to that of helper ('us against the machine'), which led to a particularly friendly and cooperative atmosphere.

In the early stages particularly, we were heavily dependent on commercially available software and, indeed, have made continued use of it throughout the year, and the types of exercise available to our students have reflected this. But these programs have been designed for simplicity of use and ease in handling by the non-computer-expert teacher in the rushed environment of the school classroom and, as such, tend not to cater for the linguistic sophistication of students at university level. This was met to some degree by the development during the year of the authoring package HILITE, which gives both teacher and student a fair amount of flexibility in picking out points of interest in a passage, giving explanations and translations, and yet remaining straightforward in use. We propose piloting other programs designed for this linguistic level during the coming year.

For each session, students were provided with more exercises than they had time for in the hour; arrangements were made for them to use one of the microcomputers in the language laboratory on an *ad hoc* private study basis if they wished to do further work on their own, and, as the session progressed, more and more students did take advantage of this facility, especially for revision purposes or when they had missed the CALL class. The individual programs were accessed not via an overall menu, but by the students typing CHAIN "...", which, as things stood then, allowed us the greatest flexibility of including or excluding things at short notice (in the coming year everything will be autobooted via menus). For each session, students were given a handout. This detailed the types of exercise (i.e. programs) available for that session, together with the texts for each program, a brief description of what was involved in each program, an indication of the theme of additional texts (from *Der Spiegel* etc.) and brief vocabulary lists where necessary. The fairly extensive use of handouts was partly a practical, indeed necessary, expedient enabling the students to know what they were doing and had done (many ticked off each exercise on completion), and partly a psychological move to give students the reassurance of something conventional to take away with them, to file at the end of their session. Over the year, the handouts built up into a reliable record of what had been covered in the CALL classes. And the use of handouts also served to help make the point that the machine did not replace pencil and paper, since several students did seem to think that the pen was now totally redundant in this technological environment.

Although it was emphasised that the students could do the exercises in any order or repeat any one as often as they wished, experience showed that they tended to stick fairly rigidly to the order on the handout, so that it was possible to some extent to manipulate their work and progress by rearranging the handout. Experience suggested that the most profitable order of work was as follows:

1. Multiple choice and gap-filling, sentence-by-sentence exercises based on specific linguistic points (*Multichoice, Gapkit*)
2. Text-based exercises, either with passages already discussed in class or with unseen but related passages, where the student's attention was drawn by the program to words or phrases of specific interest (*Hilite*); and only then
3. Vocabulary and context-based exercises, where a greater degree of randomness was allowed in the student's reaction (*Copywrite*) or the program's selection of material to highlight (*Clozemaster*): these proved to be great time-wasters, and were generally (although not always) preferred by weaker students who could look 'busy' in front of a full screen of material for a long time without accomplishing very much
4. Finally, a 'fun' exercise such as *Hangman*, with words from the current texts, with the added attraction of graphics and noises (for the sake of classroom peace and sanity, we suppressed the sound effects generated by the other programs)

No record was kept of the exercises done by students, or how often any student accessed a given exercise or text. Student scores of 'right' and 'wrong' answers were likewise not recorded. Students were informed of this, and it was hoped that this would encourage students to be intrepid in their interaction with the machine and, by making mistakes, learn as much or more from these (particularly in the case of programs which offered error help routines) as they would have learned from typing in correct answers. In the CALL class, this kind of creative mistake-making became a popular pursuit, especially amongst the better students who no longer felt the need to 'prove' themselves either to the tutor or to fellow students.

3   STUDENT REACTION

Deliberately, no record was kept of student attendance or performance, and this was made clear to the students from the start. In spite of such lack of cajoling (or incentive?), student attendance remained high over the year, and invariably participants looked surprised to be told that their hour was finished. An attempt was made to gauge student reaction by means of a (hard-copy) questionnaire, to which they could append their name or not as they wished. On the whole, reactions were positive, if not overly so. Most students ranked the usefulness of the various types of exercise in the order we had envisaged, as detailed above, as well as their enjoyability (although, predictably, most found *Hangman* most enjoyable and least useful), and most students found the hardware and the individual programs upwards of 'moderately easy' to use. With one exception, they all asked for the class to be continued for the purpose of revision in the summer term. But also, with few exceptions, the majority asked for more 'traditional' translation work and translation classes. This may represent the innate conservatism of (northern) Scottish students touched on earlier; on the other hand, it may be due to the language examination at the end of the year being at that time translation-based; it may be due to the limited, rather mechanical nature of several of the programs we have been using; or it may suggest that we have not yet got the 'mix' or the content of the course right.

4   FUTURE DEVELOPMENT

Students coming into the new German 2 class in October 1985 will have had some experience of CALL in German 1 this past year, and some will also have had experience of Brian Farrington's French translation programs, so that we may expect them (hopefully!) to take more easily than some this past year to the concept and practice of language-learning by machine. Clearly, we shall be drawing on our experience of what went down well and not so well this year, eliminating some programs and texts and adding and extending others, and changing the format of the on-screen presentation and of the handouts, particularly for the early sessions. Over the year, we have developed more home-grown material, as well as acquiring further outside programs and additional suitable texts. We are hoping, too, to use AECAL, although this will only be available in the language laboratory for private study, and we are at present exploring the possibilities of *Microtext*, with its potential for controlling both AECAL and video recorders. We are involved in an interdepartmental project looking both at theoretical and at practical aspects of CALL; and a new venture will be the creation of material (already underway) for our course in German for Beginners, where we are planning a similar integration of taught and CALL classes and materials.

All this, of course, takes an immense amount of time, and such an investment of teacher time should not be underestimated. Quite apart from actual program development, the sheer time involved in putting exercises together, sorting out suitable texts and devising appropriate commentaries, typing them into the machine, and preparing the handouts for each session, is high, since all this needs to be done thoroughly if the students are to get maximum benefit from their CALL sessions. Even with ready-made, straightforward authoring packages, it took about a day's preparation per one-hour-plus session. It is, of course, impossible to quantify objectively whether all the time and effort we (and the students) have put into this have been worthwhile in terms of improved student performance. Believing that, in the present state of the art, a computer can best — or even, perhaps, at best — reinforce or tell but not teach, we have tried to combine the established with the innovatory, integrating both the teacher into the computer classroom and the limited scope of the computer with the traditional university method of the written translation. Both approaches, it seems to us, have their place in the language-learning curriculum, and from our experience in the past year we certainly would not wish to discard one in favour of the other. We are hopeful that, by developing and improving further the type of integrated course we have initiated this year, we will make university language teaching not only more effective but also more varied and more enjoyable for all concerned.

3

Computer applications for final-year linguists

Osman Durrani, University of Durham

1 CHOOSING SOFTWARE — PACKAGE OR PROGRAMMING?

Given the poor quality of much commercial educational software — the inflexible drills, the crudely randomized multiple choice tests, and the unpredictable pattern-matching used to evaluate student input -- it was with considerable trepidation that I began to address myself to the computerization of language instruction in the Department of German at the University of Durham some two years ago. My own credentials were not good. I had no science background and no knowledge of any programming languages, be they of the high-level, low-level, or the ready-made 'authoring' variety. What follows is a record of a quest for the right computer, a clutch of programs to go with it, and a year-long attempt to monitor the responses of the group of third-year language students who were to be the first users of the new equipment. All I had at the point of departure was a dim awareness that the computer could be the most powerful tool to have been placed at the disposal of the teaching profession since the invention of the slate. And the more I realized its potential, the more difficult it became to overlook the fact that it was not being exploited to the full either by educationalists or by the software industry.

If the computer was going to be employed in language instruction at tertiary level, it would have to offer something of value not just to beginners, scientists, the post-'A' level brigade or to those requiring remedial instruction, but also to those who were nearing the end of their degree course and were, in some cases, all but bilingual. Previous experience with audio-visual learning methods led me to believe that these techniques work better with the neophyte than with the advanced learner, and least well with mixed-ability groups. Since virtually every university prose class contains a few members who have fulfilled only the minimum foreign residence requirements of their institution side by side with others who have lived abroad or come from bilingual families, conventional language laboratory programs are seldom able to offer equal rewards to all. This becomes increasingly obvious as students approach their final year. There are few laboratory courses for final-year linguists; this group seemed to be the obvious one on which to test the strengths or otherwise of CALL.

The hardware needed to be cheap, durable, easy to operate by the novice, and capable of handling programs containing large amounts of linguistic data. The cost factor ruled out a mainframe connection, and out of the micros available at the time, I opted for the Commodore 64, since it seemed sturdier than the Spectrum, and, unlike more expensive rivals such as the BBC and the Apricot, required no interfaces to be connected or operating systems to be loaded before program execution or communication with peripherals could commence. It had what seemed like an additional advantage in that it was the best-selling microcomputer in West Germany, but so far I have not been able to obtain any programs other than a few remarkably 'unfriendly' graphics adventures from that source.

For better or for worse, the Commodore 64 has acquired the reputation of being a 'games machine' just as the BBC has the reputation of being the 'number one' serious educational tool in Britain — neither verdict is fair or in the interests of the industry. The BBC has better graphics capabilities, which should give it an advantage in the games market, while the Commodore has a larger memory and better facilities for condensing programs, which make it eminently suitable for text-based language programs. Still, it is no secret that several colleges have had their applications for computer laboratories based on the latter turned down on the grounds that it was not a 'serious' machine. But now is hardly the time to question the wisdom of decision-making by equipment and finance committees in our educational enterprises.

Having selected the equipment, there is a further choice confronting the would-be arts programmer: whether to use an authoring language or a programming language [1]. The most common of the former is probably PILOT. PILOT is a very clever package enabling the teacher to type in a question, one or several answers, to allow or disallow pattern-matching when assessing student input, and to add helpful comments depending on whether the input is judged to be correct or otherwise. But ease of use is paid for in terms of inflexibility. Although PILOT accepts alternative correct answers, which in itself is admirable, it does not necessarily do so in an intelligent way. Take a question to which the answer is 'der Mann'. PILOT can easily be instructed to accept a number of alternatives, such as 'ein Mann', 'DER MANN', 'der Herr', but only if the programmer can foresee all possible correct responses (what about 'ein männliches Wesen', or even the correct answer followed by an exclamation mark?). If the computer is to be taken seriously by teacher and learner alike, it seems vitally important to preclude, as far as possible, situations in which the student can justifiably say: 'I gave it the right answer, but the computer marked it wrong'. Of course, the student ought to have said 'the teacher marked it wrong', but, paradoxically, students tend to blame the infinitely patient hardware, or even themselves, rather than the often highly impatient programmer!

Whether written in PILOT, BASIC, or any other language, the main problem encountered by teachers testing commercial language software is that of rigidity. To give a few examples of the sort of material that is currently floating round those schools lucky enough to have money for CALL:

— *Countdown with the Sinclair Spectrum* (AVC Software) rejects 'tun' as a translation of 'to do'; the program wants 'machen'. It also insists on 'husband' rather than 'man' as a translation of 'Mann'.
— *French Vocabulary: GCE 'O'-level Revision* (Rose Software) rejects 'je suis née' as a translation for 'I was born'.
— *French Vocabulary Tutor* (Hargreaves Software), expects you to translate 'mille' as 'one thousand' but not as 'a thousand' [2].

One reviewer of CALL systems actually commented, rather generously in my opinion, 'Inflexibility of matching is the norm in commercially available programs and should not be a reason for rejecting this particular package' [3]. At the other extreme, there are systems which allow an answer if it is partially correct, on the assumption that if you write 'Managoa' for the capital of Nicaragua you must know enough of your subject to deserve credit. Not so in languages, where an exercise designed to test endings in Russian recently awarded all students 100 per cent simply because it automatically marked everything as correct if the first few letters were right [4].

It did not take long to recognize that no serious programming for the advanced learner could be effected through commercial authoring packages. It was therefore a case of BASIC or bust. Most of the other major languages implemented on today's computers (FORTRAN, Pascal) lack the powerful string-handling capabilities of BASIC, which although often denigrated as a cheap and messy factotum for the beginner, is certainly more than the haven for 'Self-Appointed Instant Computer Experts' that it is sometimes cracked up to be. I would agree with Graham Davies who writes, 'Many critics of BASIC who argue that it is unsuited to the manipulation of text, simply do not know the language well enough to realize its potential' [5]. In fact, I would go further and suggest that the way we ourselves use language is similar to the execution of a BASIC program, flitting from one subroutine to another, referring to tables of variables and abbreviations, and creating new ones as we go along, rather than being able to declare them all in advance as the advocates of structured programming are always urging us to do.

One of the chief drawbacks of BASIC as a programming language is undoubtedly the so-called 'garbage collection' process which is apt to set in without warning and interrupt the smooth running of a program with increasing frequency as the program gets bigger. There are two easy ways of circumventing this occurrence: one is to avoid holding any text in memory, but to call it up from word banks within the program whenever required, and the other is to use a compiler to translate the finished product into machine language where it will be safe from prying eyes and ready to run much faster and more efficiently than it could ever run on the computer's resident BASIC interpreter.

2 IDENTIFICATION OF SUBJECT AREAS AND APPROPRIATE PROGRAMS

The next task was to identify those areas of the subject where the advanced student could be expected to benefit from computer-generated exercises. Here there was a wide range of options: vocabulary building, strong verbs, use of tenses and cases, case endings, comprehension, were just a few of the areas where the finalist continues to be vulnerable. I must confess that the production of a vocabulary tester proved a frustrating exercise, but it made me aware of one of the greatest impediments to successful programming. No matter how brilliant the program, it cannot be judged a success if your typical student response is something along the lines of 'the program was terrific and I learnt a lot during the first 15 minutes, but then the examples began to repeat themselves...' This is, unfortunately, a flaw that characterizes nearly all programs produced for schools and home users, including, I fear, such imaginative exercises as CUP's *Quelle tête!* and *Jeu de ménages* (*Kopfjäger* and *Umziehen*). Although I agree with Jones that sound and graphics are important factors in CAL, I would have reservations about any language program in which three quarters of the available RAM was used to draw pretty pictures on the screen [6].

Accordingly, the vocabulary tester *Ratemal* became a gargantuan affair with, at the last count, more than 2,200 items in four separate disk based files. Words tested ranged from the relatively commonplace ('der Lotse', 'das Steckenpferd') to obscure plants and animals ('das Ehrenpreis', 'der Lurch'), and the method used was the dreaded multiple choice. At least, the sheer volume of the program enabled it to produce an almost inexhaustible stock of examples, and one of the more complimentary things said about it was that students were learning English as well as German from it — it is surprising how many were unfamiliar with terms like 'tracery'. I went on to produce another guessing game, *Denkspiel*, based on the hangman idea, in which a word is gradually built up from clues and odd letters, until I realized that it was much easier, and also much more fun, to shift the burden onto the computer itself and write generative rather than linear programs. And it is to these programs that I should like to devote the remainder of my paper, since it is here that I feel the greatest strength of the computer lies — i.e. in its ability to produce not merely hundreds of examples, but hundreds of millions of variations from one original set of instructions.

The generative language program requires three elements: firstly, a series of word banks from which separate lexical units can be collected while sentence generation takes place; secondly, a system of blueprints for sentence construction to ensure that meaningful examples will be created; and thirdly, a set of instructions to ensure variation and to accommodate the specimen sentences within the teaching context. My first example is a program designed to test the use of the German preposition 'in'. All that is necessary is to provide a person, an activity, and a location. These elements are stored in the word banks containing around 750 words in total. There are approximately 30 sentence patterns, including questions and negated statements, some of which contain optional adverbial components. The program then runs as follows. Ten sentences are generated in which the preposition 'in' occurs with a dative singular. The user merely identifies the gender of the location and supplies the missing article, 'der' or 'dem' (sentences 1–10, below). After that, things get more difficult. Some verbs implying movement are introduced, and the user must decide whether the dative or the accusative is more appropriate (see nos. 11 and 14). These proved to be the most challenging hurdles. The final section (nos. 21–30) includes a few plurals for good measure.

1. Abends verbarg er Bananen in —— Mühle.
2. Da tanzt das Männchen in —— Ort!
3. Heute wäscht er Birnen in —— Taverne!
4. Der Jäger wohnte in —— Zelle.
5. Häufig begrub er Mehl in —— Scheune.
6. Der Bub träumt in —— Küche.
7. Das Kindlein ißt in —— Kanal.
8. In —— Schule jubelt sie jetzt.
9. Petra verbarg Käse in —— Fluß.
10. Wieso bleibt die Nixe in —— Mühle?
11. Petra guckte öfters in —— Bunker.
12. Wieder kam Jörg in —— Tal.
13. Das Fräulein kam in —— Stube.
14. Birgit will heute in —— Spital.
15. Dann tobte Ute allein in —— Höhle.
16. Das Liebchen redete in —— Dörfchen!
17. Eine Oma floh in —— Hütte!
18. Wann steckte sie Eier in —— Dom?
19. Marie geht später in —— Kirche.
20. Wieder gewann er Senf in —— Museum!
21. Der Lehrer staunt in —— Burghof!
22. Ein Mädel rauft in —— Häusern.
23. Ein Dieb ißt in —— Stollen.
24. Der Doktor jubelt in —— Haus!
25. Jutta bekam Wolle in —— Aula.
26. In —— Zimmer blieb es schwül.
27. Karin begrub Quallen in —— Sümpfen.
28. Hans stellt Beeren in —— Säle.
29. Karin verbarg Fisch in —— Palast!
30. Eine Dame staunte in —— Tälern!

This little test owes some of its success to the sheer unpredictability of the examples and the consequent sense of mystery surrounding these at times almost oracular utterances. I am still in two minds as to whether to curb the facility for producing some of the obviously more preposterous statements (e.g. no. 20). Because it is not possible to display, let alone to check each of the 100,000,000 specimen sentences, ambiguities may occur (no. 23). There are at least four remedies: 1) to weed out any words that regularly or occasionally produce ambiguities ('der König weinte in—— Fluß'); 2) to ask the users to opt for the more likely (and least offensive!) alternative; 3) to avoid computer responses of the right/wrong type in favour of something like 'I would have preferred you to put ...'; 4) to remind students regularly that the exercises *are* machine-made, and to encourage them to compile a list of any phrases that they can't make sense of. Quite often it then transpires that they have simply misread a word. The next stage will be to employ a team of experts to dredge up convoluted or nonsensical examples from recent man-made grammar books; the spirit of the 'postillion who was struck by lightning' is still alive and kicking.

After completing the first version of the *In* program, I began evolving another sentence generator with the intention of displaying and testing adjectival endings. And so, *Endspiel* began to take shape — a much more ambitious piece of programming, which provides not only a test routine but a grammar course as well. The user is introduced to the difference between strong and weak endings in each of the cases in turn, and can at any stage request as many alternative examples as she wishes. The following printout gives an idea of the range of typical constructions that the program is capable of producing.

1. Welcher laut* Jaeger mag tanzen?
2. dein gross* Anzug wird verschenkt!
3. gefaellt mir das kaputt* Radio?
4. welch* hungrige Hexe ist gerade da?
5. mancher einsam* Doktor lernt tauchen
6. im Saal eur* wackeren Witwe
7. das Hemd jenes frommen Bauer*
8. der Verkauf jenes gut* Schals
9. der Knopf d* Tochter war verschwunden
10. der Duft alt* Kohle
11. der Doktor mochte ein kaputt* Hemd
12. Wer verzeiht dem mild* Narren?
13. Opa war bei einem mutig* Onkel
14. Paul sah eine alt* Kiste
15. Gib d* Zwerg die Bluse!
16. das waren ganz klug* Plaene!
17. da sind Maries alt* Bilder!
18. Wo werden edel* Prediger verurteilt?
19. sind jen* Gnus ertrunken?
20. manche nett* Nadeln sind da
21. die Ideen beider drollig* Richter

22. die Reize der neun gruen* Felder
23. die Ladung huebsch* Messer
24. die Plaene neun zornig* Dozenten
25. die Hunde seiner brav* Studenten
26. Toni fand die toll* Wannen
27. Karl besah einige feucht* Stangen
28. die Koechin ging zu mehrer* Denkern
29. Susi hasste diese fidel* Knaben
30. Glaube dein* Dienern!

The total vocabulary of *Endspiel* is in the region of 2,000 and the number of examples it produces is to all intents and purposes infinite. Due attention is paid to those sticky indefinite quantities (bestimmte, einzelne, ähnliche, etc.) that cause problems in the plural, and where there are acceptable alternatives ('manche schöne[n] Frauen'), the program treats them as equal.

How do final-year students face up to this type of exercise? At their first attempt, only between 5 per cent and 10 per cent managed to get through a round of 30 questions without making a mistake. I felt this was about as it should be, but student opinion saw the computer as a rather cruel taskmaster. This is perhaps because, in an oral prose class, the odd slurred ending will often pass unnoticed. Those with experience of computer games will know that in order to hold the player's attention, the game has to be virtually unwinnable, and I do not see why this principle should not apply in CALL. This is not to say that *Endspiel* is unfriendly. Quite the contrary, if you accidentally hit a key twice and produce a three-letter response, you get another chance. Of course, when I started to analyse the errors in student input to *Endspiel* and *In*, I discovered that approximately half of them were attributable to word blindness rather than ignorance. While coping quite well with the keyboard with its unfamiliar function and delete keys, many students showed an alarming tendency to confuse certain words, 'Schacht' and 'Schlacht', for example, partly because the phrases had not occurred within a proper context. However, such errors tended to diminish with practice, and I feel that one of the lessons learned by the user was to look very carefully at the text before keying in an answer — a procedure which tends to pay off in other walks of life as well.

But I would not wish to leave you with the impression that I intend to transfer to the screen all those bad habits acquired in years of marking proses by the subtraction method. Revelatory and emancipatory programming — to use Stephen Kemmis's terms — are no less important than the old-fashioned instructional approach fostered by close familiarity with books and blackboards [7]. Accordingly, I wrote a routine for converting words into numerals and numerals into words. This 'billion-word-and-number-game', *Zahlwort*, produces precisely one billion words, i.e. the numerals from nought to 999,999,999, and part of the fun is being able to key in any number within these limits and watch the computer write it out — even if, on occasion, it needs almost half the screen to do so!

Another approach is that of the text maze. Personally, I find this one of the most rewarding compilations, although, or perhaps because, it is the one that owes most to the games program. But then, do not the great educators and psychologists from Plato to Piaget agree that we learn best when at play ('No compulsory learning can remain in the soul... In teaching children, train them by a kind of game': Plato, *The Republic* VII)? And so to *Schattenburg*, an almost Kafkaesque adventure in which a mysterious castle has to be entered and explored, involving comprehension and logical deduction. Unlike the commercial text adventures, it runs without a parser, and performance is not vitiated by typing errors or ignorance of options. All options are set out on screen, making progress relatively easy, though the cash prize offered to last year's students for the first correct solution has yet to be claimed, despite some valiant tries.

3   A GERMAN ELIZA — DIALOG

Finally, a few words about the weirdest member of the family, a program that actually enables a dialogue to take place between the user and the computer. Christened *Dialog*, it poses an opening question of the 'tell me about yourself' variety, and proceeds to involve the user in a conversation that can, sometimes for protracted periods of time, convey the impression that there is an intelligent mind lurking somewhere within its circuitry. It is, of course, a modified version of the ELIZA program, which, in its simplest form, can be implemented even on quite small micros [8]. It need hardly be stressed that *Dialog* is in no sense 'intelligent', but merely programmed to respond to five different elements that may occur in the user's input. Firstly, it scans the input for certain phrases to which it has a selection of stock responses. Thus words like 'vielleicht' or 'ziemlich' produce responses such as 'Ganz sicher ist das aber nicht' or 'Kannst Du das beweisen?' Secondly, it recognizes questions and produces vague, evasive answers ('Ja, wer das wuesste...') Thirdly, it rejects all one- or two-word inputs and invites the user to be more expansive. Fourthly, it identifies a small number of verbs, such as 'will', 'kann', 'muss', 'bin', and converts the input phrases into further questions or exclamations such as 'Willst Du wirklich... ?', 'Ich bin auch...'. If it is unable to latch on to anything in the user's input, *Dialog* has a number of alternatives: it asks leading questions, trots out general platitudes, teases, or, as a last resort, switches itself off. A perusal of the following printout from *Dialog* will illustrate some of these procedures, which may, from time to time, generate almost frighteningly appropriate responses:

Computer: HALLO. ICH HEISSE HEDWIG. WIE HEISST DU DENN?
John: ICH HEISSE JOHN.
Computer: NA JOHN, WAS BIST DU EIGENTLICH FUER EIN TYP? WER BIST DU UEBERHAUPT?

John: ICH BIN EIN JUNGER MANN, DER GERNE FUSSBALL
SPIELT.
Computer: OHNE FLEISS, KEIN PREIS, WIE ICH IMMER
SAGE!
John: JA, ICH BIN ZIEMLICH FLEISSIG, VOR ALLEM BEIM
FUSSBALL.
Computer: GANZ SICHER IST DAS ABER NICHT, ODER?
John: DOCH.
Computer: JOHN, ICH MUSS DICH DARUM BITTEN, EINEN
RICHTIGEN SATZ ZU BILDEN, WENN ICH DICH UEBERHAUPT
VERSTEHEN SOLL!
John: DAS SAGT MAN ABER!
Computer: BIST DU ETWA STOLZ DARAUF, DASS DU
ZIEMLICH FLEISSIG VOR ALLEM BEIM FUSSBALL BIST?
John: ICH HABE OFT KEINE ZEIT FUER MEIN STUDIUM.
Computer: WAS STUDIERST DU DENN UEBERHAUPT?
John: DEUTSCH, MIT GEOMETRIE ALS NEBENFACH.
Computer: VERSTEHST DU AUCH DEUTSCH, ODER SPRICHST
DU NUR CHINESISCH?
John: NAJA, ICH MACHE GANZ GUTE FORTSCHRITTE.
Computer: DU HAST IN MANCHER HINSICHT NOCH VIEL ZU
LERNEN.
John: BESTIMMT.
Computer: JOHN, ICH MUSS DICH JETZT SCHON WIEDER
DARUM BITTEN, EINEN RICHTIGEN SATZ ZU BILDEN, WENN
ICH DICH UEBERHAUPT VERSTEHEN SOLL!
John: BITTE, ENTSCHULDIGE MICH.
Computer: DEINE HOEFLICHKEIT GEFAELLT MIR. MACH NUR
WEITER SO!
etc.

Not being omniscient, there are obviously occasions when *Dialog* appears to get hold of the wrong end of the stick, and it is not difficult to confuse the operating system by typing in garbage. I have tried to incorporate some safety features to prevent this from occurring too frequently. The program lacks a specific teaching strategy, and I appreciate that some teachers would not wish to use it because of the risk of incorrect German appearing on the screen, although I personally would defend *Dialog* on the grounds that the final-year university student will normally spot the elementary lapses in its performance. Also, and this is a vital point to which I fear I cannot address myself in the present context, program errors do give students and teachers valuable insights into how computers process information, and not the least of the CAL expert's task is to acquaint students of all disciplines with the strengths and the weaknesses of the computer as a tool, rather than to pretend that hardware, software, and programmer together constitute an unbeatable triumvirate of experts. As O'Shea and Self point out, 'Computers ... follow their instructions without error, but it is a mistake to believe that their pronouncements are therefore without error' [9].

References

[1] For a discussion of such 'authoring packages', see Last, R., *Language Teaching and the Microcomputer*, Oxford 1984, 54–63.

[2] See reviews in *Modern Languages in Scotland. News and Reviews*, February 1984, 36–40, and June 1984, 66–68.

[3] Kershaw, P., *Modern Languages in Scotland. News and Reviews*, June 1984, 65.

[4] Davies, G., *Computers, language and language learning*, London 1982, 44.

[5] *Ibid.*, 14.

[6] Jones, B., 'Call for help — Computer-assisted language learning', in *Modern Languages* 66 (1985), 45–49.

[7] Kemmis, S. *et al.*, *How do Students Learn?*, Norwich 1977, 23–33.

[8] A German version of this was first implemented on the Commodore VIC 20 by Robert Treichler. See 'VIC — Das intelligente Programm', in *64'er. Das Magazin für Computer-Fans*, May 1985, 173-178.

[9] O'Shea, T. and Self, J., *Learning and Teaching with Computers. Artificial Intelligence in Education*, Brighton 1983, 41.

[NB Since this paper was written, most of the the programs mentioned have been converted for use on the IBM PC. It is hoped that other versions will follow.]

4

Grace—a call system for the acquisition of reading skills

Anthony F. Hartley and Fiona Motley, University of Bradford

1 PEDAGOGIC OPTIONS

1.1 Aims and objectives

One of the scientist's most frequent professional laments is the personal inability to access the contents of FL (Foreign Language) publications [1]. It is the search for an effective and efficient way of surmounting this barrier that has motivated the present project. (The terminology used in this section is consistent with that in [2]).

In general terms the purpose of the prototype CALL system described here is to enable those with a specialist knowledge of the conventions of a given subject field to acquire the conventions of language necessary to decipher foreign language texts relating to that specialism. In other words the would-be reader's schematic knowledge of the conceptual organization of the field is assumed at the outset to provide a reasonable scenario for judging the relative plausibility of competing interpretations of the reading text. Thus, pedagogically speaking, the package is seen as constituting one element in an LSP (Languages for Special Purposes) course, where the aims and objectives are tightly specified. The emphasis is on training rather than on education, which seeks to foster the capacity to deal with all language situations. The specificity in this instance is threefold. Firstly the skill element is confined to the acquisition of a reading ability, secondly the content of the texts is restricted to a single domain, and thirdly the program is valid only for a particular text type.

In specific terms the prototype, as implemented, is designed to enable chemical engineers to read German abstracts of articles on various aspects of chemical engineering, hence GRACE — German Reading Acquisition for Chemical Engineers. German is widely recognized as being an important language of publication in this field, which means that the skill is a useful one. Furthermore, the CALL activity proposed to the learner/reader is authentic in that the reading texts are genuine, "undoctored" abstracts taken from a German journal. As is characteristic of training courses, there is a high degree of congruence between the pedagogic objectives and the behavioural aims. We believe this to be an essential condition where CALL is to be the sole or principal element in a teaching package.

1.2   Strategies

Before adopting a given strategy or set of strategies to achieve the desired "target product" (here the ability to derive coherent information from a text), it is obviously necessary to take into account the learner's starting point. For the reasons given above it is important that the reader's schematic knowledge is sufficient to minimize problems of comprehending content, allowing the learning effort to be concentrated almost exclusively on the linguistic system. No systemic, linguistic knowledge is presupposed, which means that the system is designed for use by absolute beginners. This is not to say, however, that it is inappropriate for linguistically more advanced learners, such as those of 'A' level ability. Being of a general educational nature, the school syllabus goes only part of the way towards satisfying the specific training needs of this category of learner. Scientific discourse (and *a fortiori* abstracts) instantiate only a subset of the rules of the language system. While a post- 'A' level student is likely to have been exposed to all the sentence patterns found in scientific texts, the frequency of these patterns as well as the models of term formation are likely to be sufficiently novel to merit a teaching/learning effort.

The envisaged implementation is based on a mainframe. It is also possible to install it on stand-alone micro running PROLOG and with sufficient space for the dictionaries.

The 'A' in CALL can represent a whole gamut of stimuli, differing in nature and purpose. The assistance provided to the reader by GRACE is based on the principle of linear predictive analysis. The exploitation of such an analytic approach in promoting FL reading abilities is not in itself new, and we acknowledge the inspiration given by courses adopting the Integrated Dictionary Systems method [3, 4, 5]. The reader attempting to interpret a string of FL text is normally forced to consult both a dictionary and a reference grammar in order to identify and assign values to its constituents. GRACE incorporates both semantic and morpho-syntactic information in a single source, so realizing enormous savings in look-up time thanks to the very fast retrieval capability of the electronic medium. Thus the interaction between GRACE and the user is essentially collaborative [6].

It is recognized that abstracts may not be the most captivating of texts to read, but they are viewed here as appropriate material for the first stages of an LSP reading course.

2   LINGUISTIC INPUT

In order to compile the initial system dictionaries, we established a corpus comprising one hundred abstracts. This represents a total of some ten thousand tokens, of which some eight thousand are text proper and the remainder titles and keywords. The corpus was submitted to the Oxford Concordance Program in order to generate different views of the data, such as frequency and reverse alphabetical listings and selective concordances.

The word classes obey the distribution pattern normally found in scientific/technical texts. Homonymy which could potentially occur at the level of general usage is all but eliminated in the instances of use in the corpus analysed. For example, "aufbringen" is realized only in the sense "to apply", and the auxiliary "wird/werden" exclusively as a marker of mood, never of tense. The tenses observed are present and compound past, and verbs appear only in the third person. The dictionaries take due account of these simplifying factors.

The analysis of further abstracts is unlikely to result in the addition to the dictionaries of any more functors or inflections, both of which instantiate fewer values than in general language texts. Since, however, the ultimate intention is to increase the users' motivation by allowing them to input texts of their choice, there will need to be a substantial increase in the number of properly lexical entries, especially nouns, if a coverage of better than 95 per cent is to be ensured. Existing published dictionaries rather than running text offer the best solution to this problem.

It remains to be seen through empirical analysis and trial whether any extension to other scientific text types (reports, for example) will increase the complexity of the morpho-syntactic component to a point where the reader is confronted with too many choices to resolve them easily.

3   A USER'S EYE VIEW

3.1   Help

The system is designed to be self-instructional. It requires only basic computer-literacy on the part of the learner (notions such as "page" and "quit"). Likewise the grammatical metalanguage is kept to a strict minimum of traditional terms, and there is deliberate recourse to computing terminology to convey lexicographical concepts by analogy. For example, a "dictionary entry" is referred to as a "display" and a "part of speech label" as a "flag".

The first-time user is advised to scan a few, brief pages of information which are confined to explaining the dictionary conventions used and outlining noun-noun and adjective-noun compounding in German. The decision to pare to a bare minimum the information provided about the language was taken to force the students to develop and explore their own hypotheses about German, free of preconceptions. Teachers not sharing this view can always use the classroom to treat grammar explicitly.

3.2 Reading procedures

The text selected from the system's library by the user is displayed in the upper half of the screen (Fig. 4.1). The top line lists the prompts available to the reader at that level. We limit ourselves here to explaining prompts "m" and "v".

```
<F,B> <f,b> page <m> meaning <v> verbs <e> edit <q> quit <?>:
Chemisch inerter Modulmischer fuer Stroemungs- und gestoppte
Stroemungsversuche Papadakis et al haben ueber einen Quarzmischer
berichtet, der viele wuenschenswerte Anwendungen (schnelle Vermischung,
kleine   Abmessung,   hoher   Mischungswirkungsgrad,   chemische
Widerstandsfaehigkeit, optische Transparenz) aufweist. Leider ist seine
Anwendung wegen Bruchgefahr etwas begrenzt; speziell bricht er leicht an
der Verbindung der Ablassrohre mit dem Mischerkoerper. Unter Verwendung
des Stroemungsmusters dieses
```

```
haben                    Quarz+mischer            der
+<acc thing>: (to) have  m quartz                 +<nom m sg>: the;
+<past verb>: have        m mixer                  +<gen/dat f sg>:
(eg have doNE)                                     the
                         bericht+et               +<gen pl>: the;
ueber                    to report                +<verb(s) at end>:
+<acc/dat>: over,about    <verb>+et: flags 3rd     which
                         person sg present
einen                    (eg it doES) or flags
flags acc m sg: a, one   past verb
```

Pressing "m" enables the learner to request the dictionary entry for a chosen word by positioning the cursor on its initial letter. This information is displayed in the lower half of the screen. Fig. 4.1 shows the information accumulated after successive queries on "haben", "ueber", "einen", "Quarzmischer", "berichtet" and "der".

Following the golden rule, stated on the first Help! page, that only alternatives with compatible flags may be selected, the learner will find only a single path through the analysis, which gives the reading "have reported on a quarz mixer which". The compatibility rule serves to discard those significations not realizable in this particular context, here namely the other potential values of "haben", "+et" and "der".

The extent to which the constituents of compounds should be separately represented in the dictionary was decided pragmatically on the basis of their frequency of occurrence in isolation and of the perceived transparency of the resultant translation. Thus "Widerstandsfaehigkeit" is displayed as "Widerstand+s+faehigkeit", it being assumed that from the gloss "resistance" + link + "capability" a chemical engineer will be able to construct "resistivity".

The "v" key prompts GRACE to search for and identify the verbs and auxiliaries in a given sentence. We contend that this option is pedagogically and tactically useful in that it creates in the reader expectations as to the presence of arguments typically associated with the verb in question. It also has the advantage of weaning the learner away from a narrowly linear, serial processing of the text [7]. A sample entry from the verb dictionary is: entfern: to remove (x removes y from — (von [+ dat]) point z; (aus [+ dat]) container z).

All the dictionary information called to the screen is held in a reference file which can be printed at the end of the session for the benefit of learner and, where appropriate, tutor.

4   THE GRACE SYSTEM

GRACE is a menu driven program which guides the user through the selection and operation of tasks. The different tasks involved and the flow of information between the user, the processing centres and the information store are shown in Fig. 4.2. The flow is in both directions, data is read from and written to the files. There are only two reports, the unfound words list (to enable dictionary update) and the reference file already mentioned. The most important output is the flow of information back to the user via the screen.

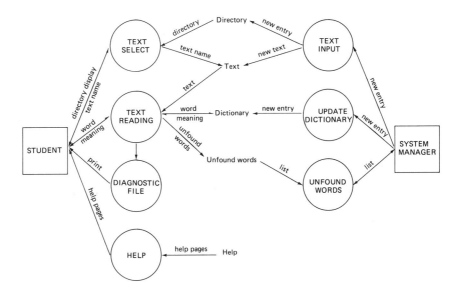

The interface with the user requires a standard character video display. It is presented in a way which tries not to detract from the task of language learning. The menu choices are displayed as numbered lists and the student invited to select an option number. A single character response (without RETURN) is all that is needed and the screen is protected from inadvertent key depressions scrolling the display out of sight. A wrong entry results in an error line at the bottom of the screen reminding the student to enter a single number within the accepted range for the menu.

The help index uses the same format as the main menu and provides a choice between different pages of advice. Selecting a help option changes the display to the first page of the relevant notes. There is a 'continue' prompt at the bottom of the screen which enables the user to read the next page or return to the help menu. Selecting option 0 in this and in all secondary menus returns the user to the main menu.

The text selection option divides the display area on the screen for different functions. The second reading screen, shown in Fig. 4.1, is the most complex since it not only controls the selection of reading options, via the prompt line, but also contains both the text used to input information, and the output flow of data in the form of meanings for selected words. In order to make best use of the limited 24 × 80 character display, the commands and prompts are restricted to one line at the top of the screen. The selection of commands is shown in short form simply as reminders, their full explanation being given in the help notes. The text, which is write protected, is displayed at half-intensity, and can be easily distinguished from the words and meanings shown below. Text is 'paged' five lines at a time to enable a student to view a whole sentence without having to change the ten line display. The meanings are written onto the lower half of the screen in three columns which are 'paged' by shifting one column left or right.

The problem of identifying words or sentences requested by the student is another function of this complex screen display. After selecting 'm' or 'v' the cursor can be moved to the beginning of the required word in the text since the write protect is temporarily removed. On receipt of the ESC character, the position of the cursor is read back from the screen. If the cursor has been correctly positioned at the first letter of a word the screen co-ordinates read in can be used to identify the word or sentence. A reverse calculation which generates screen co-ordinates is used to display verbs by changing the visual attributes of these characters to reverse video. Attributes of text characters revert to normal video on paging.

The remaining options, entering text, updating the dictionary (reserved for the system manager) and printing reports (ie the contents of the scratchpad and the dictionary entries consulted), use the main menu format and simple screens consisting of single line prompts for the information which has to be entered.

Processing required for GRACE is a simple combination of control flow where there are menu choices and transform flow for the different activities of reading and updating files. The software structure for the text selection option is shown in Fig. 4.3 and follows the notation described by Pressman [8] for data flow design which distinguishes between these two types of information flow. The boxes, or elements of the software structure, name the principal tasks which have to be carried out.

The process of requesting a reading text from the directory is unusual in that the item number must be linked with a file name. The number is looked up in a table of file names which is stored as part of the directory. Since the directory entries may be deleted or added the table has to be rewritten when these changes are made.

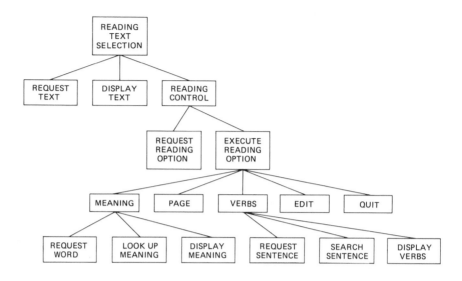

The meaning and verb functions also make use of a table which is constructed as the text is read in. Each word, in text form, is stored with a record of the word's sequence number in the text, the sentence number and a reference number which is calculated from the text line number for the word and the character position of the first letter of the word on that line. Any word requested from the screen can therefore be identified, using the screen co-ordinates, with a word in the table, and therefore with a sentence identity and a unique position in the text. When verbs are requested a sentence identity for the selected word is found and used to search through the table for words which are verbs with the same identity. These verbs are displayed on the screen using the reference numbers in the table. For meanings the text string and the word position in the text are retrieved from the table. The string is used for dictionary look up, and the word position to sort the output for the session report.

All files are held as ordinary serial files which may be edited and printed by the standard utilities. The text files can therefore be easily updated using a full screen editor and this is how GRACE enters new text. Each text is an individual file whose name is generated and stored in the directory.

5   ALTERNATIVE MODES OF USE

GRACE has been implemented as a system functioning in collaborative mode, assisting the learner in an authentic task. In its execution the learner acquires the capacity to interpret a limited subset of German texts. We have already indicated that the inclusion of other text types may not be without difficulties.

It is equally possible to envisage an implementation in an instructional mode, by the addition of question/answer routines generated by the system. This represents a switch in strategy in so far as the focus shifts from authentic reading to monitoring the student's awareness of certain structural features of texts. GRACE's existing "knowledge" could readily be exploited by grafting on instructional modules relating to morphological analysis and/or verb identification. Similarly, checks on the identification of cohesive ties could be built in at little extra cost, although defining their contribution to signalling macro-structure is an altogether more complex matter. The incorporation of question/answer (test) routines raises the matter, referred to above, of the metalanguage in which the questions are phrased. This is not a trivial aspect of CALL and the need to address it is growing with the growing sophistication of programs. The implementation of a full parser rather than of a simple affix-stripper and morph analyser would permit the non-realized values of inflections, for example, to be suppressed from the screen where resolution was straightforward. Where unequivocal resolution by the parser remained impossible, the choices could be narrowed down in order to lighten the reader's burden. In learning terms, however, this might present the same drawbacks which Widdowson cites for some priming glossaries, namely that they "relieve the learner of the essential task of interpreting the discourse for himself" and are "directed to the understanding of the particular passage (...) rather than to the development of an interpreting strategy which can be applied generally to other discourse" [2].

The computer is a powerful instrument whose potential is currently under-utilized in language teaching. But in the future one may well have to guard against the temptation to exploit this power for its own sake, keeping in mind that the purpose of CALL is to assist and stimulate a learning process which will bring the individual within reach of linguistic self-sufficiency.

References

[1] Large, J. A. (1983), *The Foreign Language Barrier*, London: Deutsch.

[2] Widdowson, H. G. (1978), *Teaching Language as Communication*, Oxford: Oxford University Press.

[3] Heron, P. (1975), *Russian-English Integrated Dictionary* (2nd edition), Birmingham: Modern Languages Department, University of Aston in Birmingham.

[4] Heron, P. (1977), *A Concise German-English Grammar Dictionary*, Birmingham: Modern Languages Department, University of Aston in Birmingham.

[5] Jelinek, J. (1974), *Japanese-English Grammar Dictionary*, Sheffield: Centre for Japanese studies, University of Sheffield.

[6] Wyatt, D. H. (1985), "Putting the Computer in its Place (in LSP)", Paper presented at the Fifth European Symposium on LSP, Leuven, August 26–30, 1985.

[7] Baltra, A. (1983), "Learning How to Cope with Reading in English for Academic Purposes in 26 Hours", *Reading in a Foreign Language*, 1 (1); pp. 20–43.

[8] Pressman, R. S. (1982), *Software Engineering: A Practitioner's Approach*, New York: McGraw-Hill.

5

CAL in Italian at the University of Leeds

Brian Richardson, University of Leeds

1 INTRODUCTION

What is normally understood by 'post A-level language teaching' is teaching a language that has already been studied at A-level. All Italian teachers in British universities do this; but most of them must also teach Italian to beginners who have shown their linguistic ability by taking an A-level in *another* language. It is with this second category of teaching that my use of computers is concerned.

It is 'post A-level', then, only in a certain sense. Nevertheless, elementary teaching of a language in these circumstances is very different from what it would be in a school. Firstly, one can assume awareness of linguistic categories — what a pronoun is, for instance, or what the subjunctive mood is. Secondly, one has to go fast: from scratch to something like A- level standard in about twenty-three weeks' teaching. One lesson of fifty minutes might cover a whole tense or a set of rules for using some part of speech. To help in such teaching I have been using a computer at Leeds for three years now, mainly in grammar drills to supplement written exercises and work done orally in grammar classes or the language laboratory. We also use CAL in other ways, for instance in Cloze tests and other text reconstruction exercises. These are of particular interest for students who already have some knowledge of the language, and have been used up to final-year level. But in this paper, I wish to concentrate on our use of computerized sentence-based drills, which I feel are still, for all their faults, a convenient and effective way of familiarizing well-qualified and well-motivated students with the grammar of a language in a short period of time.

2   A GRAMMAR EXERCISE PROGRAM

The program which runs the grammar exercises is written in BASIC and runs on a mainframe computer (when the project began, the University of Leeds did not have a cluster of micros). At first I provided a separate program for each grammar topic; this permitted flexibility of format, but it proved very time-consuming to alter them all when changes became necessary; so now one large program runs all the exercises. These fall into two types: the question-and-answer type (QA), such as transformation and substitution exercises, and the multiple choice type (MCQ). The latter is useful for variety and also because at present students are unfamiliar with the keyboard and are generally slow typists; normally MCQs are used where otherwise a student would have to type in more than two or three words. The program can be run in two modes: as an examination, with no responses given, and as a teaching session, in which guidance is given. The correct answer is given if the student has got the question wrong twice or has asked to see the answer. But after an error on the first attempt, two kinds of guidance may be given. One is produced automatically by the computer and the other can be given by the teacher preparing the exercises.

In the QA type, a wrong answer is matched character by character against the right answer.

(a)   if the correct characters are not all present, then the computer displays any characters which *are* correct, with '*' for any wrong characters and '-' for any missing characters; for example, when the correct answer is *me lo manda*, and the student gives *mi lo manda*, the response is *m* lo manda*; similarly, a student answer of *mandarano* instead of *manderanno* generates the response *mand*ran-o*.

(b)   if all the correct characters are present, then '↑' (up arrow) is used for superfluous characters and ' ͜ ' (underscore) is placed under characters which are in the wrong order; for example, a student answer of *manderemmo* instead of the correct *manderemo* gains a response of *manderem↑o*, while *lo te manderemmo* (instead of *te lo manderemo*) yields <u>lo te</u> manderemo.

At the moment the program does not attempt morphological analysis or parsing, though this is something which we hope to introduce in the future. Matching is carried out only if one acceptable answer is indicated. If there is more than one, the computer could be told to see which acceptable answer is nearest to the student's answer; but can one be sure that this is the one at which the student was aiming? However, at this level there are few occasions where alternative answers are possible.

In both the QA and MCQ types, the datafiles used by the program can include comments which are printed on certain conditions being fulfilled. These comments, which would normally refer to the grammatical principles involved, can be given either for all answers, or for all correct ones, or for all incorrect ones, or for answers with a certain pattern of letters (for example a particular ending). The comments are given in Italian as far as possible (that is, where there seems to be no danger of misunderstanding), as are all the elementary prompts while the program is running, so that the student is not jerked in and out of the target language more than is necessary — and these students, usually with an A-level in French, can understand a message like 'Il plurale è irregolare' even on their first lesson.

Example 1: from an exercise on noun plurals

l'albero	*question*
i alberi	*student's answer; correct answer is 'gli alberi'*
No, c'è un errore:	
-- i alberi (carattere mancante)	*response 1*
"Albero" comincia con una vocale.	*response 2*
Prova un'altra volta:	*another try...*

Example 2: from a multiple choice exercise on noun plurals

la moto	*singular*
1: le mote	*incorrect alternative*
2: le moto	*correct alternative*
2	*student's answer*
Giusto!	*response 1*
"Moto" è un abbreviazione di "motocicletta".	*response 2*

Example 3: from an exercise on pronouns

you have given us many good ideas	*response 1*
voi . molte buone idee	*partial translation*
ci avete dati	*student's answer; correct answer is 'ci avete dato'*

No, mi dispiace: *response 1*
   ci avete dat* (*carattere
sbagliato)

"us" = "to us"; il pronome è   *response 2*
indiretto

Prova un'altra volta: *another try...*

Help can be summoned at any time. This consists of a summary of the forms or rules being tested, in English this time for the sake of maximum clarity. The 'default' is help on the main subject of the exercise, but one can also summon help on another topic (for example, in an exercise on compound tenses, help might be needed with auxiliary verb forms). At the end, students can go through again the questions which they got wrong, and they can take away a printout recording their session.

Student connect time and marks are recorded for use by staff; but the most important feature is that all errors are recorded and counts are kept of how many times each error is made and of how many times in all a question was attempted. In subsequent classes one can thus know which points are in most need of remedial help, and one can also include appropriate comments in the datafiles for guidance in the future. To illustrate this recording of student errors, here are examples taken from recent analyses of two exercises. We see the question itself (the dot represents the position for the entry of the answer); the correct answer; any conditions for comments on answers (these are introduced by 'if', and '*' means 'any sequence of characters'), and the consequent comment on the answer (introduced by 'ca:'); and the errors, together with the number of times they were made:

Example 4: from an exercise on adjective forms
(the masculine singular form is given in brackets)

question 17
quelle automobili sono . (italiano)
answer : italiane
(freq.) (errors)
17 ITALIANI
5 ITALIANO
2 ITALINE
2 ITALINI
total errors this question = 26 out of 71 tries (= 37%)
question 18
quell'automobilie è . (inglese)
answer : inglese
(freq.) (errors)

10 INGLESA
3 INGLESI
1 INGLEAS
total errors this question = 14 out of 62 tries (= 23%)
question 19
queste automobili sono . (inglese)
answer : inglesi
if:*e
ca:Gli aggetivi in "-e" hanno il plural (maschile e femminile) in "-i".
(freq.) (errors)
12 INGLESE
1 UNGLESI
total errors this question = 13 out of 60 tries (= 22%)
question 20
non c'è . latte (molto)
answer : molto
(freq.) (errors)
10 MOLTA
10 MOLTE
3 MOLTI
total errors this question = 23 out of 69 tries (= 33%)
TOTAL ERRORS THIS EXERCISE: 196; TOTAL TRIES THIS EXERCISE: 1047 (19%)

Example 5: from an exercise on forms of the demonstrative 'quello'
question 18
. due quadri sono di Michelangelo
answer : quei
(freq.) (errors)
8 QUELLI
5 QUEGLI
2 QUEL
2 QUELLE
1 QUELI
1 QUESTI
total errors this question = 19 out of 45 tries (= 42%)
question 19
. uomini sono italiani
answer : quegli
(freq.) (errors)
2 QUEI
2 QUELLI
1 QUELI
1 QUELL'
1 QUESTI
total errors this question = 7 out of 34 tries (= 21%)

question 20
. vecchio specchio è francese
answer : quel
(freq.) (errors)
14 QUELLO
2 QUEGLI
1 QUEI
1 QUELL'
total errors this question = 18 out of 47 tries (= 38%)
TOTAL ERRORS THIS EXERCISE: 187; TOTAL TRIES THIS
EXERCISE: 751 (25%)

Errors such as 'italine' and 'unglesi', where the ending being tested is correct, suggest that 'fuzzy matching' (acceptance of such an answer, together with an appropriate reminder of the correct spelling) is a good idea. Another consideration arises from example 4, question 20. Here several students clearly had no idea what 'latte' means and what its gender is; and this suggests that a future development should be to provide an on-line mini-lexicon of the vocabulary found in the exercises. We are at present using different grammar books for our two beginners' courses, and we have found that we cannot assume knowledge of the same vocabulary for all students. It would be very helpful if students faced with an unknown word could initiate a search which provided its meaning and some basic grammatical information on it (eg gender, any irregularities).

3 FUTURE DEVELOPMENTS

Finally, a brief comment on the future of the exercises. We now want to produce a micro-based version: it is a luxury to have the storage facilities of a mainframe, but it makes the exercises hard to transfer to other potential users. But *which* micro? Most universities have clusters of BBCs, and this might seem an obvious first target. But in the longer term, universities may be looking to larger machines (such as the IBM PC, of which Leeds is establishing a cluster), so that we shall also be looking at the potential of the personal computer.

6

A sense of perspective: CALL for Russian

J. Halliday, Heriot-Watt University, Edinburgh

1 INTRODUCTION

A frequently-voiced criticism of CALL is that it is essentially reductivist: learning a language, one of the most stimulating and enriching educational experiences, is compressed into a series of drill-and-practice or gap-filling routines. Another is that software writers become so obsessed with the technology that they lose sight of the use to which their product is to be put. The end result is a piece of masterful programming which has superb graphics, animation, flashing lights and bells that ring, but which is of no discernible educational value. Sceptical colleagues look at all the ROMS, RAMS and kilobytes labouring mightily to produce a mouse, and turn away from the new gimmickry.

The aim of this paper is to show that CALL need not fall into either of these traps if a 'language-learning' rather than a 'computer-based' approach is adopted. Although it is ostensibly about CALL for Russian, the remarks it contains are pertinent to other languages as well. After briefly outlining my views on the place of CALL, I shall consider three areas of teaching in which I have found the BBC microcomputer to be helpful: guided essay writing, maximizing the use that can be made of a text, and practice with numerals. Then four typical CALL programs are assessed for their contribution to the learning process.

2   NEW OPPORTUNITIES IN CALL

One of the most important reasons for learning a language must be to establish contact with human beings and their culture. It follows from this that to speak of "communicating" or "interacting" with a computer is, in terms of language learning at least, to speak metaphorically. In another sense (ie programming), communication with the computer is in effect a performative act. Masoud Yazdani has depicted the computer of the future as an ideal teaching machine, which will enable the learner to acquire a knowledge of a language without formal instruction (this volume, Chapter 16). The only sure way of doing this is to follow his own example and live for an extended period in the country where the target language is spoken for. Since most learners are not in that fortunate position, it is likely even in the times to come that they will continue to require both some degree of formalized instruction and communication with speakers of the language. Learning the syntax of a language is a minor component of the totality of the learning experience, which is really about the acquisition of semantic and pragmatic knowledge of a humanistic nature. To lose sight of this can lead to extravagant assertions about CALL which are in fact counter-productive.

That said, the computer opens up a whole range of new opportunities. Above all, it shifts the focus from the teacher to the learner, which has to be an improvement. The teacher, or at least this teacher, is obliged to move away from the taxonomic method of presenting the language and ask what it is the learner needs and wants to know. Instead of teaching *about* the language, one can get on with teaching the language itself. In this way it is possible to resolve the paradoxical situation whereby the introduction of the microcomputer has brought in its wake a resurgence of behaviourist methods which run counter to all recent thinking in language teaching. It does not have to be the case that the latest in twentieth-century technology entails a return to the worst features of nineteenth-century pedagogy. When used in the right way, the computer offers the learner yet another approach and the teacher new and creative teaching strategies in all sorts of ways, some of them not immediately apparent.

The humble word-processor, for example, can be used by teachers without programming knowledge for the development of essay-writing skills in small groups. This activity works well where the theme of the "essay" is fairly restricted and the kind of language being elicited is not necessarily "creative." Subjects such as leadership changes in the Kremlin, reform of the Soviet education system, the morality of the French nuclear test program and so forth where there is a reasonably closely defined lexis are eminently suitable. But topics that involve a more imaginative use of language might lend themselves to this approach. Minimal pragmatic, lexical and syntactic information can be prepared in advance and recalled from disk. One student acts as "secretary", keying in the text as it is produced by the group. Since this is much faster than trying to keep a hand-written record, that student is able to participate fully in the activity of composition.

The job of the member of staff is to intervene as little as possible, requesting students to comment on errors rather than supplying "correct versions" himself, prompting a range of possible variants, commenting on the degree of idiomaticity and formality of the text, and introducing concepts such as collocability, field, tenor, mode and so on. If he chooses, he may make comments on the way the argument is developed. The "end result" (in the students' eyes) takes the form of a hard copy: this means they leave the class with a feeling of achievement because they have something tangible to clutch. Their real achievement, of course, lies elsewhere, and the production of an accurate and reasonably authentic piece of continuous prose is only one small part of it. The shared experience of contributing to a wide-ranging and vigorous discussion and selecting the optimal strategies for presenting and expressing the arguments put forward is worth a great deal. This exercise is particularly valuable if it is carried out in preparation for an extended piece of writing in the FL, and goes a long way towards meeting the common complaint of students that they are expected to write long essays on complex subjects without having the requisite linguistic experience. After this kind of practice, when students go on to write their own individual essays, they are likely to turn out a vastly superior piece of work. The participation of a native speaker enhances this exercise immensely, and can give all kinds of insight into the thought-patterns of speakers of the language. The complexity of the data files can be adjusted as required, and the activity can be carried out with students at any level. The text produced can be used for cloze-entropy work on a subsequent occasion. Naturally, such guided or shared essay writing would lend itself to support from a proper computer program for those in a position to write or otherwise obtain one.

The word-processor also enables fundamentally lazy people like myself to gain maximum value from their laborious typing (particularly if one is typing in Cyrillic), as the same passage can be used for a number of purposes with only minimal editing. There is even a pedagogical justification for this, in that it is beneficial for students to "memorize" text without rote learning and to practise certain skills without the unnecessary complication of comprehension problems. A typical "text-use" profile might look something like this: first of all, exercises involving the extraction of salient information; translation followed by questions to be answered in some detail in the FL; analysis of the structure of the text; substitution of similes; changing the degree of idiomaticity or formality of the text. Finally a range of substitution exercises such as restoring omitted prepositions, pronouns, conjunctives and disjunctives, and case-endings can be carried out, individually or in a group, using hard copy, gapping programs, or a combination of both. The programs produced by Lanchester Polytechnic are particularly useful in this respect, as the basic text prepared on their word-processing program can be easily adapted for use in gapping and substitution routines. All the texts currently being created in the Heriot-Watt *ab initio* Russian course are being edited in this way, so that computer-based activities will be a fully integrated part of the course design. Both of the above activities are pedagogically highly productive, essentially communicative and, although they perhaps do not come into the remit of CALL as conventionally considered, they are in a small way computer assisted.

Another, narrower application of the computer is in practising Russian (or anybody else's) numerals. Interpreting is an increasingly popular component of language courses, and one in which automatic response to numerals is required, both into and out of English. Previously for this exercise I used a slide projector, which had some disadvantages: it created a tense atmosphere within a small group; the speed of loading was not easily controllable; and the number of slides needed was far in excess of the capacity of the magazine. The micro enables large, clearly defined Arabic or printed numerals to be dispayed on the screen at a selected speed, with an audible signal to indicate when the time is up. Decimals, fractions, units, tens, hundreds etc. may be chosen in sequence or at random, or a combination of all can be requested. The students have simply to say the number before a 'bleep' cuts them off, and speed can be developed by decreasing the display time by seconds or parts of seconds, thus giving great precision. Students can take turns, or compete against each other (or the member of staff). A few minutes of this is sufficient, but effective, takes no time to set up and is appreciated by the consumers, who are more than aware of their shortcomings in this area. This elementary program could be improved in many ways, such as by incorporating the calculation facilities of the Exeter PALLAS programs and testing routines.

3 CURRENT CALL PACKAGES FOR RUSSIAN

Ideally, CALL programs intended for use in the context of an educational institution should be custom-built. Where this is not possible or is felt to be unnecessary, commercially available software can be incorporated into the course. Despite the status in this country of Russian as a minority language and the problems associated with generating the Cyrillic character set, a reasonable range of software is available. The morphological features of the language together with its highly inflected syntax mean that Russian is well suited to CALL techniques, a fact that was appreciated at an early stage by teacher/programmers. Apart from software written specifically for Russian, a number of well-known programs such as 'Gapkit' have been adapted for Russian, and others such as 'Lingo' and 'LingoTest' provide Russian as an option. The following programs were written by lecturers in Russian rather than professional programmers, and display the typical strengths and weaknesses of current CALL materials in general.

Russkiy vybor by R. Bivon (Wida Software) is a multiple-choice authoring package designed to check basic grammatical and lexical knowledge. The documentation supplied with the program is clear and concise. The learner has to indicate which of four possible answers he thinks is correct, using the cursor to highlight the text. He is told whether his response is right or wrong in Russian, but there is no attempt at error analysis. After a wrong response, the list of possible answers is re-ordered and he has to try again. After two wrong attempts, the correct answer floats up from the bottom of the screen to fit into the spaces left by a line of asterisks. The multiple-choice format removes the difficulty of having to type in answers in Cyrillic (of which more later). The score is permanently displayed in the top right-hand corner of the screen. *Russkiy vybor* is a very flexible program which can be used for practice with declensions, conjugations, agreement with adjectives and number, and so forth. The points being concentrated on can be contextualized, which should be a basic principle of CALL programming. The most obvious appeal of *Russkiy vybor* is to the student in the initial stages of learning the language, but given questions of suitable complexity, it could equally challenge more advanced learners. This program could be readily incorporated into a language course as a means of testing or reinforcing the material covered by students.

Russkiye slova ('Russian Words') by the same author (Wida Software) is in a different category altogether. Vocabulary tests, which on the face of it would seem to be among the easiest programs to write, are in fact far from simple, because of the irritating polysemy of words. If the program does not accept all possible equivalents, its utility is diminished accordingly. Although *Russkiye slova* allows for four translations, by the time account is taken of the articles (zero, definite or indefinite) there is not much scope for variety. The data files that come with the disk exemplify the kind of muddles that vocabulary tests are prone to. In one subject file, for example, '(Female) student' is rejected as a translation of *studentka* with '(Girl) student' being the preferred version. In another file, however, only '(Female) student' is accepted. The word *zatylok* cannot be translated as 'Back of the neck': only 'Back of neck' will do. *Brov'* is only 'eyebrow', never 'brow'; *skol'ko vam let?* can not mean 'What is your age?' but must be 'How old are you?' The learner also has to remember to indicate the aspect of perfective verbs and transitivity.

Note that these are not defects in the program as such, but are features of the data the program is reading and can be put right. The onus is very much on the teacher to ensure that confusion is prevented. One solution is to stick to items which have a one-word equivalent, but this is hardly satifactory either. There is no contextualization. And, since each lexical item is stored on a separate file which has to be read from disk, the program is slow to use — and speed is one of the few advantages a computerized vocabulary list has to offer. Vocabulary programs are not, however, entirely without virtue, and are perhaps more popular with those at the sharp end, who find they serve their immediate purposes well enough, than with their teachers. If treated with due care, a role could be found for *Russkiye slova*, especially for handling special lexical fields. A further note of caution concerns the whole question of whether it is a good idea for learners at an early stage to be typing 'in English' at all, when what they need is to completely disassociate themselves from the Roman alphabet.

Still on the grammar-and-lexis front, *Russian Irregular Verbs* by D. Adshead of Birmingham University (Carsondale Software) is a sophisticated piece of programming which is enjoyable to use but which has some shortcomings from a teacher's point of view. In the first place, the title should be *A Hell of a Lot of Russian Verbs, Quite a Lot of Them Regular*. With a data-stock of 152 items, almost all of the verb types are represented, including reflexives. It was apparently the distributor who insisted on the title, to keep in line with other language versions in the series. A more serious criticism is that the program was supplied with sparse documentation. No list of the verbs in the data-store was provided, and this information cannot be recovered from the program, as a set of rules together with coded strings of data is used to generate the forms as and when required. Nor is it possible to output the screen image on a printer via a graphics dump. There is nothing for it but to copy the 152 verbs out, which seems an unnecessary encumbrance. It could be argued that there are plenty of other sources of information on Russian verbs, but the provision of grammatical information on the verbs which actually figure in the program would have enhanced its value to the learner.

The program allows the learner to "browse" through the verb form/s of his choice (present, past, future, imperative, gerunds and participles), with the verbs being grouped into five levels of difficulty. He may then go on to test himself, with or without a time-limit. Corrections are shown at the end, along with the score. An important feature of *Russian Irregular Verbs*, which is often missing from programs, is that the accented syllable is shown on all forms. The screen display is colourful without being garish, and the characters are well-formed and clearly defined. The program is somewhat mechanical, as the verbs are not presented in context, which would presumably have added to the difficulty of an already complex programming exercise. The contextualization might also become tedious with repeated use, and this is one of the great advantages of this program: it can be used over and over again, as often as the learner feels he needs to practise his verbs.

Although it is easy to see ways in which the instructional value of *Russian Irregular Verbs* could have been increased, students enjoy using it, to the extent of not even complaining too much on the (infrequent) occasions when it marks their correct responses wrong, miscounts their score or produces an incorrect stress. It could be argued that programs of this nature do not do anything that could be performed by some more conventional means. The fact is, however, that students are quite willing to brush up their verbs on the computer from time to time, whereas the same information presented in a text-book exerts less pull on them. *How* they do it matters less than *whether* they do it.

Russian TextFill, also by D. Adshead and from Carsondale Software, is a cloze-test program which will delete from every fifth to every second word, or the whole text. The passage can be reconstructed in either a linear or a random sequence, with a time limit if desired. One of the strengths of *Russian TextFill* is that the keyboard lay-out is permanently displayed at the top of the screen. 'Help' options are provided, and at the end the complete passage is provided, as is the score. As in *Russian Irregular Verbs*, colour is used intelligently to enliven the screen without giving the user a headache. The short length of texts permitted (12 lines on one file) is something of a handicap if students are being asked to work their way through extended passages, but has the advantage of making for an uncluttered screen lay-out. These aspects of program design are not mere luxuries: the sight of an entire screen covered with tightly spaced white dots or dashes is not conducive to successful recall. *Russian TextFill* is more popular with students than some other similar programs precisely because of its attractive screen display. *Russian TextFill* comes complete with twenty well-chosen passages of increasing difficulty written in colloquial modern Russian. As it is an authoring package, new texts can be readily entered. However, there is no provision for the output of hard copy, which some users may consider a disadvantage.

Although cloze-entropy exercises are perhaps most familiarly associated with student assessment, gapping programs such as *Unifill/Rusfill*, *Gapkit* and *Russian TextFill* can also occupy an important place in the acquisition of advanced language proficiency. The abilities developed by the cloze exercise correlate closely with the high-level skills required for conference interpreting. The most appropriate form of cloze work with final year students is aural, conducted in the interpreting laboratory. Problems come, however, at an earlier stage in the students' training, at the ticklish point of transition from what is in effect a fairly straightforward form of 'oral translation' to more demanding tasks. Although students' aural comprehension on advanced texts is basically sound at this level, there may nevertheless be some residual difficulties which detract from the utility of the aurally-conducted cloze exercise. The isolation of the interpreting booth is a factor which induces further stress. It is here that the 'new technology' comes into its own. We have found that a considerable improvement results if the aural cloze activity is preceded by cloze exercises on a section of the same text, only this time carried out at the microcomputer on a group basis. The atmosphere here is less inhibiting, and once again students can benefit from the support and exchange of knowledge provided by a team endeavour. Further work could be done on an individual basis. They can then move on to their aural comprehension exercises on the passage, followed by aural cloze and then by "interpreting." This sequence takes them with minimal trauma towards the point where they can cope with interpreting proper (i.e. without any previous exposure to the text), by developing an analytical approach to text and an efficient short-term memory as well as the anticipatory techniques involved in simultaneous translation: a retentive short-term memory, sensitivity towards such features as collocation, element order, anaphoric reference, modality in its widest sense and towards communicative dynamism at all levels of the text.

The use of CALL programs of Russian would be greatly simplified if agreement could be reached by those who write and publish programs on a standard keyboard lay-out. This would eliminate at a stroke one of the minor irritations of Russian CALL: at present, there are a number of methods of assigning Cyrillic characters to the keys and life can be confusing for learners working their way through different programs. One solution would be to adopt the Soviet typewriter keyboard: this is harder to operate with at first, but would mean that users would have only one lay-out to contend with. A more recent suggestion is that the Russian computer keyboard, which is different again, should be used.

4   CONCLUSION

CALL has moved from being the province of a handful of enthusiasts to an established part of educational practice. The very size of this conference and the range and scale of what is being done in various kinds of institutions (some of them renowned for their strong adherence to traditional methods) are proof. Its present performance is clearly a weak reflection of its potential, and until such time as genuine heuristic systems for handling natural languages develop, exaggerated claims should be treated with caution. It is certainly not yet true that computers are in a position to "revolutionize" language teaching, as some of their over-enthusiastic supporters have proclaimed. But they can help us both to develop new forms of creativity in the educational process, and to approach long-standing methods in a fresh, imaginative light. In this sense, it is those who accuse CALL of reductivism who are themselves the reductivists.

7

Computers in Arabic language teaching

Colonel O. B. Taylor, Ministry of Defence and Major D. Harding, United

Kingdom Arabic Services Ltd

1 THE STRUCTURE OF ARABIC AND ITS SIGNIFICANCE FOR THE STUDENT.

Arabic is a Semitic language, of the same family as Ugaritic and Accadian, both now long dead, as Aramaic, which survives only in vestigial form, as Hebrew, and the Semitic tongues of Ethiopia, which include Amharic and the church language, Geez. Its phonemic repertory comprises 28 consonants and 3 vowel qualities, of which only one is cited in the 'abjadiyya' or alphabet. The most striking thing about Arabic to a European approaching the language is the phenomenon known as Roots and Patterns. The vast majority of Arabic words are derived from a basic sequence of 3 consonant phonemes in a determined order; this tri-phoneme sequence is called the Root. The Root can then be modified by the addition to it of prefixes, infixes and suffixes, all of which impart some semantic variation to the root meaning. These additions are not random: they are highly systematized and are categorized by grammarians as Patterns. The variations in meaning are not always predictable but in many cases there is a beautiful regularity. For example: The root *salama* produces *sallama*, a causative verb, and *tasallama*, a reflexive verb.

This system of root and pattern is most markedly observed in the verb system. Each basic root is capable of up to 14 variations, or Forms as they are called.

Form I is the base or root. Forms II — X are all in common use in both colloquial and literary Arabic, with the exception of IX, which is rare (See Fig. 7.1). Forms XI — XV are used only for poetry.

I	SaLaMa
II	SaLlaMa
III	SaaLaMa
IV	'aSLaMa
V	taSaLlaMa
VI	taSaaLaMa
VII	inSaLaMa
VIII	iStaLaMa
IX	iSLaMma
X	istaSLaMa

It is important to note that not all verbs have all Forms, but they are all capable of being modified in accordance with God's universal template for the language, so that neologisms can always be created from within the root system to reflect developments in human language. Once the paradigm of each Form has been learned — and it normally comprises past tense, non-past tense, participles and verbal noun — then it is possible to form unerringly the correct person, tense, mood, participles and verbal noun of any word in the language. Because of the perfect regularity of this system, there are no such things as irregular verbs, and it is not even necessary to insert the short vowels; in fact the short vowels, which are represented as superscript and subscript markings associated with the appropriate consonant, and a whole series of other orthographic symbols, are omitted in all works of literature save the Holy Qur'an and children's books.

Let this suffice as a brief introduction to the intrinsic nature of the language. What are its implications for the student and the teacher? In the second part of this chapter, there will be an explanation of how the computer has been used to capitalize on the advantages and mitigate some of the difficulties. Several programs for different aspects of the language have been devised, but only the more significant of these will be discussed here.

1.1 Consulting a Dictionary

The student of Arabic has a number of problems when faced with a word he does not understand, problems which are much more complex than those faced by a student of English. For example if the student of English meets the word *decomposition* what does he do? — He opens his dictionary fairly near the front with the aim of finding the D section. When he has found it he gradually refines his aim by going through each letter of the word in sequence, starting with the first one. Eventually he locates his word in bold capitals on the left-hand side of the column, followed by an entry. An Arabic dictionary does not work like that:

a) it groups together all words derived from the same root and lists the roots alphabetically. So the first thing the student has to do is to look at a word and be able to work out its root. This not only demands an understanding of the structure of the word, but may also need clues from the rest of the sentence.

b)   the sequence of the Arabic alphabet has to be remembered.

c)   it greatly speeds up the search if the conventional order in which words are sequenced under their root headword is known.

The combination of these three factors makes consulting a dictionary a fairly daunting and slow process for the learner. And of course, as for any learner consulting a dictionary, there is often a bewildering variety of alternative meanings, with little guide as to which is the most frequent or common.

1.2   Consulting a Grammar-book

Analogous problems face the student attempting to consult a grammar book for help in analysing a word. Grammar books are an asset when one is proceeding from the known to the unknown, but they are not well adapted to the reverse procedure of finding a solution to a problem. In practice, what happens is that the student, faced with a word he cannot parse, constructs a hypothesis, which is then checked on a trial or error basis in the grammar book.

1.3   Verb Conjugations

One important reason for consulting a grammar book is to verify, or indeed learn, the conjugation of verbs. As has already been pointed out, the verb system is highly structured — but it is also very extensive, and it is not easy to look up how to conjugate a particular tense of a particular verb. As in any other language, the actual verb which the grammar book chooses as its example of a particular type almost certainly will not be the verb one wants at that moment, and one has the constraint of mentally substituting the verb in the place of the example in the book. Of course, this can itself be a valuable learning technique, but a lengthy process when one simply wants a quick answer to a problem.

1.4   Plurals

In English, and indeed in most other European languages, nouns form their plurals by inflecting the ending of the word. This is not the case for a considerable number of Arabic nouns. An approximation in English might be *mouse* becoming *mice*. They are called in English "broken plurals". Fig. 7.2 lists some examples.

In the right-hand column are six different vocalic patterns of the singular — Some are accompanied by letters of increase and some are not. In the left-hand column are two forms of the plural — you will see that the first two have the same pattern and so do the last four. But of the six different singulars the first two use the same plural pattern, and the last 4 share the other pattern.

```
        PLURAL          SINGULAR
   -- -- --- ---- ----------- ----- -- --- --

        Sugharun        Sughraa
        rukabun         rukbatun

        thiyaabun       thawbun
        qibaabun        qubbatun
        rigaalun        ragulun
        kibaarun        kabiyrun
```

Figure 2

There are in fact 29 different forms of the broken plural — each one of which is created by combining the root consonants (the sequential order of which remains constant) with short vowels, long vowels, doubling of one of the root letters or the addition of a very restricted number of so-called letters of increase to form the new patterns. Each particular pattern of singular noun forms its plural using one (or occasionally more than one) of these patterns, resulting in a complex relationship between the singular forms of nouns and the 29 different plurals. Naturally, one is not expected to learn the whole of this set of rules — indeed probably nobody does learn it. One tends to learn two words instead of one — the singular and its plural, thereby avoiding the problem arising out of encountering a broken plural. But faced with a new word, one of the possibilities is that it might be a broken plural, and if it is then the problem is how to find the singular form. With experience one gets a feeling for the patterns, and it becomes fairly easy to recognise the form as a broken plural and to work out quickly what singular is hidden in it. It is precisely that experience that the learner does not have.

In this introduction, a number of problems specific to the learning of Arabic have been outlined — consulting a dictionary and a grammar book, and mastering the highly regular but highly complex verb and noun systems. The student needs help in simplifying the reference process and practice to achieve familiarity with the underlying algorithms until they become second nature. And in all these aspects of learning Arabic we believe that the computer has a useful part to play.

2   COMPUTER ASSISTED ARABIC LANGUAGE LEARNING.

Reference has been made to two possible ways in which a computer system might be integrated into a course of study — as a reference tool and as part of the teaching-testing process. Some examples of each are now provided, with the aim of demonstrating that Arabic — and indeed all Semitic languages — by the nature of the way they are structured, are peculiarly suitable for computer analysis, and thus for CALL applications.

The examples described below have been designed to run on a BBC Model B micro, using a second processor to gain additional memory. This still means of course that no program referred to is longer than about 40k (including variables). It does mean too, that a student or indeed a teaching department is not dependent on immediate access to a mainframe network.

To date, three reference programs have been developed, and to a certain — and still developing — extent they are interlinked. The programs comprise a reference dictionary, a program which will conjugate all verbs in all Forms (although it is only about 70% complete at the moment) and the embryo of a program which forms hypotheses about the grammatical function of a word from its component letters. The link between the three is the data file of the dictionary words, which can be consulted by all three programs for information needed to carry out their own processing.

The DICTIONARY is essentially a program which searches a data base and prints the results on the screen. In most languages that would probably be a little used facility, since a book would be quicker and easier to use. The Arabic dictionary program, however, enables the course developer to control the amount of information extracted from the dictionary under the headword entered by the student. This depends on the student telling the computer what stage or month or lesson has been reached in the course. The dictionary entries contain markers to restrict the output to only those meanings or derived forms of the word which are relevant to the student at that stage of the course. This should overcome the confusion faced by the student of a printed dictionary entry with far more information than can be coped with — a very real problem in Arabic. These markers — and indeed the contents of dictionary entries — can quite easily be altered.

The VERB CONJUGATING PROGRAM relies very much on the algorithmic characteristics of Arabic — one set of rules will generate almost all forms of the verb. The program has to consult the dictionary for one piece of information about all verbs in the imperfect tense — because there is no all-embracing rule to determine which vowel is used after the second root letter, and about one vowel in the past tense of certain weak verbs. If the specific verb is not in the dictionary, the program asks if the vowel which should be used is known, and if it is not, the computer tells the student that it is making an assumption that the vowel is the most common of the three possibilities and then conjugates it in that form. The start of the program is a list of different types of operation that the student can choose.

Fig. 7.3 illustrates the response to a student who has typed in the first form of his verb (in this case *kataba* — to write) and has asked for the tenth form. This has been supplied at the top of the screen on the right, and a choice of conjugations is now offered — Past or Imperfect Tenses in the Active or Passive mood. This program uses diacritics — the student has to type in the verb including its vowels, and the program responds with vowelled Arabic. The vowels are printed on separate lines from the consonants; the program therefore needs three lines of screen for one line of Arabic.

```
┌──────────────────────────────────────────┐
│         DERIVED FORM No 10               │
└──────────────────────────────────────────┘

   كَتَّبَ        FORM 10 :      اِسْتَكْتَبَ

You now have a choice:

To conjugate this verb -

   In Past Tense (ACTIVE) ..... Press A
   In Past Tense (PASSIVE) .... Press B
   In Imperfect (ACTIVE) .......Press C
   In Imperfect (PASSIVE) ......Press D


        To return to CONTENTS .. Press Z
```

```
┌──────────────────────────────────────────┐
│      DERIVED  FORMS  OF  THE  VERB       │
└──────────────────────────────────────────┘

    كَتَّبَ    ١ *         تَكَاتَبَ    ٦

    كَتَّبَ    ٢ *         اِنْعَتَبَ    ٧

    كَاتَبَ    ٣ *         اِكْتَتَبَ    ٨

    أَكْتَبَ    ٤ *         اِكْتَبَّ    ٩

    تَكَتَّبَ    ٥          اِسْتَكْتَبَ   ١٠

  Only Forms marked with asterisk are
       in the computer's dictionary

  Check book dictionary to see if the
  other Forms are produced by this verb

┌──────────────────────────────────────────┐
│      Press SPACE BAR to continue         │
└──────────────────────────────────────────┘
```

Fig. 7.4 shows the outcome of a different operation — a list of the ten forms which a first form, in theory, can generate. In practice any one verb usually generates only a selection of them. The program has consulted the computer dictionary and has discovered that there are only four forms of the verb recorded, and has issued a warning that the other forms might not exist in practice for this verb.

The third reference program is one to ANALYSE the GRAMMATICAL FUNCTION of a word. It is intended to help the student to sort out the root letters of the word, which carry the basic semantic information, from the letters of increase and other syntactic accretions, and thus come to an understanding of its function and of where to look for its meaning in the dictionary. The student types in the whole word (but without diacritic marks), and the program then attempts to match the word with a series of patterns, each of which carries specific syntactic information. In fact of course it does not try to match it with patterns which use the particular root letters of the student's word, but with the standard three root letters used for most paradigms in Arabic grammar books. The program therefore has to go through a series of steps which involve substituting the standard three radicals for the radicals of the student's word before doing the matching. This process does a lot of grammatical cheating — it relies for instance on the length of the word to give it certain information, and on the fact that an Arabic word is a sequence consonant-vowel-consonant-vowel and so on — and here again one sees the impossibility of adapting such a process to non-Semitic languages where such characteristics are of no syntactic significance.

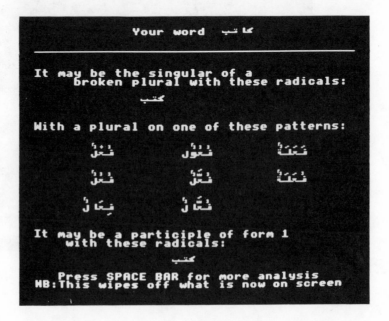

Fig. 7.5 is a simple example of this program at work. It should be emphasized that it is in an early stage of development and will never be comprehensive. It is intended to provide suggestions to the student; if it is unable to do so it will admit it, and the student then has to find a more intelligent human. The important thing is that it should not give any WRONG information — and that means spending a great deal of time using the program and debugging it, because it is impossible in practice to foresee what responses the program will give to all possible inputs.

The other programs we have been developing have been for student practice and learning. Some of them — such as cloze tests — are not dependent on the particular characteristics of the Arabic language and do not require discussion here. On cloze testing, though, it should be said that there is very good learning to be gained from the process if it is applied to a short passage which the student does again and again, but with different words omitted each time. By the time the student has seen the passage half a dozen times, each time with different gaps, and has thought about them, he knows the passage off by heart, meaning and all.

As we have indicated, one of the major hurdles which the student of Arabic has to learn to overcome is the extraction of the root letters from a word. There are obviously many ways in which exercises can be devised to practise and help a student to master this process. One program presents a sentence to the student who is then invited to type in the radicals of each word, with a view to working out the meaning of the sentence. The student chooses a word, enters a choice of radicals, and is then offered the oppportunity to look it up in the computer dictionary.

If the course has a controlled set of vocabulary, the correct word in the sentence should be in the dictionary. If the student looks up the word and it is not in the dictionary, it will be because the wrong word has been selected — unless, by chance, the correct radicals of another word that is in the dictionary have been extracted, when the screen will show that word. The course organiser could structure a program of this type so that it would issue a warning to the student at this point; alternatively, the student could be left to come to a realisation that semantically the word was a misfit in his sentence. It is also desirable in programs of this type to offer some help to the student in difficulty. This program offers two types of help: it will give the student the radicals of any one word on demand, or the radicals of the whole sentence. Alternatively it will provide the English meaning of any one word or of the whole sentence. It should be pointed out that these meanings have to be stored as part of the exercise data file — they are not worked out by the program from first principles, nor by looking up the dictionary!

Another test relies on the fact that in a sentence, the syntactic function of nouns and adjectives very often dictates their final vowel. Of course these final vowels are usually short vowels and are therefore only written in the Qur'an, children's books and language learning texts — however for our purposes they can be present. The test therefore presents a vowelled text on the screen, with certain terminal vowels omitted; the student is then given a list of seven possible options and is invited to choose.

So far we simply have a test. However, if the student makes an error, a hint is offered. These hints are generated by the program, which does a number of fairly unsophisticated analyses of the words around the target word. For example, a word governed by a preposition goes into the genitive, so the program checks back for a word which matches a supplied list of prepositions. Words with the definite article take a different form of vowelling from indefinite ones — so the program checks the front of the word for the definite article prefix, etc. The program then issues the hint or hints and invites the student to have another try. If he remains confirmed in his error, the program issues what it calls a Direct Hint. These are pre-programmed with the data file of the exercise in question, and thus should guide the student to the correct answer. If it still fails, the program supplies the answer. When the student supplies the correct answer a confirmatory learning point is offered — and this is the same message that is used for the Direct Hint. So the program has some claim to be a teaching as well as a testing process. A further development of a program such as this would be to link it to the dictionary, so that students could look up any of the words in the passage, as an aid their understanding its structure through its meaning. This has not yet been attempted, but it would not be a difficult process — mainly a matter of incorporating a number of program procedures from the dictionary look-up program into this one.

One of the first problems facing the student of Arabic is the need to master a new written notation system. Although in fact it is not so daunting as may at first appear, it is nonetheless an aspect of any course in Arabic on which both staff and students have to spend a significant part of the first term. It is, however, a study in which practice plays a notable part, and is one to which the computer can contribute. In the simplest application, the computer can provide examples of the printed forms of Arabic in a structured sequence, and provide practice in recognition both at the individual letter level and then of letters embedded in clusters of other already familiar letters.

A program of that sort has been developed, teaching, testing and revising the letters of the alphabet. It introduces the letters written in very large size — in fact occupying the space of two normal 40-column screen characters wide by three characters deep. This gives enough definition — 16 dots by 24 — to be able to draw the characters with quite good clarity. The program shows single-character size letters as well, thus providing an introduction to their use in other later programs. Because, as it will be appreciated, on an 8-by-8 dot matrix it is not possible to have such a sophisticated definition of the characters. In practice, however, students can use them quite quickly without constraint.

This program includes what might be called "Wake-up" screens — the idea is to respond to the inevitable fact that as the student is simply pressing the space bar a number of times to look at the next letter being introduced, a sort of self-hypnosis can develop, and little learning will be taking place. So every now and again, controlled by a random-number sequence, a test question is posed. The program also remembers which letters a student failed to recognize correctly in the tests, and produces them for revision at the conclusion of the test.

3   CONCLUSION

Some of the applications referred to above are part of the common stock of any Computer Assisted Language Learning system, and indeed are very unsophisticated exponents of them because of the deliberately self-imposed limitation of using a cheap stand-alone micro system. However, it is hoped that the initial thesis that Semitic languages lend themselves in a particularly accessible way to this new discipline of CALL has been justified.

8

Computer assisted reading—work in progress at the University of East Anglia

Jeremy Fox, University of East Anglia

1 INTRODUCTION

The CAL reading materials under development at UEA are intended for intermediate to advanced learners of English as a foreign language; though the approach may later also prove applicable to the study of other languages, or of English as a first language. This particular project is for the standard 32K BBC 'B' microcomputer with twin 80 track disk-drives, chosen because of its wide distribution in British educational establishments. Nevertheless, it has to be admitted that the use of BASIC on small micros imposes limitations on CAL development; and that more powerful machines using AI-oriented languages such as Lisp, Prolog and POP-11 have considerable advantages, not simply because of their bigger memories and processing power, but in particular for operations like string-handling, handling natural language, and working with flexible data structures [1, 2, 3, 4].

In this project, the methodological problems are seen as the most important. The computer presents the language learner with new opportunities, some, probably, still to be discovered. Integrating the computer into the overall language learning environment is difficult. It is the teacher who normally has this task, and the involvement of the teacher would seem to be of great importance if CAL is going to be accepted, and to develop usefully [5].

2 CURRENT PRACTICE IN THE TEACHING OF READING

The teaching of reading in 'English as a foreign language' classes has tended to move away from the traditional format of reading passage followed by comprehension questions to an emphasis on reading strategies. Students are trained to skim through a text, e.g. to get the main points, or to scan it for information relating to a particular topic. Other skills in which training is given are identifying the main theme of a paragraph, and inferring the meaning of unknown words by systematically examining the surrounding context for clues. The skills of inference and prediction are emphasised [6, 7].

The UEA Computer Assisted Reading materials adopt a number of these teaching strategies. Their primary aim is to help the learner to develop his reading skills rather than to teach language directly. Nevertheless, grammatical and lexical information is made available, under learner control, in places where it may help him or her to complete the task in hand.

As is also the case with a good deal of oral communicative teaching, the teaching of reading in TEFL is becoming more task-based. Thus in one of the UEA Computer Assisted Reading programs ('Select'), students are asked to go through a text on paper to see which of the list of questions on the screen could be answered from the printed text, and which could not. Another program ('Recognise'), requires the student to identify the wordclass of various words in a text when they change colour to green. There is a time limit, set by the student. These task-based and problem-oriented approaches to the teaching of reading are widely used in modern materials [8, 9].

The reconstruction of texts from which words or sentences have been removed is also consistent with Malone's comments about the motivating power of computer games where the players have to fill in the gaps in incomplete schemata. A somewhat similar principle is used in different forms of 'jigsaw' communicative practice: student A is given half of the information needed to complete a task, while student B is given the other half. In order to complete the task, the students have to cooperate. Here again, the task is to put together something which is incomplete.

3 HUMANISTIC ORIENTATION

3.1 Student-centredness and learner-control

An important debate has recently focussed on the relationship between 'subconscious' acquisition of language in informal contexts (i.e. 'picking up a language') and conscious learning of language in formal situations such as the classroom. An inevitable concern of designers of language learning materials has been the factors which help the student to acquire or learn the second language. ('Second' is here used to include 'foreign'). Among these, exposure to linguistic input has been seen as essential for acquisition. Krashen [11] in particular has claimed that 'comprehensible input' is the key factor. Hatch [12], on the other hand, has pointed out how, in addition to input, interaction and brainwork are also important. These discussions tend to suggest that a realistic CAL course would include both exposure to a considerable amount of language (for acquisition) and appropriate analytical and descriptive material for (systematic learning of) grammatical and lexical information etc.

The UEA Computer Assisted Reading materials, therefore, aim to give the learner: firstly exposure to a good deal of language texts stored on disk (input for acquisition); secondly problem-solving tasks in which they interact with the texts, with each other, and with the computer; and finally access to information files about grammatical rules and definitions of words (analytical material for conscious, deductive learning). This information is not automatically presented to the learner, but available for consultation on demand. This use of the computer to bring information when required, as happens in industry, for example, is seen as a way of producing a richer acquisition and learning environment.

That the information is accessed under learner control is consistent with humanistic approaches which stress the learner's personal involvement and investment in his or her learning [13]. The UEA programs also try to provide a 'user-friendly front-end', making movement in and out of the programs easy; indicating by colour-coding in the Menu which programs a student has completed[14]; making backtracking possible so that learners can go back to an earlier stage in a program; making helpful suggestions about what to do next, but not coercing the student; avoiding discourteous or patronising feedback etc. In an interesting parallel, Coombs and Alty have recently argued that expert systems should not so much seek to solve complex problems as guide their users to extend their knowledge in the problem area and solve the problem themselves [15]. Their educational model of guided discovery learning may also be relevant to CALL.

The availability of a range of information of 'Help' facilities also reflects our view that an axiom of good CAL practice is 'Thou shalt not ask a question or set a problem without providing the student with the means to find the answer'. A 'rich learning environment' in this sense is one which can supply all the information a student needs in order to complete the tasks set him or her by the program

3.2 Teacher-centredness

A humanistic approach, however, does not only involve the student. Teachers have needs, rights and feelings as well, and some may feel confused, threatened or marginalized by the advent of CAL. That the teacher normally has the coordinating role of planning the course and deciding the place of CAL in it has already been mentioned in the Introduction. In a reading course like the one described here, this makes it desirable to have authoring packages so that the teachers can choose their own texts, questions, tasks etc. and put them onto disk. In most cases, it seems likely that the most common use of CAL will continue to be within the framework of a class-based course. Thus the UEA materials are planned so that the teacher can pick and choose which programs to use in class, and which to recommend for self-access. Nevertheless, it is also intended that the course should be sufficiently detailed and coherent for the student working on his or her own.

In their report on the acceptability of CAL on Plato, Murphy and Appel [16] draw particular attention to the enthusiasm of teachers for the control it gave them over the use of the medium. The teacher's and student's roles can be seen as complementary and not conflicting: the teacher chooses the package, the texts, the vocabulary items etc for authoring into the programs. Nevertheless, within the programs themselves, the students have a large degree of freedom.

4   THE MATERIALS

The UEA Computer Assisted Reading Materials are envisaged as part of a classroom-based course, coordinated by the teacher, though self-access is also possible [17].

The first choice offered to the student is between text focus (i.e. going through a sequence of programs relating to a particular text) and skills focus (i.e. selecting individual programs to develop particular reading skills). A typical sequence might be as follows:-

1.   The student chooses the 'text-focus' route, and the program 'Select' is loaded and run.

2.   The student picks a text from those available. He or she already has a book containing all the texts in use. Reading large chunks of text from a screen is unsatisfactory in many ways (40 column display will permit display of only a limited amount of text and scrolling is 'unnatural'), and our principal aim is to improve students' skills in reading texts on paper.

3.   The program 'Select' has several sections:

   (a)   multiple choice pretest to see how much the student knows about the topic and to get him or her to think about it. Students are allowed to choose whether to answer 3, 5 or 7 pretest questions.

   (b)   a scanning exercise to find out how many of the pretest questions can actually be answered from the printed text. The student can choose whether to take 1, 2 or 3 minutes for this exercise.

   (c)   another scanning exercise to find out which questions could not be answered from the text. At this point, feedback is given on how the students did in section (a).

   (d)   practice in identifying the main theme of the passage, using multiple choice to suggest four possible titles.

   (e)   end of program, with option of returning to Menu, or going on to next program in the sequence. In fact, the student can also restart or get back to the Menu from any point in any program, by pressing 'Escape'.

4. The next program, 'Vocabulary Practice', concentrates on difficult vocabulary encountered in the previous program. It has a number of stages:

    (a) the student is asked to name a word which he or she did not understand. If this matches one of the pre-stored list, it is used. Otherwise, the student is asked to choose from the list of anticipated problem words. In the first text ('Mystery of the Great Pyramid'), these are 'monument, erected, masonry, discrepancy and oriented'.
    (b) The next stage is practice in guessing the meaning of the word in context. The first step in this, following Clarke and Nation [6], is the identification of the wordclass. The student now has a choice between:

    (i)   going straight on and guessing the wordclass
    (ii) getting some practice in the skills of guessing wordclass by playing one of the appropriate games, e.g. 'Recognise'.
    (iii) using the built-in lexicon by pressing 'C' for examples in context, or 'D' for a definition of the problem word. Let us imagine that the student is working with the word 'masonry'. Pressing 'D' for definition will give:

    The pieces of stone in a building. The art of shaping and fixing these pieces of stone.

Pressing 'C' for examples in context gives:

    The quality of masonry in the old stone castle was extremely good. With the replacement of stone by other building materials, good masonry is hard to find nowadays.

    (c) Whether or not the student uses these information files, or does some extra practice in wordclass-recognition, the point will come when he or she has to decide the wordclass of 'masonry'. When the choice has been made, the student is offered access to the grammatical information files Noun-, Verb-, Adjective- and Adverb-Identification. These information textfiles, displayed under student control (but with suggestions from the program), give basic grammatical information about the wordclasses in question. Eventually, it is hoped that students will be able to refer to them from any point in any program. When reading them, students can go back to previous screens, rather like turning back the pages of a book.

(d) Finally, the keyword is shown in context. If it had been 'monument', to take another difficult word from the Pyramid passage, the word would appear, highlighted in a different colour, in the following extract:

> This impressive monument, standing high on the plains of Giza, was immortalized by Shelley with the words: 'Two vast and trunkless legs of stone stand in the desert. Near them, on the sand, half sunk a shattered visage lies....'

The question is asked: "What would be impressive and stand high on the plains of Giza?" and the student can try to answer, or see a set of contextually acceptable alternatives, e.g. 'building, tower, structure, erection, edifice, pyramid'. Each of these alternatives is displayed in context in the frame sentence. Students who wish to can use the program to memorize these contextual alternatives.

Thus the 'Text Focus' involves a sequence of reading activities relating to a chosen text. The 'Skills Focus' path offers the student a range of programs to practise particular reading skills, such as skimming for gist, scanning for particular information, recognising wordclass, and speeded reading. Among these skills-based programs, 'Shift' concentrates on features of discourse structure by asking the student to discover from where in a text certain extracts have been removed. Both the extracts and the texts are given in book form, and the student refers to them constantly. After picking an extract to work with, the student selects a likely paragraph to house it. The computer displays the chosen paragraph, and the student selects a likely position for the extract to be inserted. The computer inserts the extract in that position so that the student can see how it looks.

The program here works as a sort of elementary word-processor. It also offers fairly detailed feedback if students make mistakes, drawing their attention to features (usually lexical) of the discourse structure:

> You've chosen the wrong paragraph. Consider the linking of 'energy' and 'sun' in the extract. Scan the text to find a similar linking.

The final category of programs are the information files on subjects like wordclass, together with word definitions and examples. Eventually, one would hope to be using on-line dictionaries, thesauruses and corpuses. This seems a promising area for further work.

5 CONCLUSION

CAL does appear to be a medium well-suited for training in reading strategies. Two features in particular characterize these materials:-

— they are based on techniques already in use in the teaching of reading, but try to use the computer only when it has a special contribution to make. The use of CAL when a good teacher with an overhead projector could do just as well has been justifiably criticized [4].

— they try to exploit the computer's powers for information-processing to produce a rich and flexible acquisition/learning environment in which the learner can find the information he or she needs to complete the learning tasks successfully.

References

[1] Harvey, B. (1984), "Why Logo?" in [18].

[2] O'Shea, T. and Self, J. (1983), *Learning and teaching with computers*, Brighton: Harvester Press.

[3] Sloman, A. (1984), "Beginners need powerful systems" in [18].

[4] Thomas, Jenny (forthcoming), "Adapting dBase II: the use of database management systems in English language teaching and research" in Leech, G. and Candlin C. (eds), *Computers in English language teaching and research*, London: Longman.

[5] Fox, J. D. (1984), "Computer assisted vocabulary learning — a humanistic perspective', in Knibbeler, W. and Bernards, Marij (eds), *New approaches in foreign language methodology — 15th AIMAV Colloquium*, Department of Applied Linguistics, University of Nijmegen.

[6] Clarke, D. F. and Nation, I. S. P. (1980), "Guessing the meaning of words from context: strategies and techniques", *System*, 8:

[7] Grellet, Francoise (1981), *Developing reading skills*, Cambridge: Cambridge University Press.

[8] Davies, E. and Whitney, N. (1981), *Strategies for reading: students book*, London: Heinemann Educational Books.

[9] Hosenfeld, Carol (1984), "Case studies of ninth grade readers" in Alderson, J. C. and Urquhart, A. H. (eds), *Reading in a Foreign Language*, London: Longman.

[10] Malone, T. W. (1981), "Toward a theory of intrinsically motivating instruction", *Cognitive Sciences* 4: 333–369.

[11] Krashen, S. D. (1982), *Principles and practice in second language acquisition*, Oxford: Pergamon.

[12] Hatch, Evelyn (1983), *Psycholinguistics*, Rowley, Massachusetts: Newbury House.

[13] Curran, C. A. (1976), *Counseling-learning in second languages*, Apple River, Illinois: Apple River Press.

[14] We are indebted to Michael Johnson (personal communication) for this idea.

[15] Coombs, M. and Alty, J. (1984), "Expert systems: an alternative paradigm", *Int J Man-Machine Studies* 20, 21–43.

[16] Murphy, R. T. and Appel, L. R. (1977), *Evaluation of the Plato IV computer based education system in the community college*, National Science Foundation Contract No. NSF C731. Princeton, New Jersey: Educational Testing Service.

[17] For a more detailed account of the UEA reading programs, see Clarke, D. F. (forthcoming), "Computer-assisted reading: What can the machine really contribute?", *System.* 211–220.

[18] Yazdani, M. (ed), (1984), *New horizons in educational computing*, Chichester: Ellis Horwood.

9

Analysis of conjugation mistakes in French verbs on a microcomputer

Monique L'Huillier, Brunel University

1 INTRODUCTION

The treatment of verbs is probably the area of grammar that has been covered more than anything else in Computer Assisted Language Learning. In this respect, verbs are associated with drill, and drill is associated with kill! And yet, the treatment of verbs in CALL need not be deadly; there is more to the testing of verbs than the plain right/wrong drill approach, particularly as today, we tend to cope with variations in the learner's responses, although the ultimate objective is still accuracy.

Before discussing the program, it may be useful to consider some of the criteria for CALL packages. Certain features of user-friendliness which were not always present in early packages, can now be expected; for example :

— tolerance of upper/lower case, except when the difference is significant (e.g. in German),
— tolerance of extra spaces between words,

and, most important of all,

— a facility to input all necessary diacritics.

Unless conjugated verbs, or indeed vocabulary, are presented in the context of a short sentence, they are tedious to learn and often difficult to retrieve when needed. For instance: "j'allais, tu allais, il allait etc." learned parrot-fashion does not necessarily help the student who wants to say in French: "How about going to a disco tonight?". It is often a surprise to learn that it is the imperfect tense which is required: ("Et si on allait...")

Sound, graphics, animation are all good ingredients for an adventure game, but whether it is necessary to turn a Language Laboratory into an amusement arcade for post 'A' Level students in a vain attempt to sustain their interest is a moot point. Similarly, there is no need to be over facetious in the design of responses. "Ce n'est pas la bonne réponse, imbécile", or words to that effect, may prove to have a totally unwanted reaction.

The conjugation of verbs, as opposed to the use of tenses, can easily be computerized. It is when a grammatical decision involves a personal choice that it is difficult to use the computer to test it. A good example of this is in the use of the subjunctive. The following examples were taken from a French translation of Seymour Papert's *Mindstorms, Jaillissement de l'Esprit*.

a)   "Pour les besoins de la discussion . . . supposons que cette condition *est* réalisée..."
b)   "Cette objection exige qu'il lui *soit* fait face sans détour."

For a computer to attempt to explain why in the first example there is a case for the somewhat unorthodox use of the indicative, whilst in the second there is not, is likely to mean a lot of programming for little reward, at least for the present. In the same way, it is not a good idea to accept almost anything from the student, on the grounds that so long as it is understandable it is acceptable. After all, even French children often do not have innate knowledge of grammar and, to a lesser extent, of vocabulary: these are learnt at school, not just from the parents or the environment. A student who says "Hier je vois mon parents" has probably not made a stylistic choice. On the other hand, one who says "Si j'aurions su, j'serions pas venu", probably has!

2   THE PROGRAM

The present package is an authoring package, but dedicated to a morphological treatment of verbs. The idea is that it should be easy to use whilst enabling teachers to produce good material in a minimum amount of time. (There exist too many very sophisticated authoring packages that have put people off because they were too complicated and, in one case, a three-day course was recently advertised, just to learn how to use the package!)

At the basic level, this program deals with the conjugated verbs in terms of stems and endings. It is extremely easy to implement in that all the teacher has to do, after inputting each example, is to specify the stem. The program reads the student's answer from left to right and from right to left and it also counts the letters. Thus it works out what constitutes the stem and what constitutes the ending. It then gives the appropriate error message: "error in stem" or "error in ending", rather than just saying "wrong", which is annoying, particularly if there is only a letter or an accent missing. It works for all simple tenses, imperfect, future, conditional etc. For compound tenses like the perfect tense, the distinction is made between the auxiliary and the past participle. The teacher specifies the auxiliary and the message is: "error in the auxiliary" or "error in the past participle". It is assumed that the grammar or vocabulary will have been covered in class by the time the student sits at the terminal, so lengthy and cumbersome presentations of the subject on the VDU can be avoided.

At the second, more sophisticated level, the message is called the tutor's message. This second level is necessary because two broad types of verb mistake can be distinguished:

1) A spelling mistake in the stem or the ending, or in the auxiliary or past participle. For example, if the verb is 'aller' and the tense asked for is the perfect.

> Computer: Hier, Paul et moi XXXXXX au théâtre.
> Student: somme allés

The basic message here is adequate:

> Computer: There is an error in the auxiliary verb.

2) The wrong tense is used. For example, 'faire', imperfect.

> C: Albert XXXXXX le ménage quand Marie est entrée.
> S: ferait

Here, two tenses are confused because they look similar. The tutor's message could be:

> C: Vous confondez avec le conditionnel.

Similarly 'faire', conditional.

> C: Il XXXXX plus jeune s'il se coupait la barbe.
> S: faisait

The tutor's message could be:

> C: Vous confondez avec l'imparfait.

And 'croire', imperfect.

> C; Vous ici, je vous XXXXX à Honolulu.
> S: croyez

The tutor's message can be:

> C: Regardez bien la phrase, le sujet n'est pas 'vous' mais 'je'.

(which is more useful than a plain "error in ending"). Now we enter the 'chamber of horrors' with 'aller', conditional.

> C: Cette robe XXXXXX bien avec mes nouvelles chaussures.
> S: allerait

The basic message here would be: "error in stem" but a better hint could be given with:

> C: Voyons! ALLER est un verbe irrégulier!

And 'boire', perfect.

> C: Il XXXXX trop de bière, il va être malade.
> S: a buvé

Here, a plain "error in the past participle" might sound a little weak, so you could say instead:

> C: Quelle horreur que ce participe passé!

We could of course have decided to have both messages:

> "error in stem"

and

> "you are confusing with..."

but this message was considered a little ponderous and it was decided that a tutor's message would take precedence over any message concerning the stem/ending or auxiliary/past participle. In other words, the basic message only appears in the absence of a tutor's message.

The idea of the tutor's message is not to cover all possibilities, i.e. to accept any anagram of the correct answer. This would be tedious for the teacher to work out, and not always helpful for the student. For instance, if you look at the following example for 'aller', subjunctive:

> C: Il faut qu'il XXXXX chercher sa grand-mère à la gare.
> S: aleil

If the computer's answer is:

C: Nearly there but the letters are in the wrong order.

The point is evident! The idea therefore is not to cater for everything or anything, but to input error messages corresponding to genuine errors commonly made by students, and which deserve a special message. What about 'dire', present:

C: Qu'est-ce que vous XXXXX?
S: disez

Here there is room for a humorous response if required, such as:

C: Ah! Vous êtes tombé dans le piège. DIRE est irrégulier avec 'vous'!

But if this proves too time-consuming, the program will simply say:

C: error in ending.

The tutor's error message is particularly useful for the so-called "advent" verbs, i.e. those that are normally intransitive and therefore conjugated with 'être' in the perfect tense, but which can have a transitive meaning, and therefore be conjugated with 'avoir'. For instance, 'sortir', perfect:

C: Catherine, tu XXXXX le chien aujourd'hui?
S: es sortie

Your message can be:

C: 'sortir' est transitif ici, il faut utiliser AVOIR.

Or it could have been:

C: Regardez bien la phrase: 'chien' est le complément d'objet direct de 'sortir', il faut utiliser AVOIR.

The tutor's message should correspond to the emphasis given by the teacher to this particular point of grammar. If a tutor's message for this particular example had not been provided, the program would simply have said:

C: error in auxiliary and past participle

which would not have been as informative. Another example:

C: Catherine, tu XXXXX le chien aujourd'hui?
S: a sorti
C: Attention, regardez bien le sujet.

This may be judged more useful that a bald statement, such as 'error in auxiliary', because of the juxtaposition of 'Catherine' and 'tu'.

The tutor's message should appear whenever an error is predictable, particularly if it is a relatively minor error in the eyes of the student, like a missing accent for instance. Let us look at 'aller', perfect:

C: Hier, Paul et moi XXXXX au théâtre.
S: sommes alles
C: N'oubliez pas l'accent aigu!

(instead of "error in past participle", which could be misleading). And:

C: Hier, Paul et moi XXXXXX au théâtre.
S: allés
C: Ah! L'erreur classique: vous avez oublié l'auxiliaire.

That is if the students, as is often the case, have a tendency to forget the auxiliary. But, in the absence of a tutor's message, the basic message still is:

C: I think the auxiliary is missing.

3   TRANSLATION

Once the error message has been dealt with, another useful feature would be not only to present the verb in the context of a short sentence, but to give its translation in English. It would be wrong here to choose examples whose structure is such that they can be translated literally. On the contrary, as will be seen in the examples there is seldom exact mapping between all items in the source language and items in the sentence in the target language; the sooner students get used to this, the better. Efforts have been made to try and keep the subject matter plausible, whilst taking every opportunity to introduce one of the less expected meanings of a hackneyed verb. (This principle has already been used in the Logifrench series, and has been very well received).

C: Catherine, tu *as sorti* le chien aujourd'hui? (Catherine, have you taken the dog out today?)

where 'sortir' is no longer 'to go out' but 'to take someone or something out'. And:

C: Il *ferait* plus jeune s'il se coupait la barbe. (He would look younger if he cut his beard.)

where 'faire' is no longer 'to make' or 'to do' but one of the meanings of 'to look' (or, to an English ear, 'to look' is one of the meanings of 'faire'!)

Teachers who have been consulted are equally divided on the vexed question of whether to have the instructions, commands etc. in English or in the foreign language. As a result, the present preliminary version offers an abominable mixture of both!

4 CONCLUSION

It it is clear that interesting and even amusing things can be done in the treatment of verbs, without being either too didactic or too trivial. In conclusion, I would like to thank Mr David Martland of Brunel University, who is responsible for the software package to support the courseware mentioned.

10

Computer assisted learning or computer inhibited acquisition?

Brian Farrington, University of Aberdeen

1 PROBLEMS WITH CALL PROGRAMS

The main part of this paper could be described as a sort of cautionary tale. I want to describe a CALL program that I developed recently, which produced some rather disconcerting results in terms of what people learned, and didn't learn, from it. I shall try and draw some conclusions from this experience, and suggest ways in which CALL materials might be able to avoid the effect that I seem to have discovered.

The program is called GENDERS, and it is supposed to teach French noun gender. It works on an Apple and on a BBC B, and can be used on three levels of difficulty or sophistication or whatever. It is a type of Drill and Practice program. When it was first designed, not very many years ago, but, all the same, at a time when CALL in this country was still in its infancy, the only materials available, commercially or otherwise, were Drill and Practice. It seemed then that the majority of these materials could be criticized on five counts.

Firstly, as regards subject matter — what they were supposed to teach — these materials seemed to cater for a very limited public of learners and to be designed essentially for beginners, and with the written language in mind. This seemed a serious disadvantage, since in the early stages of learning a language it is accepted practice to lay more emphasis on speech than on writing. Consequently there was a danger that introducing the computer at this stage could be an irrelevance. Also, as regards subject matter, the materials seemed to be very error-orientated, that is, that rather than inviting the learner to function in the language, they just provoked him or her into making mistakes, which the system could then correct. (My own program did not avoid this particular blemish itself). Maybe more importantly, the exercises I saw seemed to concentrate on linguistic areas which were not necessarily those which a native speaker would consider of primary importance. This is, of course, not a point that concerns just CALL: it is an interesting experiment to take a text written by a learner in, say English, and to give it to two groups of people, one composed of non-native teachers of English, and the other of native English speakers, asking them to underline the mistakes one, two or three times in order of gravity. The differences to be found are often quite striking.

The second main failing of these materials was that they seemed to bear little resemblance to any imaginable model of how the native speaker knows her own language. This was a main failing of many early language laboratory materials: those exercises in which the learner was invited to alter some grammatical element, as, for example, by putting a sentence into a different tense. (A native speaker very rarely has to resituate an utterance in a different time-frame, but if ever it does happen he or she, as likely as not, does it by rephrasing the utterance completely, sometimes without changing the tense at all). In the language laboratory, the move to produce materials that were "contextualized" was of course a reaction in this direction, and produced exercises that approximated more closely to what the language was like when it was being used. But it is not just a matter of context: there is a question of the cognitive processes involved too.

The third failing of these materials was that though considerable ingenuity had gone into their design in many cases, the ingenuity was all to be found in the programming. The actual linguistic content was uninteresting. It seemed to me that if you were developing an entirely new medium for processing language in the interesting interface between the language and the learner, you ought to be discovering new patterns in the language phenomena themselves. If you didn't, then you were probably not innovating enough, and merely mechanizing the traditional.

Fourthly, most of the materials made no effort to instruct at all, let alone teach. Authoring languages, authoring systems, and the materials produced with their help had scanty provision for presenting new knowledge to the learner. Where there was such provision, it taught about the language rather than teaching the language itself.

Finally, on a lower level of generality, but a point of some importance all the same, almost without exception these materials were written entirely in English. In fact for most of the time that the learner was sitting in front of the computer, the screen was at least three quarters covered with English words.

It could be remarked at this juncture that all these criticisms are in no way intended to support the view that Drill and Practice exercises in themselves are of little help to someone trying to learn a foreign language. This is not my opinion: I think that Drill and Practice is of some limited use, and indeed that something the same can be said of Computer Assisted Learning as a whole. If, however, we are to have Drill and Practice, for that matter if we are to have CALL, then it should be as good as it can be made. The five criticisms outlined above can be turned inside out, as it were, to give five general principles for the construction of worthwhile instructional CALL materials. These are not the

Tables of the Law, I hasten to say. But they are the principles I set for myself to try and follow.

1. The subject of an exercise should be relevant and central to the problems of someone trying to learn the language, and the exercise not simply exist because it was easy to program.
2. The exercise should be based at least on an attempt to appreciate what it is in the native speaker's competence that guides him/her in that particular linguistic area.
3. More time should be spent studying the linguistic data involved, than on mere programming. CALL is a powerful new medium: it deserves something better than the adaptation of Stannard Allen or Whitmarsh to trendy graphics.
4. The exercise should contain information about the linguistic data being processed, so that the learner can use it to obtain new knowledge. In other words one should aim a little higher than a mere mechanization of "Please hear me my grammar homework".
5. A CALL exercise should oblige, and stimulate, the learner to interact with the system in the language being learnt.

2 SOME SOLUTIONS

The five principles outlined above were distilled as I struggled to design a CALL exercise that would be worthy of the medium. First of all, regarding the subject matter, I chose what is certainly the most enduring difficulty for an English speaker learning French, namely noun gender. It is, admittedly, somewhat of an old-fashioned problem these days, and one that makes little difference to a learner's communicative competence. It seemed attractive firstly because it was difficult to see how you could teach people to get the gender of nouns right, and secondly, because, probably for that very reason, it was not dwelt upon in most of the manuals I could find. Most French courses indicate certain categories of nouns that fall under one or the other gender, or list the most frequent troublespots. Some provide pieces of largely irrelevant information, such as that "nouns derived from Latin have the same gender as their Latin original". Everything consulted saw the problem uniquely in terms of the written language; none attempted to deduce a system of rules, or encouraged the learner to try to establish one. Yet it is clear that there is a system, that the phenomenon is not haphazard, and that the answer is probably to be found by examining the most frequent words in everyday use, and looking for a pattern there.

This brings me to my second point, that an exercise should be related as far as possible to whatever it is in the native speaker's competence that guides him/her in that particular linguistic area. How is it that French native speakers know the gender of nouns? I thought I had found an answer as I interrogated my French acquaintances and watched what they did whenever I asked them about a word that was, as it were, on the fringe of their competence. Certain words were much more likely than others to cause people to hesitate, and by people I mean lively, talkative, ordinary speakers and not amateur, or for that matter professional, grammarians. Invariably these were words which for reasons of chance, collocational or phonetic, only rarely occurred in environments where the gender was audibly marked. It was all a question of how tightly woven, so to speak, the texture of the language was at those points. Put more simply: if you ask a French native speaker the gender of a word and there is any uncertainty, he or she will try it with an adjective. That was the way I should make my exercise work. If the learner didn't know the gender of one of the nouns the system threw at him/her, the computer would present it in context with an adjective or other form that drew audible attention to the gender.

Regarding the third point, namely that the main effort should go into processing, and understanding, the linguistic data involved, it is true that the program itself is a very simple one. It just presents the learner with twenty words picked at random from a file, and asks him/her to indicate the gender by typing CE or CET or CETTE. As far as the language was concerned there were two fairly time-consuming jobs to be done. First to decide what words to include, and then to find contexts that go with them. If the exercise was to be at all serious, it would have to have access to quite a large number of words. But what words?

An obvious answer would be to concentrate on the hard words, the indeterminate ones, the ones that after years of learning French we still get wrong. That would be to make the classic mistake of the traditional grammarian and give more importance to the exception than to the rule. It would be particularly unhelpful here where we do not yet know what the rules are. Therefore the exercise was initially made on two levels, and the words selected from a frequency count. The first level contained all the nouns in the initial list of *Le Français Fondamental* [1]; the second, which was a longer list of just under 350, contained all the nouns found in the *Dictionnaire du Français Fondamental* [2]. It is easy to criticise *Le Français Fondamental*, but it remains the most useful frequency count of French, and the only one based on the spoken language. Since these are, as near as has ever been calculated, the words that French people hear and use most often, they are, first, the most important words for a learner to use correctly, and also, and more importantly, since they are the nouns most often heard, they are the ones from which native speakers, learning their own French language, must learn the rules from. In all the two main files contained just under 600 nouns, each one with appropriate context. There is a third file, which is much shorter, and which is constructed on a different principle. This was added afterwards, and contains conventionally "difficult" words of the sort mentioned a moment ago, masculine nouns ending with -e, feminine nouns ending in a consonant, nouns beginning with a vowel which rarely collocate with an audibly marked adjective, learned or otherwise infrequent words.

One interesting fact that was noticed while compiling the list of contexts, mostly single adjectives or past participles, was the small number of these which are audibly marked for gender, and consequently the large quantity of contexts in everyday speech in which distinction of noun gender is neutralized. The principle was to find for each noun a context, adjective or past participle, in which the gender was marked audibly as well as visually, and also which was in common use, and therefore useful to learn in its own right. For some words it was extremely difficult to find such a context at all, and certainly very hard to find one that it might be useful for a learner to notice, and maybe remember.

The fourth point was that the exercise should if necessary teach the learner something he or she did not know. In an exercise such as this one, which is not presenting the learner with a new chapter of grammatical information so much as darning the threadbare patches of his/her knowledge, there was obviously no point in putting lists of words and contexts on the screen. But it did seem useful to help, or indeed oblige, the learner to memorize the genders and contexts that he or she did not know. So when a wrong answer is received by the system the following annoying routine is followed. The context appears on the screen for a few seconds, and disappears. In order to proceed the learner has to type it from memory. It was hoped that this brief visit, on the part of a carefully selected collocation, to the learner's short term memory would mean that a substantial proportion of the words and contexts thus typed out would end up by being remembered.

Finally all the instructions as to how to work through the exercise are of course in French, and the system comes up with a variety of comments on the learner's responses. These are for the most part fairly flippant, with a jocularity reminiscent of some early CALL materials, but it was decided that this would be acceptable, as long as they were in the target language. In any case the remarks that the system produces are all useful colloquial French expressions.

To recap briefly, the system picks twenty words at a time from the file, and presents each word on the screen, inviting the learner to type CE or CET or CETTE. If the gender is right the next word appears. If it is incorrect then the learner is presented with the word and a context in which it is audibly and visibly marked for gender.

>   System: GUERRE
>   Student: CE
>   System: CETTE GUERRE FROIDE

This context disappears and the learner then has to type it in from memory before the exercise can proceed. There is a simple scoring scheme, and if at any point the learner types "T" a translation of the word or context is given.

Now I come to the disconcerting effect that I have mentioned. The exercise was given to our First Year students in Aberdeen. Where possible I watched them working through it or discussed it with them after they had worked at it for half an hour or so. A number of them remarked to me that one effect of working through this exercise was that they felt as a result less sure of the gender of the nouns that had been presented by the system than they had before doing the exercise. Nobody likes to find that their clever teaching gimmick actually has the result of leaving the learners with less knowledge afterwards than they had before they started. So I investigated more systematically and found that a significant number of the more thoughtful students and colleagues had noticed a similar effect. Also I had to admit that I had noticed something of the same sort happening myself as I worked on the material for the data files. Finding examples, typing out the contexts, trying out the exercise itself over and over again had had the effect that words, of which I certainly had known the gender before, suddenly set me hesitating. And the more I thought about them the less sure I felt as to what gender they were.

I am not sure what explanation to suggest for this effect. It could be that the exercise generated the same sort of uncertainty that can occur over the spelling of certain words. Or that the learner is affected in the same way as the water-spider in Belloc's rhyme, who

> "Skims across the water's face
> With ease, celerity, and grace,
> And if he ever stopped to think
> Of how he did it, he'd sink."

Or, more significantly, it could be the result of an unhappy interference between formal and informal learning.

3   CONCLUSIONS

Most applied linguists agree that language learning involves separate processes, whether they are to be seen, as by Ellis [3], as two types of learning, informal and formal, or as two qualitatively different, and entirely separate things, one of which is not called learning at all, as in Krashen's distinction between 'acquisition' and 'learning' [4]. Though there are many linguists who would not accept Krashen's claim that the two sorts of learning are entirely independent of each other, it is not at all clear, if a transfer of knowledge takes place between the two, how this happens, or how one type of learning can influence the other. In commonsense terms, formal learning gives the learner explicit knowledge, a conscious cognitive grasp of the linguistic facts: this knowledge eventually becomes automatic, implicit, but how this transfer is brought about, or occurs, is not at all understood.

What seems to happen with GENDERS is that the formal learning is actually undoing the work of acquisition. One thing that seemed to confirm this explanation was that the effect was more noticeable in the case of words in the third level file, which was not compiled on the basis of any frequency count but made up, synthetically so to speak, of conventionally 'difficult' or 'tricky' words. It was as though summoning the partly internalized, partly implicit, knowledge back into the glaring daylight of formal, conscious, explicitness was too much for it. If this explanation is right, then it suggests that there is a sixth general principle, more important than the five enumerated above, which is that, if Drill and Practice exercises are to be used then they must be integrated very carefully into the rest of the coursework, in the hope that the effect may be counteracted by intensive contextualization.

I have suggested elsewhere [5] that the very term CAL is unfortunate for various reasons. One of these reasons is that, by implying the existence of a separate entity, the term CAL gives substance to the notion that learning assisted by computer is a different type of learning to any other, and that something happens between learner and computer that does not happen in other circumstances. We need to remember that though the computer may be the most powerful resource available to a teacher, it is still only a resource. There may come a day when computer-based systems can take charge of language learning. I personally do not believe this, but one thing is certain: that day is not yet here.

To return to French noun gender, it may be that this is best learnt in an entirely different way. How, in fact do French people know the gender of nouns? In the first scientific study of the phenomenon ever undertaken, Tucker, Lambert and Rigault [6] make the point that "The French speaker's skill with grammatical gender appears to represent an aspect of rule-governed behaviour which may be largely influenced by recurring environmental regularities". I can remember, if you will excuse the anecdote, coming to something like the same conclusion when my two French children were small. I used to try them with nonsense words (Viens voir les grufles au fond du jardin) and try to get them to come out with an utterance which specified the gender of the neologism ('C'est quoi un grufle?'). It seemed clear that a fairly powerful system of regularities was guiding the choice of gender word. Tucker et al. analysed a corpus of nearly 32000 nouns, the word-list of the Petit Larousse dictionary. Some of their conclusions are extremely interesting, and they do confirm that this is indeed an example of rule-governed behaviour. It seems to me, however, that while analysis of the language as a whole, or a very large sample, as here, may show many significant regularities, the patterns by which a French-speaking child acquires the main rules are probably much simpler, since they depend on a very much smaller vocabulary.

A short study being undertaken at the moment in Aberdeen will analyse a 200 page transcript from the Nuffield Child Language Survey [7]. The nouns are to be transcribed in IPA, and then sorted according to word-ending, frequency and gender. It is hoped that this examination of a representative sample of nouns actually used by children of 8 to 10 years old will give an indication of the major regularities behind gender categorization. This in itself could provide the raw material of some useful exercises, which even if they are not CALL exercises in themselves would merit the name of computer assisted learning, since that is what they would effectively be.

One possible strategy would be to build the rules, when they are discovered, into a program for Exploratory learning. The idea then would be to make use of the ideas put forward in Johns [8]. Johns describes a program, written for a Sinclair ZX81, which "knows" the rules for the formation of plurals for nouns in English, or at least most of the rules. The object of working through the program is to discover how much the system does know, and to use it to "puzzle out" the underlying regularities of the target language [9]. Such a technique applied to the learning of French noun gender would not be suited to remedial learning, or to self-access for that matter. It might be best exploited by being incorporated in some sort of language game. It would probably not be much help with the gender of anomalous words such as GENS, or that of words like AXE which French people have to learn explicitly anyway. But if it were possible, using the research I have described, to approximate to a model of the competence of, say, a 7 year-old native speaker, and to impart that to a learner we would have done something entirely new, and therefore worthy of this marvellous new medium.

References

[1] Gougenheim, G. et al. (1956), *L'Elaboration du Français Elementaire*, Didier Paris.

[2] Gougenheim, G. (1958), *Dictionnaire Fondamental de la Langue Française*, Didier.

[3] Ellis, Rod (1985), "The L1 = L2 hypothesis; a reconsideration", *System* 13, 1.

[4] Krashen, S. (1981), *Second Language Acquisition and Second Language Learning*, Pergamon.

[5] Farrington, B. (1984), "Computer-Assisted Language Learning, an Overview", *AFLS Newsletter* No 9.

[6] Tucker, G. R. et al. (1977), *The French Speaker's Skill with Grammatical Gender*, Mouton.

[7] Nuffield Foreign Languages Teaching Materials Project Occasional Papers No 39. Language Materials Development Unit, University of York.

[8] Johns, T. F. (1982), "Exploratory CAL: an alternative use of the computer in teaching foreign languages", *Computers and ELT*, British Council.

[9] Corder, S. Pit (1973), *Introducing Applied Linguistics*, Penguin.

11

New approaches to computer aided language learning

Jonathan Barchan, University of Exeter

1 THE POTENTIAL CONTRIBUTION OF AI TO MODERN LANGUAGE TEACHING

Before discussing the potential contribution of Artificial Intelligence (AI) techniques to CAL in general, and Modern Language Teaching in particular, a few suggestions are proposed as to why computers should be used at all to aid teaching:

1) The computer can save the human tutor's time by correcting 'simple' errors. Even at University level, first-year students are apt to make relatively straightforward errors to which a computer program should be able to draw their attention and offer remedial advice, thus freeing the human tutor for more advanced work.
2) The computer is always available and has unlimited time and patience.
3) The computer is currently able to attract a good deal of student interest which hopefully helps to increase their motivation. It can even help to make some useful but not very stimulating tasks more interesting.

However, AI techniques and approaches have much more than this to offer Modern Language Teaching. Some of the potential advantages to be gained by their use are:

1) The whole AI approach seeks a knowledge of the natural language which it is attempting to teach. This is in contrast to the 'dumb' conventional approach to computer-based tutoring systems. The fundamental difference between the two is that the latter is usually supplied in advance with the right (and possibly wrong) expected answers from the student but has no knowledge of what makes one version correct and another incorrect, nor of the processes involved in reaching these solutions; but in the former case, the sort of Intelligent Tutoring Systems (ITS) which AI techniques can produce possess, to a greater or lesser degree, a set of rules which attempt to provide this knowledge.

2) Less human input is required to prepare and re-prepare tutoring tasks since, for example, there is no need to tell the system which answers are right or wrong as it is able to deduce this for itself.

3) As an extension to 2) above, it is not necessary for the human expert to anticipate every possible student error.

4) AI techniques should enable a good ITS to recognise the cause of an error which it detects in the student input. This should permit it to generate helpful remedial advice, rather than just telling him/her that their answer is 'wrong' and stating what it should have been, as is so often the case in traditional systems.

5) The knowledge base and inference mechanism supplied by an AI system provides a kernel around which such further tutoring aids as a user model or a teaching strategy can be based. This seems to be an essential prerequisite for such further developments since there does not appear to be much use in having a good model or strategy if the program is weak in the knowledge of the domain which it is purporting to teach.

Work has been undertaken at the University of Exeter to produce such systems exemplifying the application of AI techniques to the teaching of Modern Languages. To date two such projects are under development with the intention of more to follow. It should be mentioned that these systems have been developed in the Department of Computer Science in close cooperation with the Department of French and Italian. It is of the utmost importance to make clear from the start that these programs are designed as TOOLS for teaching Modern Languages: in no respect is it envisaged that they should attempt to replace the human teacher, nor is it claimed that they alone will actually teach a language. Any reference to their trying to teach a language should therefore be viewed in this light and interpreted as their attempting to aid in language teaching as a helpful tool to supplement certain aspects of the course. Furthermore, both programs described below are only kernels around which a powerful tutoring system could, and should, be built if they are actually to be used as part of a course

2 FRENCH GRAMMAR ANALYSER (FGA)

The 'French Grammar Analyser' (FGA) program [1] began as an attempt at a rational reconstruction of FROG [2]. However, as we intend to show, we have made significant improvements to the theory behind the previous work, in addition to incorporating some of the best ideas to be found in FROG.

FGA resembles FROG in two important respects: firstly, it shares the teaching strategy of allowing the entry of sentences in free French which are then parsed and errors reported, rather than traditional 'drill-and-practice'; and secondly, the implementation language is Prolog [3]. FGA is basically an exercise in pattern matching along the same lines as FROG, but in the sophistication offered by Prolog differs radically from earlier 'dumb' versions such as Last's [4] and Farrington's [5].

Four distinct design features typify FGA's goals and strengths:

1) it has been designed for future work;
2) robustness is of prime importance in parsing;
3) only a subset grammar and dictionary for French is provided;
4) it generates constructive error messages for teaching purposes.

We now examine each of these aspects and their implications.

1) *Future work*: In order to ease the task of future extensions, we have gone to great pains to write FGA in a highly modular fashion. This sort of 'open-ended' approach to programming is held to be of particular importance in the field under consideration: because no finite solution can (yet) be seen in the area of natural language parsing, the author of any system must recognise the need for further development and extension of his ideas by someone else in the future and should design his program accordingly. It is our opinion that, although Imlah and du Boulay recognised and drew attention to this requirement, in practice we have succeeded better in realising it.

2) *Robustness*: Like FROG, FGA anticipates grammatically incorrect input and the need to parse successfully such input to its best degree, rather than simply giving up. There is also a need to handle grammatically correct but unanticipated structures. When a seemingly erroneous lexeme, word group or structure is encountered there are, effectively, two different explanations: if we take the case of an individual word, it may appear in the dictionary but be incorrect in some sense, or it may be potentially quite correct but not in the dictionary. The same holds for structures and the grammar. We are particularly aware of this latter danger when attempting to cope with unknown words, resorting to intelligent guesses dependent on position and spelling to identify their most probable identity and attributes and also informing the user of the assumptions made. To this end a pre-parse section is employed whose task is to make all

possible guesses about the role and characteristics of an unidentifiable lexeme. The subsequent parse phase is thus greatly simplified since all words can be treated as if they were 'known'. It will not have to generate alternative solutions, but rather can simply select from among the alternatives provided by the pre-parser as necessary.

3) *Subset grammar and dictionary*: FGA, like FROG and all other attempted natural language parsers, is based on only a subset of the complete French grammar and dictionary. In fact, FGA's subset is more restricted than that of FROG. However, it is felt that the latter may have tended to be somewhat over-ambitious in the extent of its attempted coverage of the language and thereby lost the generality, clarity and modularity considered so essential in 1) above. Given the constraints within which the work must be done, we think it better to produce solid work on a small subset alone than to attempt too much with a larger cross-section and end up with grammar rules, parsing mechanics and so on permanently intertwined on an 'ad hoc' basis. We further believe that it is reasonable to hope that thorough analysis of a subset implies that in principle the ideas (with necessary modifications) should provide a sound platform for tackling progressively larger sets of the whole. For example, the pre-parser's guesses as to the likely identity of an unrecognised word based on its spelling alone achieve some ninety percent success rate. This shows the potential for future development.

4) *Error reporting*: The top-down grammar used by FGA's parser permits expected incorrect structures to be incorporated into the grammar with an appropriate error message tag. The program can thus be used in a rigorous environment such as drill-and-practice if so desired. The result is a system which is capable of trapping the more mundane mistakes on its own while allowing a useful message to be generated for a particular purpose.

An unsuccessful parse is still able to communicate those mistakes detected before the failure to the error reporter. Furthermore, although the program does not implement a least-cost error analysis, the door is left open for such a future improvement. Finally, the power of the 'dual direction' of Prolog is utilised to generate correct forms from incorrect ones. The user can then be informed of what such-and-such an incorrect word 'should be', hopefully thus providing a most useful teaching lesson.

In summary, it must be stated that many of the best ideas behind FGA were encouraged by those in FROG and that many of the criticisms levelled against the latter should be viewed in this light. We consider FROG to be an excellent introduction to the use of AI techniques in the sphere of computer-aided language learning, and FGA to have concentrated on and clarified many of the most progressive features of its forerunner with a view towards future development in this area.

3 LANGUAGE INDEPENDENT GRAMMATICAL ERROR REPORTER (LINGER)

Drawing on what we regard as the most powerful aspects of FROG and FGA, work is currently being undertaken to try to produce a 'Language INdependent Grammatical Error Reporter' (LINGER) to be used as a computer-aided language teaching tool. While FROG and FGA can deal only with French, a language independent program would, it is hoped, be equally at home with any language, given a grammar, dictionary and set of error messages appropriate to that language. The motivation behind the project lies in the apparent duplication of effort in research involved in the separate development of tutoring systems for languages which share so many common features.

Initial research has been limited to Western European languages only — French, German, Italian and Spanish — while some thought has been given to the particular problems posed by English. These languages, all more or less closely related to Latin, share certain common characteristics which may facilitate the production of a sufficiently general 'shell' capable of parsing, and recognising mistakes in, sentences in that language. It is not claimed that these similarities would remain were an unrelated language, such as Japanese, to be included in the group. Particular interest centres on the two languages of French and German since they both resemble and differ from each other in many respects.

Many difficulties are encountered in the attempt to produce such a language independent system. To take just one example, consider determiner-noun agreements in French and German. In the former language we have to consider both gender and number agreement; but the situation is greatly complicated in the latter since the case (nominative, accusative, dative, genitive) of the noun group must be taken into account as well, which involves information about the function which it is playing in the sentence as a whole.

The objectives of the research are as follows:

1) Interaction with the student should be in the form of free sentence entry, as is the case in FROG and FGA. Typed input is parsed and any grammatical errors are recognized: initially, in common with its predessors, LINGER will only deal with the syntax of sentences, though it is hoped that further development will lead to the inclusion of some form of semantic checking. This allows the greatest degree of flexibility and variety of possible applications to which the system might be put, although considerable thought would be required to decide how precisely it should be configured for actual use with students.

2) The system should have the kind of knowledge of the language that it is attempting to teach which AI techniques are able to offer, as outlined above. Specifically, it should be capable of producing legitimate sentences based on the roots of the words encountered in the student's input through the use of the grammatical rules applicable in the particular language. Any discrepancies between

the computer's and student's versions could thus be commented upon and corrected.

3) Stress has been laid on simplicity in the design of the system: the dictionary and grammar should be writable by a linguist rather than by an AI specialist; the shell should be intelligible, maintainable and expandable to allow future enhancement.

4) A great deal of attention has been paid to one area of weakness shared by FROG and FGA: the difficulty of distinguishing parser from dictionary from grammar from error reporter. A goal has been the specification of dictionary, grammar and errors in a clear and logical fashion such that they are easily intelligible both to the language independent shell and at the same time to the human teacher, which obviously eases his/her task in 3) above.

5) LINGER has been designed to be as general as possible to permit its application to as yet unanticipated languages. It is hoped that it might be put to use outside traditional natural languages, such as computer languages or toy languages designed for a specific purpose (e.g. as a front-end to another computer language) where it is still necessary to check grammar. To this end as few presuppositions as feasible about grammar rules have been incorporated so as not to preclude any unusual cases: for example, the shell has no knowledge of the existence or characteristics of nouns, verbs etc., but the grammar and dictionary files supply all the necessary information about their behaviour in an individual language.

6) The final objective of the project will be to determine the feasibility, or impracticality, of the production of language independent tutoring aids as an alternative to the development of individual computer-based tutors for each and every particular language, and to compare its effectiveness with language dependent systems.

4 CONCLUSION

The progression from traditional CAL to FROG to FGA to LINGER can be summed up as an increasing movement away from programs constructed to perform a specific task towards tools of ever greater generality. The objective is to produce systems of great flexibility which possess a knowledge of their domain and which can be put to a wide variety of potential uses according to the imagination of a human tutor and the needs of students. From a technical point of view, the movement is also away from procedural-type programs with implicit knowledge representation towards declarative programs which exhibit an explicit knowledge representation of their domain through clearly distinguishable and intelligible data structures. This is an important step along the path to producing powerful computer-based teaching tools and should be of benefit not only to Computer Assisted Language Learning but also to the more general field of Computer Assisted Learning as a whole.

The author gratefully acknowledges the support offered by SERC.

References

[1] Barchan, J. , Woodmansee, B. and Yazdani, M. (1985), "A Prolog-based tool for French Grammar Analysis", *Instructional Science*, Vol. 14.

[2] Imlah, W. and du Boulay, B. (1985), *Robust natural language parsing in computer assisted language instruction*, Cognitive Studies Programme, University of Sussex.

[3] Clocksin, W. and Mellish, C. (1981), *Programming in Prolog*, Springer-Verlag.

[4] Last, R, (1979) "On-line computer-assisted Modern Language learning", *Modern Languages* Vol. 60.

[5] Farrington, B. (1985), *A Micro-Computer program for checking translation at sentence level*, University of Aberdeen.

12

Help levels in CALL materialS

Dennis Ager, Aston University

1 INTRODUCTION

This chapter aims to classify and systematize knowledge about communication with learners in CALL programs. It is particularly designed to review ways in which help is provided for such learners, and to examine the nature of the help.

Help is provided for learners in a number of ways that are not immediately obvious when the particular program is run. The conception of the program itself, and the clarification of the approach to be adopted in specifying how to teach, test or practise the particular grammar point, vocabulary item, manipulative or communicative skill involved are fundamental, but program design and efficiency are also important.

The presentation of instant help as the student works through the material is more obviously the concern of the present paper, which will hence be concerned mainly with questions of instructional discourse, levels of help and triggers causing help to be provided.

The research background to this paper lies in a mixture of work on discourse and discourse analysis [1], on computer education [2], and on student learning in foreign languages [3], together with a gradually increasing flow of works dealing more directly with CALL (referenced in the bibliography to Ahmad et al. [4]). From all these it is evident that CALL on microcomputers is a developing area in which many practical and theoretical problems remain to be solved, among them the significant one of discovering ways of ensuring that programs actually help students learn.

2 ASSUMPTIONS

The assumptions from which we start are by now more or less axiomatic in British CALL materials, and we shall not therefore provide supporting argument for their adoption. Most of them derive from an approach to language learning and teaching which places a high value on communicative ability, defined as the ability to interact meaningfully with other human beings within the infinite diversity of human experience. The microcomputer is not **yet** a fully interactive device in this sense: the major part of currently available software does not use videodisc or computer-controlled recorders and thus loses even the visual and the audio aspect of direct communication, let alone the gestural and situational ones which underly sociolinguistic meaning.

1. CALL is for students: this means

    — learning not teaching
    — learner control
    — reinforcement and not innovative learning

2. Help is for individual students and is supportive: it is not intended to replace initial teaching. Likewise too much help can be overwhelming, and students should in general be able to select the amount of help they receive.
3. The design of a standard one-off CALL program normally falls into one of the following types:

    a. Grammatical explanation of an item, or explanation (or translation) of a vocabulary item, followed by exercises, themselves followed by a quiz. Example: CLEF
    b. Test of a grammatical point or vocabulary item followed by correction and help. Example: EDUCA2.
    c. .A situation is presented, followed by a quiz, an invitation to create appropriate text, or a simulation. Example: LOAN, HAMMURABI.
    d. Text creation: generative programs in which the student assembles meaningful language from building bricks such as words or stems and endings.
    e. Heuristic programs following for example storage paths for information held in the computer. Example: GETRAENKE
    f. Text and guidance, leading to exercises, quiz or manipulation of the text. Example: STORYBOARD

We should perhaps note Higgins' [5] list of the manipulative possibilities: deletion, insertion, reordering and substitution. These fit neatly into applied linguistic orthodoxy, but exclude skills of direct relevance to foreign language learning, particularly if bilingual exercises are contemplated or if training in the skills themselves forms part of the course objectives. Such obvious manipulations as translation, summarizing or expanding text, and rephrasing (as in stylistic changes or intra-language varieties translation (discourse to discourse transfer)) need to be added.

Authoring systems, template programs or tutors' aids are not included in the above list, although naturally they offer examples of instructional dialogue which can often be varied to suit the preferences of courseware writers. Example: QUESTIONMASTER

There are many other ways in which CALL programs can be, and have been, classified: according to their main purpose, their intended users, their internal characteristics and by many other criteria. The purpose of the present classification is merely to indicate the range of possibilities so far realised; there is little doubt that innovation and modification will in the future add to the list and cause us to revise our understanding of the field.

3   BACKGROUND

3.1   Program design

Support for student learning is an integral part of the design of any educational materials. Hence materials producers must anticipate student approaches to the material, anticipate problems and ensure that the student interacts with the materials in the way intended — or that the materials are flexible enough to cope with a variety of student approaches.

We are frequently told that computer-assisted learning, and particularly CALL, is ipso facto interactive, perhaps most baldly by the Kennings:

> "An essential feature of CALL material is that it is conversational, interactive" [6]

In the present paper let us limit ourselves to considering ways in which program designers do — and could — interact directly with students within an individual program. Although the nature and style of the student's responses is important in considering the whole picture of interaction, we consider that so few widely available CALL programs are actually fully interactive in the normal, rather than in the Kennings' sense, that it would be impossible to systematize student response across the whole field. The only fully interactive, conversational language learning system is the dialogue between teacher (or teacher as informant) and student; if this were not so the claims to replace teachers by machines might have some substance. CALL systems can model some types of interaction and imitate some types of conversational interchange, but they still lack so much that makes inter-human conversation real, that only in certain limited cases have we yet obtained anything other than language-like behaviour and human-like behaviour.

We deliberately leave general program design considerations on one side, and do not consider the role of the program within the total learning experience of the student. Hence the help to which students are entitled in selecting programs, in deciding whether to use the computer at all, in using the program to their own advantage, and help which students are entitled to expect from good design of their overall learning experience, is not included in the present paper.

Likewise the integration of CALL programs into the classroom is not part of our concern here. Using the computer as an intelligent blackboard, in direct support of the teacher, contrasts strongly with what is now the normal use of CALL: the student or small groups of students working by themselves.

3.2 Personalization

We also leave out of account the whole question of humanizing programs and personalizing them. Kenning and Kenning [6] point out how much more friendly it is when the computer can address help messages to the student by name, and how personalizing address enables freer interaction. Similarly Paramskas [7] describes the CLEF use of students' names; however others (e.g. [8]) consider such matters trivial in the context of individualizing instruction, and see as more important such matters as learner control of pace and path.

Programs such as ELIZA which attempt to simulate natural dialogue are too complex for most CALL environments, but randomization of messages is quite common, with the program selecting from a range of alternatives to a straight "no" : "*Not quite!*", "*Not really!*", "*Incorrect!*", "*Sorry, it's not that one*", "*Hard luck!*", "*Have another go*", "*Well, not really!*".

4   TEACHER ROLES

Higgins & Johns [9] briefly comment on roles the teacher adopts in the process of teaching foreign languages: manager of routines, responder, facilitator, model, informant. This rather more elaborate list supersedes simplistic contrasts between teacher as magister and teacher as pedagogue [5] which reflects the dichotomy noted by those opposed to the "totalitarian classroom", and who prefer to see teachers in the role of informants and guides.

Language teaching has always suffered from the necessity for teachers to play God. In many other subjects it is much easier to enable students to learn: in geography, history and the social sciences by reading for themselves and discovering data; in the sciences by experimentation, discovering laws and principles; and in the arts by performance. In languages students generally have to be told, and have to listen while they're told, so a simple elimination of the teacher is much less likely. It is not surprising that orthodox teacher training in languages assumes active oral interchange in the classroom, with the teacher developing the expertise of pupils by constantly questioning, presenting, representing and manipulating the form of the question and the material being learnt. It is precisely the form of the information, the medium as well as the message, which is important.

5   INSTRUCTIONAL PATTERNS: DIALOGUE, MONOLOGUE AND LEARNER STYLES

Rushby points out that most educational interaction in computer-assisted learning has been dependent on the insights of programmed learning [2]. The 'standard' sequence involved in this approach assumes that a text, or a frame of some other information cast as a minimal step, is presented to the student; that questions based on this data are provided for the student to answer; that if the answer is correct, reinforcement or other approval is immediately provided and the student moves on to the next step or phase, whereas if the answer is wrong the student is diverted to a re-presentation of the material, to an alternative presentation of the material, or to some other re-teaching sequence and is not allowed to move on to the next step until he has demonstrated mastery by a re-test.

In this process the 'trigger' which determines the path to which the student is directed is the answer he gives to the question or questions posed at the conclusion of the learning sequence. In computing terms this trigger can be a simple, complete or partial match of the answer with a stored correct version, based on a keyword match; or it may be a much more complex affair involving a syntactic analysis of the student response to determine the degree of acceptability of the answer.

Programmed learning can be an inflexible instructional approach; indeed, in order to work effectively according to the theory, it should impose complete barriers to progression until mastery of earlier stages has been achieved. It hence contrasts sharply with notions of student self-paced learning and particularly with the concept that the student should decide for himself whether he repeats the exercise he got wrong, whether he should review material he clearly is not sure of or whether he should be allowed to by-pass what's good for him. Such simple and frequent devices as the "Press C to continue" instruction, enabling slow readers to be slow, hence contrast with such concepts as timed reading slots and forced branching. Nonetheless the basic concepts of programmed learning — itemized learning, sequenced learning, item testing and branching — are now accepted as axiomatic. It is clear from any review of actual programs, too, that the idea of splitting language into small teachable units has been accepted as normal [4].

Learning styles were also reported on in Rushby, with four approaches being identified: the instructional, revelatory, conjectural, and emancipatory [2].

Whether an understanding of the nature of these helps or has affected the way in which CALL writers operate does not clearly emerge from the programs we have seen: most dialogue between program and student seems based on common-sense principles rather than on any deep understanding of learner psychology. Thus for example there are different views on the value of graphics, sound, colour and other arcade goodies in instructional materials, with some authors discovering that not all students are positively motivated by them and that some indeed are negative towards such enhancements.

Likewise the idea that the computer can act as drudge, rehearsing the boring bits of language learning (in monologue) while the teacher gets on with the interesting bits in face-to-face exchange (dialogue), while superficially attractive, does not seem on the face of it destined to lead to interesting and exciting programs.

Certainly instructional/tutorial programs — or aspects of programs — in which information is passed to students contrasts with the quiz (revelatory ?) in which knowledge is tested, and with the untested or rehearsal aspect of programs (conjectural ?). It is by no means essential that any individual program contains any of these.

It is perhaps the emancipatory aspect which is less frequently met: students are not generally encouraged to use the computer as an equivalent to a personalized dictionary to aid rapid look-up while they carry out an exercise on paper, and the idea of recording personally useful information of value in the learning process (bibliography, useful quotations, time and learning management) has not been widely pursued, although such programs, along with development of the essay-writing and text processing skills, might be the next stage.

Likewise recent language learning theories do not do much to help program design: Krashen's Monitor Theory does not really do much to help programmers to understand their craft, except to make it clear that CALL is all about learning rather than acquisition.

6 CLASSIFICATION OF HELP PROCEDURES

6.1 Indirect help

Indirect help is defined as assistance which the program designer thinks might be of use to the student; it assumes that the student may not necessarily ask the right questions — or enough questions — and hence is more subtle than the direct form of help which provides immediate answers to questions posed by the student.

6.2   Instructional dialogue

6.2.1   *Presentation of programs*

Program presentation is itself a form of assistance to students: pleasing presentation of information, intelligent use of reading aids such as colour and highlighting, the supportive use of sound and graphics, all aid or speed up comprehension by the student of what he is supposed to do when faced with a keyboard and a screen. Although many young people these days are quite familiar with arcade games and the ways in which they expect interaction to take place, not everybody is, and in any case neither the arcade tradition nor the computing tradition is necessarily appropriate for student learning needs.

Nonetheless there are aspects of program presentation of an even more basic type which present unnecessary difficulties to students: unexplained flashing cursors or other prompts, oversimplified messages, unclear instructions: the list is endless. And poor program design leading to unnecessary slowness of execution or limits on flexibility can be matched by poor program conception leaving the poor student wondering what it is exactly the program wants him to do or what it is exactly the program intends to teach him: some programs are quite amazingly frivolous in conception and purpose and look more like gimmicks than serious learning aids. Although at the moment CALL is a novelty for many, if it is to be successful it will have to be accepted by the student body at large as having a valid purpose and function.

6.2.2   *Menus and selection*

Menus of choices are now the normal way in which students initially meet the computer. The irritating blank screen and meaningless prompt is reserved for the programmer, and students are faced with choice, whether keyed by number or letter. This is the user-friendly approach and each menu is characterised by a selection process, including an abort facility, an explanation of the menu options if they are at all complicated, access to further help if needed, and a simple process of getting things moving once the selection has been made.

The user-friendly approach is not always taken to its logical conclusion, however, and some menus do not contain the necessary "finish" option; if they do, some untidy programs do not reset the machine to its original neutral state, but leave it in the program's colour mode and perhaps with other machine features set (e.g. character sets).

Word-based menus are the obvious way of presenting choices. If it is a matter of a simple binary choice, a simple question appears, often at top or bottom of screen, together with an indication of how to signal the response (Another go ? Y/N). Likewise if a binary choice is offered at some point within the program, the normal way of accepting the response is to check for only one of the possibilities, assuming any other response to equate to the other. Since the aim of the menu is to act as a gateway to other things, the least time and space spent on it the better, so keys, even for multiple-choice selections, are usually numbers of single letters.

Menus are not at all rare in commercial programs and systems such as word-processors or data-base systems. The menus in Wordstar or in dBaseIII are models of their kind, providing whole hierarchies of help, including explanations of what the next menu contains, of the intention and result of selections, and providing a whole range of possibilities. Icon-based menus (as for example on the Macintosh) will enter CALL soon.

6.2.3 *Selection of language*

One immediate problem faced by the program designer is whether to communicate with the student in English or in the foreign language. Solutions will depend on the intended audience; but the problem with CALL is that much material is used by those for whom it was not intended, and that at the present stage of use of material it is not always easy to predict how the material will be used.

A further choice to be made is that of 'you' versus 'we'. Does the computer address the student as an opponent or as a member of the group? Again, no simple answer can be provided: it may well be appropriate in teaching English as a foreign language to mature, motivated adults to assume that we are all on the same side in this learning business; teaching to less well-motivated younger pupils can not necessarily be quite so flippant nor so matey. In any case, the authority figure has occasionally to make itself felt: the computer (i.e. the program designer) presumably does know more than the student, and know it better, so occasionally it must be possible to say that 1 is right whereas 2 is plain wrong.

The style in which interaction takes place is of major importance. The authoritarian statement (computer as judge) of a message such as

No, that's not what I want

or

Your answer is incorrect: The correct answer is...

contrasts with the impersonal, yet friendly, message style of

Hard luck ! What you should have said is...

Nonetheless the overall opposition of computer as judge to computer as guide, reminding us of the various roles of the teacher, has to be clearly visible. Paramskas [7] shows that one way of doing this is to vary the style according to the severity of the error. In CLEF he points out that it was decided to cater for three types of error: flubs, insignificant errors, and significant errors. Flubs (typing errors, extra spaces and other oddments caused by spastic fingers) were merely discarded, while insignificant errors such as a single missing letter, double letters where a single one had been expected, single extra letters provoked a question

Typing error?

on the screen. The significant errors, those which bore on the point being taught or significantly affected the norms of the language — verb endings, agreements — provoked a comment such as

The ending is right but the stem is wrong.

Programming for this type of language selection and varying the style of program response in this way is evidently costly in anticipation time, in programming design time and in space, but the idea of variation in response is worth following up.

6.3   Clues

In many cases the program will be designed in such a way that the student is encouraged to make constructive guesses at the correct solution to a question. In these circumstances it is necessary to be able to provide clues to the correct answer.

Such clues may consist of providing part of the answer (some letters in a word — see Soemarmo [10]) or in providing visual support (a picture of a pen or a tree). Partial matching of an answer, as in Soemarmo, in effect treats anything in certain parts of the answer as irrelevant to evaluation. The process is equivalent to that carried on in spelling checkers such as SpellStar, and is rich in possible adaptations to other areas in CALL.

6.4   Background information

Background information which can be provided includes for example a complete list of all the irregular verb forms, translations of texts, data on rainfall, a map of Germany, or other indirect help from which the student must then make a choice.

In some cases the computer can be used to assist the student by providing derived or calculated information. This is a straightforward matter if numerical information is called for: if a student is learning the Russian number system for example it is a simple matter to provide considerable help by varying the numbers and carrying out numerical operations in order to provide visual clues to the language use he is acquiring. Derived verbal information is harder, but nonetheless possible: even within the confines of a small microcomputer program it is possible to store the various bases of the French verbs, store the personal endings, and combine the two by the application of fairly simple rules. More complex derived help depends mainly on memory available within the computer and on questions of opportunity cost in space, programming time and value.

Strangely, what might seem like obvious forms of help for linguists are not very frequent: few dictionary packs and only rarely even the possibility of a specialized or personalized vocabulary or special purpose word list. Nonetheless Ahmad et al. report on dictionary programs of this type, containing also the option of reviewing, or testing, knowledge not merely of the words contained in such dictionaries but also in frequency dictionaries, thus permitting the student to review his knowledge of the 1,000 most frequent words in language X [4].

Again phraseological dictionaries are a straightforward matter and frequently used by professional linguists; they are not frequent in CALL.

6.5   Gratuitous help

In some programs it may be of interest to provide more help than is strictly called for. If a student asks for the translation of "chip" the computer may provide, and in most cases normally will provide, only the word required in the related text; it may nonetheless be thought worthwhile indicating that "chip" has other meanings for which different words will be needed in French.

Likewise additional information of a non-linguistic nature may well be provided in cases where the student has asked for help in formulating an answer.

6.6   Direct help

The assumption behind direct help is that the assistance is provided on a straightforward basis: the student asks for the translation of a word and it is provided; he asks for a one-letter clue and it appears.

One-letter, one-word or one-line answers are the simplest form of help; they are familiar from well-known programs like STORYBOARD and its derivatives, where students are encouraged to press a key to reveal one letter, one word or the whole text. Often a range of such options is provided and the computer can make available any part of a stored text, or select from other stored information for display.

The simplest form of direct help operates where a stored text or stored answer (which may be quite short) is matched with a student response, and where the student requests display of the stored answer or part of it. This is a straightforward matter, assuming that the program permits learning of this type and does not regard it as cheating; it may well be that scores will be kept of those who request such direct and obvious help, or request it too often, in order to keep track of the learning process.

The most complex form of direct help of this nature is probably the provision of a word in support of translation or of quizzes seeking the correct morphological form. Assuming that the information is stored already, but not in the form of a list of direct answers to each question, it may be necessary to provide some form of look-up table to identify and match the request and the answer.

6.7   Help screens

If the length of the information requested is longer than one line it may be preferred to provide a help screen, containing previously stored text which will be shown direct to the student in response to his request. Clearly the information may be as long or as short as necessary, may be stored within the program or separately on disk to be loaded and displayed.

Program designers need to ensure that students can find where they are in this loop; there might be some danger in diverting attention away from the main learning point by providing too much information or by not reminding the student of the point at which he requested help, particularly if the student is encouraged or able, in more complex programs, to request additional help from within a help screen itself. The situation is somewhat similar to the levels of search involved in bibliographical searching, or in a program like CARDBOX, where it is possible to request a search history if matters get too complex.

Different levels of help can easily be provided by allowing access to different screens. Thus GERAD [4] has 2 screens, one on German strong adjectival endings and the other for the weak endings. Here students themselves select which they want, but the idea that a different level of complexity might be made available, as with a different level of arcade game, is worth pursuing.

6.8   Reference to external sources of help.

Micros are not good at storing large amounts of text, and in any case their screens are not the best medium for extensive reading. Hence if large amounts of text should be scanned to provide help in the learning program, or if it is clear that basic or elementary learning has not been satisfactorily covered, the student is sent to an outside source (book, teacher, informant) to obtain the information he requires.

7   HELP TRIGGERS

7.1   Voluntary

The usual trigger is the letter H for HELP, I for INFORMATION, D for DATA or whatever other mnemonic is thought appropriate. This approach is obviously satisfactory for numerical programs, but much less so for textual work in which letters are part of the normal expected input. Hence the use of Escape keys or a function key. One of the extra keyboard signs such as the asterisk, square bracket or plus sign is often preferred depending on machine possibilities.

If different types of help are required it may be necessary to specify a range of triggers: asterisk for a letter, plus sign for a word, ampersand for the full text, as in STORYBOARD derivatives.

During quiz sessions requiring one figure or one letter answers the rest of the keyboard becomes available again for access to help, and it seems quite common to adopt a simple code such as Q for quit, A for assistance or abandon, N for next question and so on.

7.2   Forced

Various methods of forced branching to help routines are in use. The simplest perhaps is dependent on score: five wrong answers in a row obliges a jump to a help routine. Score triggers of this type can be made quite sophisticated; thus Hickman (EDUCA2) repeats only those parts of an exercise which have been failed.

Even without keeping a numerical score the computer can keep track of wrong answers and force a branch. Such recapping procedures can also be random; assuming a student has failed 5 per cent of a quiz, he can be obliged to review that 5 per cent plus a proportion of the other material in order to ensure that his wrong answers were not merely random.

Triggers of this type operate very much as did the triggering procedure in programmed learning, with branching possibilities to alternative material and, if wished, a refusal of reentry to the normal program until satisfactory performance is recorded on the renewed test.

What the student does after being obliged to branch in this fashion is again dependent on the program's requirements: help can be specific, directed to the point which has been found to be incorrect; more general, providing alternative exercises to those originally failed; or can provide extra tuition, displaying additional teaching material.

8   PROGRAMS REFERRED TO

The programs referred to in the text above are listed here with a summary of their purpose, and the name of the publisher:

dBase III (purpose: Data-base) — Ashton-Tate
CLEF (purpose: French language) — G. Holmes / University of Western Ontario
EDUCA2 (purpose: French grammar) — P. Hickman
LOAN (purpose: English) — T. Johns
QUESTIONMASTER (purpose: Authoring) — Hutchinson Software
SpellStar (purpose: Spelling check) — Micropro
Wordstar (purpose: Wordprocessor) — Micropro
ELIZA (purpose: Interaction) — Weizenbaum

GETRAENKE (purpose: Decision tree on drink types) — Ahmad & Rogers
HAMMURABI (purpose: Simulation)
STORYBOARD (purpose: Text deletion) — Wida Software
CARDBOX (purpose: Data-base) — Caxton
GERAD (purpose: German adjectives) — Ahmad et al.

References

[1] Stubbs, M. (1983), *Discourse analysis*, Blackwell.

[2] Rushby, N. (1979), *An introduction to educational computing*, Croom Helm.

[3] Brumfit, C. J. & Johnson, K. (1979), *The Communicative approach to language teaching*, OUP.

[4] Ahmad, K., Corbett, G., Rogers, M. and Sussex, R. (1985), *Computers, language learning and language teaching*, CUP.

[5] Higgins, J. (1983), "Can computers teach?", *CALICO Journal*, 1, 2, 4–6.

[6] Kenning, M. J. & Kenning, M-M. (1983), *An Introduction to computer-assisted language teaching*, OUP.

[7] Paramskas, D. M. (1983), "Courseware-software interfaces: some designs and some problems", *CALICO Journal*, 1, 3, 4–6.

[8] Curtin, C. & Sinall, S. (1984), "Programming for learning", *CALICO Journal*, 1, 5, 12–16.

[9] Higgins, J. & Johns, T. (1984), *Computers in language learning*, Collins ELT.

[10] Soemarmo, M. (1983), "Programming for misspelled extended input", *CALICO Journal*, 1, 3, 31–36.

13

CALLS: Computer-assisted language learning simulation

David Crookall, University of Toulon

1 INTRODUCTION

Two developments have recently caught the imagination of language teachers: computers and simulations. When these two are combined, we have a potentially powerful educational methodology; indeed some of the most interesting CAL software is in the form of simulation. In L2 (Second language) education, teachers are beginning to follow suit. However, the use of computers in L2 instruction still remains more widespread than the use of simulation — witness the many conferences on CALL, whereas there have been none on simulation in L2 instruction.

Some most interesting CALL programs have been developed in recent years, and the whole field is becoming diversified; for an overview see Higgins [1]. Simulations existed long before computers were invented, but became associated with computers as soon as these came on to the scene; indeed it was a major game theorist, Jon von Neumann, who designed one of the first modern computers (EDVAC — see Randell [2]). At first, simulations drew upon the power of computers to crunch numbers (e.g. to carry out complex calculations in business games). Then, in the early 1980's, simulations were designed explicitly for the computer; their shape was determined by the capabilities of the computer (its demand characteristics). More recently, there has been a movement back again towards using the computer as a peripheral aid in simulation.

Many CALL programs remain drill-based or computer-oriented, and at this level they are valuable for they provide instant feedback and are tireless. However, computers themselves cannot provide social interaction, in which language is used as a means of communication. One of the simplest definitions of simulation is "the model in operation" [3]. Simulations are thus ideal vehicles for L2 instruction, for they can invent or replicate social situations, and thus encourage participants to use language as a means of communication, rather than consider it as an unapplied 'object of study'. Computers can be used to assist situational, language-generating simulations.

Computerized simulations come in many forms, from weather or chemistry simulations, to those (such as are described below) in which the people participating have full control over simulation events and interact with each other rather than with the computer. It is the participant who is important, while the computer plays a background role; for a discussion on these varied participant and computer roles in simulation see Crookall and Martin [4].

Jones says "a real company uses a computer to minimize the problems of data generation and control" and suggests "that such a role for the computer is appropriate for realistic simulations" [5]. In the two simulations described below the computer is used, not to provide a mathematical model, nor as a motivator (to brighten up an otherwise drab exercise), but as a peripheral, but nevertheless vital, tool (e.g. word processing) in an essentially human situation. As a general rule, when social and communicational processes are important learning objectives, such as in L2 instruction, the learning potential is highest in those computerized simulations where the participants, rather than the computer, have control over events, and where inter-participant, rather than computer-participant, interaction predominates. The less the computer detracts from the human dimensions of simulation contexts, the greater the scope for using language communicatively. Two examples of this kind of simulation follow: one, NEWSIM, is described briefly; the other, ICONS, in more detail.

2 NEWSIM

News institutions have inspired a number of media simulations. The basic procedure consists in items of information being handed periodically to participants, who then edit them to produce either a simulated front page of a newspaper or a simulated radio or TV news programme. However, published manual media simulations are based on 'news' items which are inevitably old or second-hand (e.g. newspaper cuttings); some are even based on fictitious items. NEWSIM is a 'real' news simulation; it is based upon 'raw' or unedited information that has not yet even appeared in newspapers or on radio or TV. NEWSIM methodology accesses, within the classroom, 'raw' news, by tapping one of the real media's actual news sources, i.e. the press agencies' radio transmissions, which are used by the media the world over. News items are thus obtained at the very same time in the classroom as they appear on the real newspaper and TV studio teleprinters. In NEWSIM, it is this raw material that participants have to process. Examples of press agencies are AFP (Agence France Presse), AP (Associated Press), and MAP (Mutuelle Africaine de

Presse), and there are some 200 operating round the world. News agency despatches are sent out via shortwave RTTY (radioteletype) transmissions, and can therefore be picked up using suitable equipment.

While the simulation is under way, participants are seated away from the screen, and the news items are handed to them on hard copy printout. The computer's role here is to act as a teleprinter to produce news items; the participants are absorbed in the problems of putting a front page togther or producing a broadcast news bulletin. The computer has no bearing on the processes or outcome of the simulation, except in that it provides the raw material which permits the simulation to be run in the first place; the computer helps to make the simulation more realistic amd immediate. Participant editors work in a team, much as they would do in a real editorial office, and are thus concerned, not with screen presentation (which if anything is rather dull), but with all the complexities of media issues and social aspects of working in groups, thus encouraging L2 fluency. The other function of the computer is word-processing for the writing of their front pages; here if anything, the computer makes the task easier, and allows students to concentrate on accuracy. Students have full control over what they do, and all interaction is between themselves as people with a job to do; in fact participants can forget there is a computer in the room, vital though it may be. As in real life, they will notice the computer only if it breaks down.

The basic equipment needed to run NEWSIM is: a shortwave general coverage communications receiver capable of picking up SSB (single sideband) transmissions, a good antenna, a RTTY (radioteletype) interface unit, a microcomputer with appropriate software, and a printer. Technical notes on picking up international radio transmissions will be found elsewhere [6], as will a full discussion on NEWSIM, with details on equipment and suppliers [7].

3 ICONS

3.1 Overview

ICONS (International COmmunications and Negotiations Simulation), employs a powerful methodology: some twenty university teams round the world participate in month-long international relations simulations. Each team represents a different nation in the scenario; a certain number represent their own country; at the moment they are to be found in: Argentina, Canada, England, France, Israel, Japan, and USA. The majority of the country-teams are currently located in the USA, but more non-US teams will be joining in as the simulation develops.

The communication process involves each team sending its messages in the language of the nation it represents, and therefore receiving messages in foreign languages. Thus, ICONS provides a natural laboratory both for the development of foreign languages as a vital instrument of communication, and for the exploration of culturally defined (often divisive) issues. Teams representing their own country provide a culturally authentic perspective, while those representing other than their own country are forced to see the world in a new cultural light.

Communications between these country-teams are assured by a variety of computer technologies, which allow the simulation to run in real time. Local microcomputers (equipped with word processors, telecommunications software and modems) are linked via international telecommunications data networks (national packet switching systems connected by satellite) into a central mainframe (situated at the University of Maryland and equipped with sophisticated and easy-to-use software).

Simulation sessions last about one month; at the moment there are two sessions a year: one in the Spring, and one in the Autumn. A scenario, which launches the game, outlines the state of the world, inspired by present-day facts, but includes new data. For instance, in the May 1985 scenario, situated in the simulated October of 1985, Iraq had mined the Straits of Hormuz. Throughout the simulation, an electronic newspaper, "The Diplomat", projects new data into the simulation, and also plays its role as an ordinary newspaper: interviews, commentary, etc.

ICONS was developed by Jon Wilkenfeld and Dick Brecht at the University of Maryland [8] and is based on POLIS, pioneered by Bob Noel at the University of California at Santa Barbara [9]. European coordination for ICONS exercises is provided by David Crookall at the University of Toulon.

3.2   Fields and applications

There are three major fields — foreign languages, international studies and communication technologies.

3.2.1   Foreign languages

It is generally acknowledged that students learn more efficiently when the L2 learning experience is made real, when it is taken out of its usual purely academic setting, and when the student must actually function in the L2. Very often this means students studying abroad or within some kind of domestic total immersion environment. ICONS may be considered as a kind of semi-immersion environment, for during the time of the simulation teams become foreign language saturated. Typically, more than 3000 messages, many over a page in length, will be exchanged during a five-week exercise. Another important feature of ICONS is that it is both multilingual and multicultural. Seven languages are already used: English, French, German, Hebrew, Japanese, Russian and Spanish; and some of these languages emanate from, culturally authentic sources, e.g. Spanish messages are written in, and transmitted from, Argentina.

There are two main modes of L2 implementation in ICONS, and these correspond to two broad types of skills: translation and reading. The basic process involves each team sending its outgoing messages in the language of the country it represents, and therefore receiving incoming messages from the other teams in their languages.

One mode involves translation sub-teams, attached to the policy team. These sub-teams translate incoming L2 messages into their policy team's mother tongue; native speakers attached to US-based teams representing foreign countries also translate the policy team's outgoing messages from English into the foreign language of the country they represent in the simulation. For instance, native Russian speakers attached to the Soviet Union country-team (situated in the USA) translate the Soviet Union's messages into Russian before they are transmitted.

The other mode involves reading the incoming messages directly in the foreign language, and writing their outgoing messages in their own language. For instance, French nationals in the France country-team read the incoming messages directly in the foreign languages and write their outgoing messages in French. Both modes may operate in parallel, while central translation facilities are provided for teams not able to handle certain foreign languages. Reading is widely recognized as one of the most important L2 learning activities, yet it often remains hampered by a lack of motivation. Within the context of ICONS, reading incoming L2 messages is self-motivating: they are addressed personally to team-members, not written for an ill-defined and anonymous audience. In order to become effective actors in their own (simulation) world, students actually want to read the messages, many of them several times over; all team-members are directly and urgently concerned with every incoming message. Reading for fluency and for accuracy are integrated in a natural way; the large quantity of written material received provides extensive L2 reading, while the importance of many details encourages intensive reading.

In ICONS, foreign languages become a vital instrument of communication. Within the framework of this simulation, a foreign language is no longer an abstract system devoid of meaning or consequence; it becomes a purposeful, authentic, and communicative activity, a means for negotiating realities. The state of the world depends upon a full understanding of foreign language messages; this remains valid in both modes of operation.

Inter-cultural communication, too, is an important factor in motivation. Foreign languages become links between participating nationalities; e.g. students in France know that messages received by the team representing Argentina were written by Argentinians themselves. The social-psychological aspects of second language learning are well documented, e.g. Gardner [10], Giles and Byrne [11]. Negative attitudes to foreign languages are not uncommon, and may be perceived as a threat to one's self-image, and the effect of this on L2 learning can be catastrophic [12]. ICONS goes some way towards combatting this. First, students begin to realize they are part of a global family, and this helps them to see their L1-L2 (i.e. first language to second language) relationship in a truer perspective. Second, students also realize that their own L1 is an important L2 for their colleagues abroad. For instance, the French team takes great care in writing, because they know that their messages represent their language abroad, and that they are used in ordinary L2 classes (e.g. by the teacher of French in Japan), and this makes students more receptive to the L2. In short, students from different countries help each other to learn a foreign language, and this in itself is highly motivating, apart from involvement with the simulation activity itself.

3.2.2   International Studies

ICONS is an LSP (Language for Special Purposes) simulation, for it provides a natural laboratory for the study and practice of various disciplines in a complex world of international relations. Participants explore and tackle foreign policy and diplomatic issues in a wide range of areas, such as: superpower relations, human rights, European integration, the Middle-East conflicts, NATO, North-South relations, OECD, world economic policies, international trade, Third World problems, environmental threats.

Students are confronted by practical, real and urgent international issues in a context which provides an authenticity of experience unobtainable by other means. The vital skills exercised in this field will include: understanding and analysis of complex situations, diplomacy, policy implementation, articulation of ideas, decision making. For a fuller discussion on these aspects, see Wilkenfeld [13]. The simulation also develops other valuable skills, such as team work, creativity, interdisciplinary thinking, which are put into practice 'on the job' in a real situation. A few examples of messages sent during the Spring 1985 exercise will provide a glimpse of the topics.

[Note. The top line of each message gives the following information: recipient, sender, date (real) and time, message number, key(s). These are provided automatically by the central mainframe.]

To france From newspaper Date 4/23/85 1035 Msg 524 Key [news]
THE DIPLOMAT — SPECIAL EDITION — Fall 1985 SOVIET LEADER TO VISIT FRANCE
It has just been announced that Soviet Premier Mikhail Gorbachev will be in France tomorrow for a state visit.... This will be the first meeting between the two leaders since the funeral of the late Soviet Premier Konstantin Chernenko 16 months ago. THE DIPLOMAT will be holding a historic press interview with both Gorbachev and French President Francois Mitterand tomorrow.

[Note. Chernenko's replacement by Gorbachev was built into the game scenario of October 1984, some six months before the real event. Between the previous and the next message, a new system was set up starting from zero, which explains why the next message number is smaller then the previous.]

To s.arabia From france Date 4/30/85 1821 Msg 327 Key [human]
En reference a votre message 135 du 29 avril .... La France souhaite agir de la maniere la plus energique pour la suppression de certaines dispositions repressives en vigueur dans de nombreux pays du monde selon ... Amnesty International. Nous estimons en effet indispensable de purger les systemes repressifs des peines afflictives et infamantes ... . Nous estimons qu'il est du devoir de tout Etat de droit de ne pas confondre barbarie et repression penale. ...
To france From argentina Date 5/9/85 1338 Msg 866 Key [human confer]
Argentina acepta gustosa participar en la Conferencia de Derechos Humanos el viernes 10 de mayo a las 15:00 gmt. Esteramos esperando con mucha ansiedad para tan importante conferencia.
To france From iraq Date 5/9/85 1656 Msg 895 Key [confer][gulf]
Please accept our regrets for being unable to attend the human rights conference. Our war obligations, in defense of the sacred homeland, require all our energies at the moment, along with our diligent peace efforts. Our human rights positions are already on the table from the last conference, and we await positive developments in Iran and Syria — key violators of political rights in recent years. Might we ask you as well to use all your influence in convincing Iran to accept the eminently reasonable peace terms now on the table. ...

3.2.3   Communications technologies

The communications technologies in the simulation are a vital component, both as a flexible, user-friendly support system, and as a training instrument. The computer technologies used allow the simulation to run in real time, with twenty or more teams situated in different parts of the world, and at the same time provide students with an efficient and motivating training environment. All universities are linked and communicate via:

a) a local computer terminal, consisting of a personal microcomputer (with word processor, communications software, modem and ordinary telephone line);

b) an NUI (network user identifier) on one of the national telecommunications packet switching networks, such as DDX-P (Japan), PSS (UK), Telenet (USA), Transpac (France).

c) a central mainframe at the University of Maryland, loaded with special software, called POLNET, written in C and running under the UNIX operating system. This has two main functions:

1)   During the simulation, it acts as an electronic mailing system for diplomatic communications allowing students and faculty to maintain continuous contact throughout the exercise; a special facility also allows the setting up of real-time teleconference sessions, where all participating teams can log on and communicate simultaneously.

2)   After the session, it becomes an on-line retrieval system, allowing searches to be made on messages sent during the simulation. Despite (or because of) the sophistication of the various technologies employed, most of them are transparent to the participants, and the whole system is easily learned.

3.3   Effectiveness

To sum up, ICONS improves the teaching and learning of a number of foreign languages; it promotes international studies and related social sciences and develops a wide range of skills; and it gives practical experience of computer technology. Through the use of a fully tested, relatively inexpensive, and easily replicable methodology that incorporates computer technology, interactive student learning simulations and important international issues, a whole range of foreign languages are brought to life and used communicatively. With the aid of the new communications technologies a real world situation is simulated among students in different higher educational insitutions around the world. The authentic use of foreign languages is linked with critical aspects of international affairs. More information on this simulation will be found in Brecht et al. [8].

4   CONCLUSIONS

Perhaps a final word can be left with Leopoldo Schapira, who runs the ICONS team at the University of Cordoba, Argentina. This is a message he sent after a recent exercise: "The main conclusion of our participants is that it has been a great success. Students and staff are more than happy to have played. We have all acquired a lot of knowledge and experience. Through telecommunications we have felt a sensation of belonging to mankind and an increased belief that we all have to dialogue to solve problems. ICONS has proved to be an adequate forum for our students to realize that they can be agents for a better world." Rather than passively watching the running through of a drill-type exercise, or being mesmerized by flickering photons on the screen of a typical computer game, participants in a computer-assisted language learning simulation concentrate on using language to negotiate the realities of their social situation. The computer-assisted simulation allows the human elements and social dimensions of the 'real' world to develop, and thus encourages students to use language naturally, purposefully and meaningfully — as a means of communication. "There are enough clearly identifiable advantages to justify optimism that computer simulations will play a major part in the far reaches of computer-assisted instruction" [14], but only as long as we are clear about what we wish them to achieve, are aware of their limitations, and recognize the importance of human interaction in the L2 learning process.

References

[1] Higgins, J. (1983), "The state of the art: computer-assisted language learning", *Language Teaching* 16:2.

[2] Randell, B. (ed) (1981), *The Origins of Digital Computers (3rd edn)*, Berlin: Springer-Verlag.

[3] Lehman, R. S. (1977), *Computer Simulation and Modelling: An Introduction*, Hillsdale NJ: Lawrence Erlbaum.

[4] Crookall, D. and Martin, A. (1985), "Participant and computer roles in simulations", *Simulation/Games for Learning* 15:2.

[6] Crookall, D. (1984), "Rigs and posts: radio reception technology for FLL", *System* 12:2.

[7] Crookall, D. (1985), "Media gaming and NEWSIM: a computer-assisted, 'real news' simulation". *System* 13:3.

[8] Brecht, R. D., Noel, R. C. and Wilkenfeld, J. (1984), "Computer simulation in the teaching of foreign language and international studies", *Foreign Language Annals* 17:6.

[9] Noel, R. C. (1979), "The POLIS methodology for distributed political gaming via computer networks", in [16].

[10] Gardner, R. C. (in press), *Social Psychological Aspects of Second Language Learning*, London: Edward Arnold.

[11] Giles, H. and Byrne, J. L. (1982), "An intergroup approach to second language acquisition", *Journal of Multilingual and Multicultural Development* 3:1.

[12] Ball, P., Giles, H. and Hewstone, M. (1984), "Second language acquisition: the intergroup theory with catastrophic dimensions" (in [15]).

[13] Wilkenfeld, J. (1983), "Computer-assisted international studies", *Teaching Political Science* 10:4.

[14] Versluis, E. (1984), "Computer simulations and the far reaches of computer-assisted instruction", *Computers and the Humanities* 18.

[15] Tajfel, H. (ed) (1984), *The Social Dimension*, Cambridge: University Press

[16] Bruin, K., de Haan, J., Teijken, C. and Veeman, W. (eds) (1979), "How to Build a Simulation/Game" (Proceedings of the 10th ISAGA Conference, August 1979; Netherland: Leeuwarden).

14

The potential of computerized interpreting in teaching

D. R. Stewart, Liverpool Polytechnic

1 INTRODUCTION

This paper arises out of collaboration, as language advisor and computer programmer, with Captain Keith W. Lindsay of the Department of Maritime Studies at Liverpool Polytechnic on a research project funded by the Marine Operations Research Unit (MORU) of the Department of Transport to investigate means of reducing the risk of collisions at sea, and of overcoming the language barrier in communications.

2 THE RESEARCH PROJECT

The underlying assumptions, based upon years of experience and investigation, were:

    i)   that seafarers, including watch officers, speak a very wide variety of native languages and that relatively few of them are fluent in languages other than their own

    ii)   that a prerequisite for the overcoming of the language barrier would be the compilation, in one natural language, of a lexicon of the message components used in collision avoidance: these might be single words, expressions or abstract concepts such as 'negative'. This lexicon would have to cover all possible contingencies while keeping its own size to a minimum

iii) that it would be difficult, if not impossible, to induce all the watch officers in the world to learn the contents of the lexicon in the natural language chosen

iv) that sea voyages on average are rather long and the use of collision-avoidance terminology is usually limited to leaving and entering ports and negotiating narrow seas. This means that even people who mastered the lexicon would tend to forget parts of it in the intervals between the occasions when they had to use it [1].

v) that, conversely, native speakers of the native language chosen for the lexicon (probably English) would have to be constrained to use ONLY the lexicon and no other elements of their native language when dealing with collision-avoidance situations [2].

The conclusion which ultimately was drawn from these assumptions, after experimental verification, was that a computer network would be desirable for ship-to-ship collision-avoidance messages. Each ship would have a computer terminal and be linked to other ships through primary and secondary radar. Each ship would have appropriate software and peripherals. It would send out any message it wished, within the scope of the lexicon: the user would press the appropriate key for each message component. The component would appear on the VDU in his own language, or, to be more precise, the official language of his ship. When the message was complete, another key would be pressed to despatch the message to the appropriate ship. Assuming the two ships had a common language, the identical message would appear on the VDU of the receiving ship. If the language of the receiving ship differed from that of the transmitting ship, the message would be translated into the language of the receiving ship. Therefore the end result would be the same in either case — a message in the receiving ship's own language.

Before the computerization stage was reached, however, there were two factors to consider. These presented the dilemma of whether "to communicate or not to communicate", and, connected with this a decision that a computerized system of communication would be more acceptable and more widely useful than a radio-based one. In order for ships to navigate safely past or around each other they must be aware of each others' intentions, that is, how fast they intend to go and in which direction, either in absolute terms or in relation to other ships or to man-made or natural hazards. How is one ship supposed to know what another will do? Mainly, by the assumption that the other ship(s) will obey the rule of the road at sea. It may seem a simple matter to agree that ships will use the rules to solve whatever problems those rules can solve, but will have to communicate with each other to solve other problems. It is not, however, as simple as this. Until recently the official attitude of governments, drilled into seafarers through regulations, seems to have made mariners hesitate to engage in ship-to-ship communication. Directives have tended to stress the harm that can be done if one ship induces another to break the rule of the road and the dire consequences that could ensue for the seafarer responsible. The result has been an atmosphere of extreme caution, with everyone taking as their watchword "if in doubt, remain silent". Yet, while it is obviously true, in itself, that no watch officer should suggest that another break the rules, it is apparently by no means true to say that silent obedience to rules by all ships can eliminate the risk of collisions completely. Therefore, there is a need for ship-to-ship communication, used judiciously and with discrimination. One of the first objectives of Lindsay's research was to find out the conditions under which officers would think it sensible to engage in ship-to-ship communication and would be willing to do so. His method, in this and all subsequent experiments, was to ask a number of experienced merchant navy officers to take part in an exercise in which they resolved one or more collision-avoidance problems of a kind which had occurred in real life. Some exercises used the simulator in this case while in other cases, pen and paper were used in conjunction with charts and drawings. The conclusion drawn from these first experiments was that officers, who at first were chary of using ship-to-ship communication at all, were by the end of the exercises generally willing to use it, where appropriate, subject to the following conditions:

   i)   it had to be quite clear who was talking to whom.

   ii)   while there was no objection to a conversation in which one ship addressed two or more, it had to be impossible for ships not taking part in the conversation to overhear or eavesdrop. Ships which overhear others' conversations are apt to act precipitately or anti-socially on the information overheard.

   iii) the need to deal with collision-avoidance messages could not be allowed to interfere with other activities on the bridge OR to congest the radio channel (channel 16) that would be needed for initial calls of any other kind, or for distress calls.

   iv) language problems had to be overcome.

Regarding identity, the most obvious aid to certainty is for every speaker to refer to his own and other ships by their call-signs, especially when first making contact or first referring to them: personal pronouns or possessive adjectives, used without antecedents, are even less helpful in ship-to-ship communication than on terra firma.

Assuming the means of communication is VHF radio, however, the use of call-signs does not in itself solve another problem, namely the fact that, given the 'right' atmospheric conditions, one ship might be able to receive collision-avoidance messages from another 500 miles away. Such messages are at best useless and at worse actively misleading. Moreover, there is no way of preventing eavesdropping, apart from insisting that it should not occur, when radio is used. The use of a computerized system of communication based upon radar has an impact upon both these problems. It limits the possibility of ships inadvertently making contact when they are really too far away from each other for the contact to be useful, because radar only operates as far as the horizon. It makes eavesdropping almost impossible: only a dedicated 'hacker' could penetrate the bona fide network. Additionally, the use of the computer network to produce the collision-avoidance messages on the VDU, when compared with VHF radio communication, has all the usual advantages of the written word over the spoken — permanence, clarity, freedom from noise, incapability of inflicting its own noise upon other transmissions or normal conversations, freedom from problems arising from differences of pronunciation, intonation and so on. To sum up this section: the subjects of the experiment expressed to the experimenter the reasons for their reluctance to communicate with other ships for purposes of collision-avoidance. He managed, in general, to persuade them that, given the right safeguards and provisos, such communication could after all be useful. In particular, he found that their objections could partially be met by an insistence that every ship identify itself before communicating, but that the objections could be much more comprehensively overcome by the establishment of computerized machine translation networks.

The lexicon has been given the name "Ship-Write CA". The stages by which it and the concomitant computer software were developed were briefly as follows. The experimental subjects were in all cases EITHER qualified and experienced ships' officers OR students of maritime studies, i.e. intending officers.

a. Subjects were asked to deal with various collision-avoidance problems which were simulated, in English, using whatever words and phrases naturally occurred to them. The words and expressions they used were noted and from this body of raw material, this 'corpus', the initial version of the lexicon was distilled.

b. With the help of academic staff at French maritime colleges, this version of the lexicon was translated into French.

c. An English and a French group of subjects were asked to take part in a comprehension test to measure their ability to understand simulated ship-to-ship dialogues in Ship-Write CA. The results obtained, in terms of subjects' ability to grasp quickly and correctly the nature of each problem and its solution, were found to be very similar, generally, for both nationalities.

d. To obtain fuller experience of how a series of dialogues between two ships would develop, the experimenter asked three different subjects to work through the same series of exercises with him, passing pencil and paper messages to each other. All the messages were recorded on an Apple computer disk.

e. A print-out of the output of a computer program which translated messages from English to French was given to a number of French subjects. They were asked to examine it critically and suggest amendments. While they never found the French versions difficult to understand, they were able to suggest some more natural-sounding or polished translations. The computer program was amended to incorporate these suggestions, along with some others from D R Stewart.

f.   A systematic series of messages for computerized translation was compiled to prove that the program coped successfully with all the relevant grammatical contingencies. Here are some examples of what was involved.

1)   The English infinitive had to be translated, according to context, *either* by a straightforward infinitive *or* by 'de' plus the infinitive, if that infinitive began with a consonant, or alternatively by d' tagged onto the beginning of that infinitive, if it began with a vowel, *or* by 'doit' plus the infinitive *or* by 'pour' plus the infinitive *or* by 'que' before a proper name and a subjunctive after the name.

2)   The English 'to depart', which incidentally appears to be used by mariners where landlubbers would say 'to leave', had to be translated according to context EITHER by the appropriate variant of 'quitter' OR the appropriate variant of 'partir'. In conjunction with point 1) this created ten permutations.

3)   The English 'to cross' sometimes had to be translated by the appropriate variant of the French verb 'passer' (literally, to pass), not by the appropriate variant of 'traverser'. This again created ten permutations.

4)   The English intransitive verbal expression 'to keep clear' was translated by the reflexive expression 'se tenir à l'écart'. This created a need to use 'me' rather than the dictionary form 'se' in certain contexts.

5)   Adjectives or adjectival phrases generally had to follow the noun they described in the French version.

6)   Sometimes 'de' was required in French where no word 'of' was used in English. For example 'anchorage position' had to become 'position de mouillage', literally 'position of anchorage'.

7)   'To the' had to be translated either as 'au' or 'à l' ', according to what followed. There was, mercifully, no need for the other two forms, 'à la' and 'aux', which exist in the full French language.

The MORU asked us for a brief confirmation that such a computerized translation system could be extended, with appropriate adaptations, to the Spanish language. After investigation, we were able to give this assurance. This particular research project is now complete, and at least one similar project is likely to follow.

How does "Ship-Write CA" fit into the whole spectrum of machine translation and machine assisted translation? What follows is from an article written in the summer of 1984 for the Department of Maritime Studies of Liverpool Polytechnic:

The characteristics of "Ship-Write CA" as a 'language' are clarity and functional simplicity. It does not permit the user to introduce extraneous verbiage. Even phatic speech is eliminated. There is only one way of expressing each message, except perhaps where the laws and relationships of mathematics create alternatives. Dialect, archaisms, jargon, slang and unusual phraseology are avoided, which considerably aids comprehension. Sometimes the message components, the irreducible units from which generative activity starts, are several words long. For example, "Ship-Write CA" treats 'I am manoeuvring with difficulty' as an indivisible unit. It provides no opportunity to build other sentences around the word 'manoeuvring' or the phrase 'with difficulty', because no such opportunity is necessary for "Ship-Write CA" purposes. Where possible, concepts such as 'negative' are used instead of specific words like 'no' or 'not'. All this keeps the 'language' "Ship-Write CA" simple and thus makes it easier to translate [3].

3   SHIP-WRITE CA IN THE WORLD OF MACHINE TRANSLATION

The proposed Ship-Write CA software and hardware will constitute an Machine Translation (MT) system, because the translation process will be completed without human assistance. The most salient characteristics of the Ship-Write CA system will be as follows:

(1) It will operate in 'real time'. Both computer response time and human response time will be crucial. In linguists' terms, the system will be for *interpreting* rather than *translating*. In this it is unusual and possibly unique. It contrasts with 'while-you-wait' systems where after a lapse of, say, two minutes a computer might produce a translation of 800–1500 [4] words or a 'batch' system, where the user inserts the input and collects the translation hours or days later [5].

(2) There are no facilities for individual users to 'pre-edit' their messages, that is, to adapt the wording of the text for ease of translation before submitting it to the machine. This is, however, not surprising, because the creation of Ship-Write CA was a definitive pre-editing operation upon the whole corpus of messages that would otherwise have been possible. Potential users will be trained in the composition of Ship-Write CA messages.

(3) 'post-editing', the process whereby human translators improve upon the computer output, will be impossible in the real-time situation. Fortunately, the need for it will be eliminated. Recipients of messages will be trained to grasp promptly the meaning of any 'raw'

translations produced by the system, e.g. telegram style messages or those where words are in brackets and the reader has to decide from the context whether to include them in the current message. In most respects, however, translations will be 'polished'. Ship-Write CA will have fewer possible messages to translate than most MT or MAT systems, but it will have an available translation for all of them. In MT and MAT a program which covers all possible contingencies in this way is very unusual, probably unique.

(4) Any future updating of Ship-Write CA will have to retain the above characteristics. Any changes will no doubt be preceded by extensive consultations with users but it will never be possible to permit users to amend the Ship-Write CA software themselves. This contrasts with the kind of system which allows for 'dictionary updates' by individuals according to their requirements [6].

How do other MT and MAT systems compare with the proposed Ship-Write CA system? Generally, what they illustrate is the essential nature of computers and of human language. Computers are tireless and completely dependable in the performance of any task which can be reduced to a series of simple operations of certain kinds. Thus they perform calculations or sorting tasks far more rapidly and somewhat more accurately than even the most diligent human being. On the other hand, they are totally unimaginative, except in so far as they have been programmed to 'show imagination'. This is why they frequently mortify programmers and users: they do exactly what they have been told to do, not what people think they have told them to do. Human beings have the opposite strengths and weaknesses to computers. They can, for example, guess obvious exceptions to generalized statements. If told that 'Education Guardian' appears 'every Tuesday', they assume this excludes cases where the Tuesday happens to be Christmas Day or Boxing Day, when no British national newspapers are published. The informant, unconsciously perhaps, assumes his interlocutor will guess the exception. A computer, by way of contrast, has to have every exception to a generalized statement expressly inserted into its memory. The need *consciously to realise every exception to one's inadvertent over-generalizations* can make almost any computer programming task more difficult than one at first expected. It makes the task of devising a truly comprehensive program for the translation of one natural language into another effectively impossible. Human creativity in the use of language will always be ahead of human ingenuity in programming for every conceivable contingency — for every metaphor, literary allusion, deliberate misquotation, euphemism, vulgarism, laudatory or pejorative term, connotation, rhyme, rhythmic device or pun (whether monolingual or interlingual). Linguists and computer scientists, mindful of all this, treat MT and MAT as earlier generations treated earlier inventions, such as the railway. They differentiate between texts (cf. railway traffics) for which the new invention is already suitable, those for which the invention will become suitable as it develops, those which can be made suitable for the invention, those which on reflection need no attention at all and disappear through the operation of the laws of economics and those for which the invention will never be suitable. In deciding to which of these categories a text for translation belongs, human reactions can be a good starting point. If the experienced translator says that he did a job 'automatically', similar texts in the future will almost certainly be suitable for MT or MAT. The 'automatic' job nearly always involves specialized material [7].

Various investigations into the nature of specialised language have been undertaken. The aim has not necessarily been to facilitate MT or MAT; the findings have primarily been used to decide which subset of a natural language to teach non-native researchers or students in one specialised area. Since, however, the findings corroborate the practical experiences of translators and MT or MAT experts, they are worth quoting. L. Hoffmann and his collaborators in Leipzig (GDR) found that 1,225 lexemes would cover 84.1 per cent [8] of a sample of Russian medical texts. After adding to this total various 'internationalisms' with meanings obvious to the specialist and various meanings deducible from a knowledge of grammar and/or of medicine itself, the percentage of the sample comprehensible to German medical students rose to 90–93 per cent. Similarly, in physics, 1,114 lexemes covered 87.5 per cent of the sample and internationalisms and grammar knowledge could raise coverage to 93 per cent. C. Puchta [9] suggests two reasons why physics has such a small vocabulary:

a)   because it relies so much on mathematics to express its ideas
b)   because it tends to define all its words more precisely than they are defined in everyday speech, making almost every one into a technical term stripped of all ambiguities.

The comparable coverage figures in certain other subjects were as follows:

— Chemistry 80.03% or 95.45%
— Marxist-Leninist Philosophy 84.3% or 90.7% [10]
— General History 65% or 72.2%

Clearly, History, as a subject, relies less upon specialized and closely defined vocabulary than the natural sciences or medicine. Its range of grammatical structure will also be broader. Marxist- Leninist Philosophy has a similarly restricted vocabulary to a natural science because it sets out, rightly or wrongly, to be 'scientific' in aproach, analysing the workings of politics and economics and of society, using precisely defined specialized terms.

At Hanover's Technische Universität, Professor Halbauer has paralleled Hoffmann's work with his own scheme for narrowing down the range of vocabulary needed to understand Russian texts in each scientific speciality. He argues that the more esoteric the specialization is, the more it will repeat the same words. In some cases as few as 200 words can be sufficient for an understanding of a highly specialized text [11]. The Germans' views on the smallness of the vocabulary which will prove adequate seem rather optimistic when one considers the size of Elsevier's specialist dictionaries (published in Amsterdam and elsewhere).

These principles, however, do seem to hold good:

    a)   specialist scientific language uses a narrower range of vocabulary and a narrower range of grammatical structures than normal language.

    b)   the meaning of specialized terms has been precisely defined by experts whereas the same cannot be said for normal language.

The OECD applies these principles to MT in its *International Road Research Documentation*. Using a vocabulary of a little under 4,000 words it produces word-for-word partial translations between English, French and German. Words not in the specialized computerized dictionary are left untranslated but the finished result usually suffices as a substitute for an abstract or a way of conveying the gist of the original. The output could be readily postedited if required [12].

In Canada, METEO trades upon the repetitive nature of the language of weather forecasting to do about 38 per cent of the required translation from English into French by computer. This percentage may increase in the future. (see below) [13].

The US Air Force Russian-English translation centre at Dayton, Ohio covers a wide range of technical fields, using a computer with no pre-editing and very little postediting. The quality of work in physics, chemistry and electronics is high. In political science it is not so high [14]. At first sight, this last point contradicts the Leipzig findings. The explanation probably lies in the nature of the input. If it had been heavily theoretical the problem would perhaps not have arisen. The principle that specialized material, full of technical terms, is easier to translate by computer than general material remains unchallenged. Such specialised material is the most obvious example of work for which the computer is essentially suitable from the start.

In its perfectionism, however, the USAAF system ventures deeply into the second category of work — that for which MT or MAT becomes suitable as the system develops. To achieve its standards the Air Force has built up a database of about 92,000,000 words of text which can be searched for examples of the use of a homograph. The program has built into it a series of 'flags' to highlight words or expressions which may be inaccurately translated because the programming was so hard. All this is necessary to raise the product from a 'raw' translation to a polished one.

The firm Weidner sells a system [6] which has to be developed by the user. Only a basic vocabulary is supplied with the original software. The build-up of the 'dictionary' is left to the user. Similarly, one's own dictionary of synonyms for the target language can be developed. Thus the owner of a Weidner system is able to make it suitable for translating more and more varied material. At any given moment, however, his software will only cope with words and expressions already entered in the dictionaries. Therefore, if he wants to use the system, he will be well advised to pre-edit potential texts for translation. He will then be treating the texts as belonging to the third category of material, the kind that can be made suitable for the computer.

Some large organizations regard virtually all their material as being in the third category. For example, Rank Xerox, who use the Systran system, control input very strictly, believing this is more conducive to quality, consistency and clarity than trying to amend the computer's actual operations or the output. Xerox start from the advantage that their material is technical (cf. above) but they also impose a set of 'writing rules' upon their technical authors, who must use 'multinational customized English'. These procedures serve the same purpose as pre-editing, but are more fundamental in approach [15]. Similarly, General Motors of Canada, who translate service and operators' manuals for diesel locomotives, cars, etc., insist that their technical writers adhere to certain 'guidelines for writing style'. Additionally, they believe in pre-editing. Since they also emphasize post-editing [4], their control of input may not be as firm as at Xerox.

The EEC use Systran at their offices in Luxemburg. In 1981 it covered approximately 3 per cent of the total translation work done by the EEC at Luxemburg and 1% of the total translation work of the EEC [16]. Meanwhile, a new system, Eurotra [17], is being developed. In contrast to Xerox, the EEC allow 'free', i.e. uncontrolled input. Perhaps this difference is inevitable. Employees of a firm can be told unequivocally to produce a required type of input. To persuade all authors submitting documents to the EEC to conform to similar rules, without offending them or their countries, would be very much more difficult. Moreover, rules would be harder to devise because the subject matter is so much more varied. Yet the time may come when the member states resolve to surmount these difficulties (which are human and social rather than linguistic or computational) in order to increase the use that can be made of MT or MAT.

Returning to the weather forecasting system METEO, it does appear remarkable that, at least until 1981, input was not more controlled — firstly, because statements about the weather presumably call for a limited set of precise terms and secondly, because there is little need to connect the essential data together into whole, grammatical sentences. Perhaps a fully computerized weather forecast translation system will be devised in the future.

To sum up this section, the way to make material suitable for computerised translation is to control and/or pre-edit it. Ship-Write CA's form of 'pre-editing' is the most drastic and effective of all. The user can only employ the message components built into the software.

Some aspects of a translation task may turn out not to be required after all. This often applies to the post-editing of a raw computer translation. People can often guess what a raw translation means: they use their imagination. They often prefer to do this rather than to wait or pay for postediting [18]. This is very much a case where the computer and the human complement each other.

What kind of work can never be suitable for computer translation? Generally, any work where a raw translation will not suffice for the purpose and which cannot be translated in a *fully* satisfactory and definitive way, even by non-computerized methods. This is the kind of work which translators most enjoy because it uses all their skill, knowledge and creativity, justifying the claim that translation is an art [19]. In the future translators will find increasingly that their work *either* falls into this class *or* has some connection with MT or MAT, whether in the form of programming, consulting with programmers, building up dictionaries and databases, working with systems analysts or postediting. The translator will enjoy such work more than he would have enjoyed doing the whole translation without recourse to the computer [20].

4 CONCLUSION

To the extent that other MT and MAT systems have inherently more complex tasks to perform than Ship-Write CA, they must be more elaborate and more dependent on human intervention. At the same time, many users and developers of systems could arguably rethink their strategies in the light of the basic facts about computers and human natural language. Ship-Write CA does, in the present author's view, have a lesson for such developers or users. It can be summed up in a line of Goethe's poem 'Natur und Kunst' (Nature and Art): 'In der Beschränkung zeigt sich erst der Meister' that is, 'mastery is only revealed by working within restrictions'.

Finally, how can the outcome of the project benefit undergraduate teaching on modern language courses? I do not believe that computerized interpreting in itself is the be-all and end-all, but I do believe that a sound introduction to the whole field of MT and MAT could form a very useful element on a degree course, perhaps as an option. Certainly, this would increase the vocational value of the course because more and more commercial and governmental organisations are making use of MT or MAT. Nevertheless the proposal to introduce the MT and MAT element on to the course might meet with initial misgivings. Some linguists are still 'afraid' or mistrustful of the machine and its peripherals and software, although these feelings are being overcome as the value of word processing for academic and administrative work is realised. It might, however, still be argued that language learning is essentially an intuitive matter, that computer programming is very much a matter of logic and that few people combine within themselves the right mix of intuitive and logical abilities.

Yet language learning, even without computers, involves a judicious combination of one's intuitive and logical faculties — and this applies equally to translation and critique of translation. The middle part of this paper — about the various kinds of MAT or MT and their strengths and limitations — is not just a statement about what computers and their programs can or cannot do. It is also, perhaps more fundamentally, a survey of some of the main registers and situational levels in human language. It is not possible to take a piece of natural language and decide how completely or how successfully it can be translated by computer without some fundamental thought about the nature of the sample of natural language involved. This will be all the more true of any attempted critique of a computer translation: students will have to detect and account for peculiarities or errors in the translation and the most usual explanation will almost certainly be that the software has over-simplified the task, failing to take account of all the exceptions to its rules. An appreciation of the strengths and limitations of MT or MAT should enhance students' appreciation and awareness of the different kinds of human language. At the risk of exaggerating, one could go a little further. It seems reasonable to say that by appreciating, for example, the nature of scientific language, one is appreciating something of the very nature of science. The fact that everyone, regardless of nationality, defines a term like 'valency' in the same way before using it IS a fact about the nature of science, not just a circumstance that eases the translators' task. The other side of the penny is that it would be rather a dull and uniform world if non-scientific language, including literary language, did not use more intractable vocabulary of the kind that finds its way into dictionaries of synonyms, and if people did not occasionally use language in playful, creative and imaginative ways. It can reasonably be claimed that an understanding of this kind of language and of the relative difficulty of translating it, is in effect an understanding of aspects of human creativity itself. All this should make the language graduate whose course has included MT and MAT a very broadly educated person.

To conclude, here is a suggested outline syllabus for an MT and MAT option. It assumes that students have already started studying at least one foreign language and that they will carry these studies to degree level. It further assumes that they have already received at least an introductory course in general linguistics:

1) Introduction to computers. Study of BASIC.
2) Analysis of relationship between (a) computers and natural language and (b) the computer's 'thinking' and human thinking.
3) Study of various kinds of MT and MAT, their strengths and limitations.
4) Study of existing MT and MAT programs.
5) Practice with M(A)T: exploring the interaction of programming needs, linguistic concepts and the grammar, vocabulary and nuances of specific languages. (M(A)T can here include the investigation of possible new areas for computerized interpreting.)
6) Pre-editing and post-editing.
7) Critique of computer (aided) translation. This item should enable students to assess what they have achieved and point the way forward for their future endeavours.

References

[1] For a general treatment of the problem of 'Remembering and Forgetting' see R. H. Thouless *General And Social Psychology*, University Tutorial Press Ltd., 1960 pp. 140–143. Regarding the specific problem of oblivescence in language learning, it is generally agreed that gaps between language lessons or opportunities for practice should be as short as practicably possible. For example, if five lessons per week are envisaged, it will be better to have one on each school day rather than more than one on some days and none on others.

[2] For a similar case relating to German and Russian Language associated with railway construction see L. Hums, 'Zur Russischen Terminologie des Eisenbahnbaus' in the book *Fachsprachen und Sprachstatistik*, edited by L. Hoffmann, Akademie-Verlag: Berlin, 1975 Chapter 8.

[3] For a fuller treatment of the linguistic concepts involved see J. M. Y. Simpson, *A First Course in Linguistics* (Edinburgh UP) (1979) or N. Smith and D. Wilson, *Modern Linguistics (The Results of Chomsky's Revolution)*, Penguin, 1979.

[4] Taken from the talk 'System Performance And Effective Post-editing' given by S. Sereda (General Motors of Canada Ltd,) at the conference on 'Practical Experience of Machine Translation' sponsored jointly by ASLIB (London) and the Translators' Guild of the Institute of Linguists, held at the Kensington Hilton Hotel, London, 5–6 November, 1981. Proceedings of the conference were published by North-Holland Publishing Co., Amsterdam, 1982. The conference was attended by the present author.

[5] At the ASLIB/TG conference (see note 4 above) Ian M. Piggott (EEC Commission) spoke of a time interval of 2 days for batch work for the EEC in his talk: 'The Importance Of Feedback From Translators....'

[6] One such firm is Weidner. At the ASLIB/TG conference (see note 4 above) its products were described by M. Hundt (Mitel Corporation, Ontario, Canada) in his talk, 'Working With The Weidner Machine Translation System'.

[7] In a lecture to staff and students of the Department of Languages, Liverpool Polytechnic, c. 1979, a professional translator, Mr Jonathan Griffin, cited diplomatic language as a register he had found he could translate automatically.

[8] L. Hoffmann, 'Häufigkeitswörterbücher der Subsprachen von Wissenschaft Und Technik'; in L. Hoffmann, *op. cit.* (chapter 2).

[9] C. Puchta, "Einige Besonderheiten russischsprachiger Texte der Physik"; in L Hoffmann, *op. cit.* (chapter 4).

[10] R. Schneider: "Einige Besonderheiten der Fachsprache russischer Texte der Marxistisch-Leninistischen Philosophie"; in L. Hoffmann, *op. cit.* (chapter 5).

[11] See article by H. K. in newspaper *Hannoveraner Generalanzeiger* dated 26th April, 1977, entitled 'Ohne sprachlichen Ballast Fachrussisch in elf Tagen'.

[12] See paper by P. Canisius on "Automatic Partial Translation In A Multilingual Information System" in proceedings of the *Third European Congress on Information Systems and Networks: Overcoming the Language Barrier* (Luxemburg 1977) (K G Saur, London) (2 vols) (pp. 259ff).

[13] Taken from talk on 'The Meteo system' by B. Thouin (Computational Linguistics Consultants Ltd., Montreal, Canada) at the ASLIB/TG conference (see note 4 above). Barrier (Luxemburg 1977) (K. G. Saur, London) (2 vols) (pp. 259ff).

[14] Taken from talk on 'Quality Control Procedures in Modification of the Air Force Russian-English MT system' by Dale Bostad (US Air Force Foreign Technology Division, Dayton, Ohio) at the ASLIB/TG conference (see note 4 above).

[15] Taken from talk 'Coping with Machine Translation', by J. R. Ruffino (Xerox Corporation, Webster, NY, USA) at the ASLIB/TG conference (see note 4 above).

[16] Taken from the paper by B. Lavorel, read by B. McClusky (Head of English Translation, EEC Commission) on "Experience in English-French Postediting" at the ASLIB/TG conference (see note 4 above).

[17] Taken from the talk 'EUROTRA: An Attempt to Achieve Multi-Lingual MT', by Margaret King (Director, ISSCO, University of Geneva, Switzerland) at the ASLIB/TG conference (see note 4 above).

[18] Taken from talk 'Types of Translation and Text Forms in the MT Environment' by Professor J. Sager (Modern Languages, University of Manchester Institute of Science and Technology) at the ASLIB/TG conference (see note 4 above).

[19] Jonathan Griffin (cf. note 7) derives his greatest pleasure, as a translator, from dealing with poetry.

[20] At the ASLIB/TG conference (see note 4 above):

  (a) B. Thouin, in talk mentioned under note 13, said translators no longer quit out of boredom or dissatisfaction once computers are introduced.
  (b) N. Bevan (National Physical Laboratory) said in his talk, 'Psychological Factors and Ergonomics', that MAT would remove tedious aspects of translating and leave the interesting work for the translator to do. He also recommended that postediting be done on a word processor linked to the MAT system.
  (c) G. van Slype in his talk, 'Economic Aspects', reassured members that MT and MAT would not cause unemployment among translators because demand for translation was so great.

15

Computerized information retrieval system for undergraduates of Spanish

P. J. Gummery & P. M. Crompton, Manchester Polytechnic

1 INTRODUCTION

Neither of the authors of this chapter is a computer specialist; it is in fact only nine months ago that we first had "hands on" experience of computers. The development and adaptation of the software has thus been entirely in the hands of the Polytechnic Computer Services Department, especially Margaret Raffel and Brian Horn, to whom we are especially grateful. Thus this chapter seeks no more than first, to describe this development; second, to describe the system as it now operates; and finally, to indicate possible future developments.

In November 1983 a Project Assistant was appointed to archive and index a colossal backlog of Spanish periodicals and magazines. Although publishers' indexes to many periodicals exist, these are often unhelpful as regards the cross-referencing of articles, the sub-indexing of topics, the limited time-span they cover, and the selective interests of undergraduates. There was an obvious need for a simpler and quicker method for making efficient use of an expensive uncoordinated mass of potentially useful material.

Almost every University and Polytechnic library in the U.K., as well as a number of national newspapers and weekly publications were consulted, to find out what systems, if any, were in use. In the commercial sector, only *The Daily Mirror* had experimented with a computerized archive system which was later abandoned. In Higher Education, computerization had been attempted only at the Polytechnics of Newcastle, Bristol and Oxford and at the University of Nottingham. (This situation may have changed considerably since the date of the enquiry.) Reference was made by several libraries to the work being conducted at the Polytechnic of Newcastle and this provided a starting point, for without its help, this project would never have been realized. Help was forthcoming from the library, computing and language staff, and above all from Ms Jackie Barrie, who had started to archive Spanish periodicals by computer. The project must be considered an adaptation of the pioneering system used at Newcastle — albeit with extensive developments — based as it is on the use of a non-hierarchical, key-word system to select and recall articles of interest to the user.

Three major features were seen from the beginning as essential. First, the system must be available to all students of Spanish, with such simplicity of operation that no training was necessary; second, it would be impossible to 'harm' the system when consulting records: third, no cumbersome records or instructions should be needed when using the system. With these conditions in mind, the outlines of the Newcastle project were discussed with the computing staff at Manchester Polytechnic.

The information required for each newspaper entry was determined as 100 characters for a maximum of 8 key words (averaged at 12 characters per word); 170 characters for each newspaper headline; six digits for the day/month/year code; 4 digits for newspaper code; 10 for page references, and so on. We thus calculated a maximum of 350 characters for each newspaper entry. Using one newspaper only, El País, we determined by a preliminary survey that each daily edition contained about twenty articles which would be of interest to students and staff on the courses we teach. Therefore, El País alone provides around 7,000 useful articles per annum, requiring 2,500,000 characters of storage space ($350 \times 20 \times 360$). Although our ambition is to have all papers, magazines and journals on the computer index, it has so far been an uphill battle just to bring El País up to date — a task still not completed.

By March of 1984 the first part-time project assistant, Ruth Harrison, had catalogued about four months of newspaper, and the programmers were ready to start development work. After many meetings to discuss the best way to organize the information, a very basic system was set up using the Polytechnic's PRIME 850 computer and DACOLL terminals. This prototype system allowed one person at a time either to add records or to look up information. This has gradually expanded to allow one Administrator, who has access to all the functions of the program; four adders, who can add records onto TRANS files which have to be checked from the Administrator's file before being transferred to the main file; and six users who can look for records from the main file and take a print-out of the available information.

This limited access keeps tight control over the information and the format of the information which is stored on the file. The format of the keywords is especially important as the program does not allow the computer to offer similar forms for comparison if the exact word is not found; therefore if an incorrect form is used no records are found. To minimize this problem a keyword list is produced and is available on request to all the students using the system. There is no facility within the program at the moment to allow a list of keywords to be shown on the screen. The keywords are in Spanish as it is intended for the original language to be used in indexing all periodicals, avoiding the confusion that would arise from the use of English, with consequent retrieval of irrelevant material from other languages. Also given that some concepts and names of organizations may have no proper equivalent in English, and all the users of the system have some knowledge of Spanish, it is simpler to retain the Spanish forms. 'España' is not used as a keyword since it is assumed that all the articles concern Spain in some way and would, therefore, all need to be indexed under 'España'. Each article may be indexed with up to eight keywords allowing a general description such as politics for example, and then more specific details. Thus an article concerning laws on reform would be indexed under reform, laws, then perhaps education, a minister's name and perhaps a region in Spain. Any one of these keywords will call up the article. This multi-reference system enables a very wide search to be made initially by using a very general term, which can be narrowed down as the amount of information on a given topic is revealed. A prior knowledge of the keywords is an advantage as it will obviously speed up a search, but more important is to have a clear idea of the type of information required. An essay on recent social changes in Spain, for example, must be broken down into categories such as juvenile delinquency and drug abuse, feminism, unemployment etc. The newspaper archive can only provide the details for an essay where a framework has already been set up.

The scope of a general search may be reduced by imposing a time scale. If no date is given, the computer automatically sorts through all the records on the file. However, if information about a certain event is required and its date is known, a search can be made for just that period.

2   USING THE SYSTEM

When the Administrator logs in, the following options appear on the menu:

— *Option 1*
 This has the same format on the Administrator's file and the TRANS files. The computer asks for one piece of information at a time, starting with the keywords. As each section is filled in the computer prompts for the next. The name of the paper and the library, where all the papers are stored, automatically default to 'PAIS' and 'A' for Aytoun Library where the project is based. These can be changed by typing in other details instead of pressing 'return'. If the record is satisfactory the response 'Y' (yes) is given to the question 'is this record acceptable' and the operation repeated with the next record. If the last record 'L' (last) is selected, this allows the computer to reformat the keywords and shorten any which are longer than twelve characters. If, however, the record is not acceptable 'N' (no) is chosen and it is corrected, or 'Q' (quit) which deletes the record and allows it to be restarted.

— *Option 2*
This allows a search by keyword, and also a search by record number. The record number appears in the top right hand corner of a record on the screen. This type of search is run by the Administrator if a problem has occurred but the exact record number is not known. A start and end number are given, then the records are displayed four at a time on the screen and a print-out may be requested.

— *Option 3*
This option allows the updating of individual records if a mistake has been left and noticed later or if the format of a keyword is changed. This operation is carried out in the same way as correcting a record when it is added.

— *Option 4*
To delete records. The record number has to be typed in, which causes the record to be displayed on the screen. This is to ensure the correct record is deleted. Records are deleted one at a time when the right command is given.

— *Option 5*
This option was introduced to remove any 'errors' which may appear in the records. If any odd characters are located they are replaced with spaces.

— *Option 6*
This connects the Administrator with the TRANS files. Each file is accessed separately and must be completely emptied on to the main file before it is possible to log out. Any records which are found to need updating are left in the file until the accurate ones have been transferred. Before corrections are carried out the option to delete any records is offered. The records left in the file at this point then appear one at a time on the screen to be corrected and are automatically transfered when they are acceptable to the Administrator.

Thus, to consult the system, virtually no knowledge of its workings is required. Even the slowest learners — usually lecturers, not students — can retrieve information effortlessly over and over again without any danger of damaging the system. Volunteers with a little more expertise are recruited to add information; but note that nothing can be added to the main file until it has been checked and verified by the Administrator. The system works.

3 PROBLEMS AND FUTURE DEVELOPMENT.

First, time. At least two hours are required to retrieve the minimum information from one newspaper, first formatted on a 5 × 3 inch index card, and then archived by month, year, etc. A further hour is required to access the cards into the computer, either directly into the main file, or via the transfiles. There is no lack of enthusiasm on the part of undergraduates to help with the accessing side; but strict monitoring is required to ensure a standardization of key-word use, perhaps the weakest link in the organisation of this project. Even with a full-time project assistant, it is an enormous task to complete the backlog of information retrieval; the first mistake was not starting with current issues.

Organization is the second problem: strict coordination is required to make the system work, and when research resources are increasingly hard to obtain, full-time help cannot continue indefinitely.

Our third problem is one of space: physical space to store newspapers (until a full microfiche archive is obtained) so that they are easily accessible to students and staff; and computing space to store an increasingly massive data bank. So far the project has been fortunate in having an allocation on the PRIME which can cope with needs, and there are always terminals available for use. Yet in the not too distant future additional space will have to be provided from our own resources.

The final problem is funding. This has been hitherto a relatively low-cost operation, using available facilities to the full, but nevertheless absorbing a significant fraction of Faculty research funds, even with the full co-operation of the Library, Department and Computing Centre. In fact, most efforts over the past six months have been devoted to an entirely different project designed to create finance for the computing archive project.

If all this reads like a tale of woe, it is a minor worry compared with the immense impact the archiving system has had on undergraduate and postgraduate work. Students can now find, in seconds, material which previously would have taken hours to find — if indeed they had bothered to try. Newspapers are jealously hoarded and at last, read! The machinery seems to fascinate the students (perhaps a consequence of their "space-invader" days); but the result is that more newspapers have been read in the last nine months than in the previous ten years.

4   DEVELOPMENTS

First, a refinement to the system: for both adders and users, there is a need for an extra menu item of index words, rather than the present cumbersome printed list. It will need to have an alphabetical sort capability, and if possible be self referencing. Within the Polytechnic, there is a desire to expand the system to include French and German periodicals. A parallel archiving system has been developed by colleagues in the Faculty, designed for texts and critical articles. The two systems run together will allow staff and students an unrivalled archiving service, both general and individualized.

Following the pioneering work of Oxford Polytechnic in French, the system could be opened to outside users, but preferrably by on-line consultation, rather than printed monthly subscription.

Finally: is it too much to hope that in the not too distant future a co-operative of institutions could establish a comprehensive archive of a given academic area, each institution undertaking to archive one periodical, and sharing the the archives of others? There would be little need to make each system compatible; an external consultation would simply require a brief resumé of the individual system used. The resources required to establish a completely autonomous system may well be impossible to obtain; a co-operative venture could provide unimaginable benefits. [Recently, an experimental on-line access for external users has been introduced. For full details please contact the authors.]

Appendix 1   A Sample Session

SPANISH NEWSPAPER SYSTEM
OPTIONS AVAILABLE
1. TO ADD ENTRIES
2. TO LOOK AT ENTRIES
3. TO UPDATÉ ENTRIES
4. TO DELETE ENTRIES
5. TO VERIFY TITLES
6. TO PROCESS TRANS FILES
7. TO QUIT
SELECT Option (1,2,3,4,5,6 OR 7)
Option 1. screen shows-
Enter the INDEX WORDS
TITLE
CONT
DATE START PAGE CONT PAGES
PAPER LIBRARY
When the record is complete the computer asks:
IS THIS RECORD ACCEPTABLE (Y,N,Q OR L) >
Option 2 TO LOOK AT.
DO YOU WANT TO SELECT A RANGE OF RECORD NUMBERS (Y/N)
Y >
THERE ARE 4000 RECORDS IN THE FILE
ENTER START RECORD NUMBER 3699
ENTER END RECORD NUMBER 3701
3 RECORDS SELECTED
Records are displayed, followed by the question:
DO YOU WANT ANY PRINTED OUT ? (1,2,3,4 OR ALL)
DO YOU WANT TO SELECT ANOTHER RANGE ?(Y/N)

Option 3 TO UPDATE
SPANISH NEWSPAPER ARTICLES FILE UPDATE
ENTER RECORD NO.
Record appears on the screen ready to be updated, after which
you are asked:
IS THIS RECORD ACCEPTABLE (Y,N, Q OR L)
When the record is correct you can update another or return,
automatically, to the main menu.
Option 4 TO DELETE
ENTER RECORD NUMBER YOU WISH TO DELETE
PAPER PAIS
DATE
PAGE
CONT
TITLE
LIBRARY A
KEYWORDS
OK TO DELETE RECORD ? (Y/N)
Option 5 TO VERIFY TITLES
SPANISH NEWSPAPER ARTICLES FILE TITLES CHECK
ENTER RECORD NUMBER
Title is displayed on the screen, followed by:
NO ODD CHARACTERS FOUND
DO YOU WANT TO CHECK ANOTHER RECORD
Option 6 TO PROCESS TRANS FILES
SPANISH NEWSPAPER SYSTEM
PROCESS TRANSACTION FILES
1. TO ADD RECORDS FROM TRANS1 TO NEWS-FILE
2. TO ADD RECORDS FROM TRANS2 TO NEWS-FILE
3. TO ADD RECORDS FROM TRANS3 TO NEWS-FILE
4. TO ADD RECORDS FROM TRANS4 TO NEWS-FILE
5. TO RETURN TO MAIN MENU
SELECT OPTION (1,2,3,4 OR 5)
ADD1
THIS OPTION ALLOWS YOU TO SELECT RECORDS IN
TRANSACTION FILE FOR
TRANSFER TO NEWS-FILE. YOU CAN ADD RECORDS DIRECTLY
AT FIRST
PROMPT OR YOU CAN UPDATE THEM FIRST.

Screen shows 4 records which may be marked for transfer or saved to be
updated first. You are asked to wait a short time while the computer carries out
the instructions. When all records have been looked at, you are asked:

DO YOU WANT TO DELETE ANY RECORDS

When all the records have been processed you are automatically returned to the main menu. To leave the system chose option 7 which logs you out.

16

The ideal teaching machine

Masoud Yazdani, University of Exeter

1 INTRODUCTION

This chapter may seem rather out of place in a book on the art of modern language teaching. My only personal interaction with what, for many readers of this book, is an important endeavour has been a negative one. I first arrived in Britain 10 years ago without having much knowledge of the English language. On arrival, I registered at a school respected for its teaching of English as a foreign language in June of that year. By the following August I was very disturbed by the quality of teaching at the school and this did not seem to be untypical of most other schools in the same town. Most other students viewed the lessons as part of their summer holiday in Britain and treated them accordingly. The most disturbing fact for me was that teachers seemed to share this attitude.

Having decided that I was not going to learn much English this way, and being unaware of any better school, I aproached the best of the teachers for private tuition. During the first session I explained my frustration with the affairs of the school and bluntly asked the teacher if he was capable of teaching me any English. He smiled at me knowingly and replied that "languages are learned and not taught". He advized me not to worry too much about the language and to proceed to the next part of my education, which was to study computer science at university.

This I did and, after 10 years, I seem to have forgotten my goal of learning English. In the process, I have also moved away from my initial concern with computer science to a new field of study known as Artificial Intelligence.

AI is concerned with the mysteries of intelligence and computers are sometimes used in this endeavour as a tool [1]. The concerns of AI include a desire to know "how people learn" and "how people teach". During the past five years I have been trying to build systems which are capable of a limited amount of intelligent behaviour in the domain of teaching of arithmetic skills [2, 3] and, more recently, languages [4].

First and foremost I have to admit that my prime interest is in the discoveries which might occur about the nature of the "learning" and "teaching" behaviour than in actually building useful teaching or learning tools. Nevertheless, I have to admit to a certain level of irresponsibility in offering the results of the research in progress to practising teachers, in case they may be able to put them to good use. The real motivation behind this irresponsibility is a desire to put the theories to the acid test. However much we work in the laboratory on the development of general theories, we cannot ignore the fact that such theories need to conform to the practices of the world outside. What better source of feedback can we have than by putting our theories to the test in areas where humans themselves welcome involvement. This work therefore differs in motivation from that of the more traditional computer assisted learning, where the needs of the practising teacher, the limitations of the computing devices available, and the dynamics of educational practice have had to be of primary importance.

2   COMPUTER ASSISTED LEARNING

Computer Assisted Learning (CAL) has followed an evolutionary path since it was started in the 1950s with simple "linear programs". Such programs were influenced by the prevailing behaviourist theories [5] and the programmed learning machines of the previous decade. It was believed that if the occurrence of an operant is followed by the presentation of a reinforcing stimulus, the strength is increased. To this end a computer program will output a frame of text which will take the student one small step towards the desired behaviour. The student then makes some kind of response based on what he already knows, or by trial and error! Finally the program informs the student whether he is correct; a stream of such steps is known as a "linear program". The student may work through the material at his own pace and his correct replies are rewarded immediately.

In the 1960s it was felt that one could use the student's response to control the material that the student would be shown next. In this way students learn more thoroughly as they attempt problems of an appropriate difficulty, rather than wading their way through some systematic exploration. The "branching programs" therefore offered corrective feedback as well as adapted their teaching to students' responses. However the task of the design of the teaching materials for such systems was impossibly large. This led to the birth of "author languages", specific languages suitable for the development of CAL material.

In the 1970s a new level of sophistication was discovered in the design of CAL systems where, in some domains such as arithmetic, it was possible to generate the teaching material itself for the computer. A random number generator could produce two numbers to be added together by the pupil, and then the results of the computer's solution of the addition and the student's addition process would be compared in order to generate a response. Such systems need only therefore to be given general teaching strategies and they will produce a tree of possible interaction with infinitely large numbers of branches. Such generative systems could answer some of the questions from the students, as well as incorporate some sort of "difficulty measure".

By looking at the algorithms for CAL, developed over the last 30 years, we see that they have improved on the richness of feedback and the degree of individualization they offer the students. However, they are all basically forms of "learning by being told". Although CAL seems to have improved beyond expectation in computational sophistication from its humble beginnings as a replacement for the programmed learning machines, it still suffers from a behaviourist and reinforcement theory of learning.

In generative systems there is a mismatch between the program's internal processes (computer architecture) and those of the student's cognitive processes (rules and tables). None of these systems have human-like knowledge of the domain they are teaching, nor can they answer serious questions of the students as to "why" and "how" the task is performed.

3 INTELLIGENT TUTORING SYSTEMS

Workers in AI have been aware of the importance of teaching along with other human activities. Intelligent Tutoring Systems were the first examples of a radically new approach to educational computing [6]. While CAL has tended to be basically drill and practice, Intelligent Tutoring Systems have aimed to be diagnostic. The following incorrect subtraction and addition

```
   170          033
 — 093        + 179
 ——————       ——————
   187          102
```

will not result in the message 'wrong, you lose a point' being printed on the screen, but will lead to a correct diagnosis of the pupil's error in forgetting the borrow or the carry over.

These systems succeed by containing clear articulation of knowledge involved in a narrow domain. One such system DEBUGGY [7] performs as well as, or rather better than, human teachers in diagnosis of misconceptions of pupils when performing subtraction.

There have been two major criticisms levelled against such sophisticated systems. Such systems "have not yet been incorporated within a remedial program, with which students can interact to improve their subtraction skill; nor has it yet been presented in such a form as to be usable as a diagnostic aid by any mathematics teacher" [8]. The major reason behind these shortcomings has been the complexity of the task involved. Even in such a narrow domain, such as subtraction, there are numerous ways in which a pupil can make mistakes. Therefore a program such as DEBUGGY would be beyond the power of a modest school microcomputer. However, as the cost of hardware is declining, it has become possible to offer some of this level of sophistication to the school teacher. Attisha and Yazdani [2] use a taxonomy of possible errors which children make in addition and subtraction in order to provide remedial advice, similar to that of DEBUGGY, using a school microcomputer. Furthermore, Attisha and Yazdani [3] have extended this work to cover multiplication, which is by nature more complex than subtraction. In multiplication the pupil could make mistakes due to various reasons: problems with the multiplication table, with the multiplication algorithm, or with the addition of subtotals. When errors in any two of these areas are combined, the result could appear to be nothing more than carelessness (random) to the best of human teachers. However, the computer system provides exercises in order to isolate different areas of difficulty and diagnose the problem.

4   EXPERT SYSTEMS

One novel way of teaching a subject such as Physics or Medicine would be to produce an Expert System which would behave like a skilled physisist or a medical consultant [9]. It is claimed that the trainee can then observe the knowledge and the line of reasoning of the program and learn by it so that trainee doctors, for example, could simply be asked to look over MYCIN's shoulder as it sets about solving its problems [10]. This is because:

— MYCIN can explain in English what it is doing.
— MYCIN's decision-making processes are similar to those which students are supposed to develop.
— MYCIN's representation of medical information is in a human-like manner.

MYCIN is one of a number of AI's commercially viable propositions called an Expert System. Such systems are experts in a very narrow domain of knowledge to a degree that, within their domain, they can match the performance of human experts, and possibly exceed them.

The GUIDON program [11] is one application using existing expert systems such as MYCIN for educational purposes. Clancey argues that, although MYCIN-like rule-bases are a good means of transferring knowledge from a human expert to a human trainee, the rules in themselves are not sufficient. He proposes adding two further levels: one a "support" level to justify rules, and the second an "abstraction" level to organize rules into patterns in order to transfer such systems into a tutorial medium. Further, he argues that such systems still need teaching expertise of a general kind and natural language competence to carry out a coherent dialogue with the student. Fig. 16.1 shows the overall structure of the program.

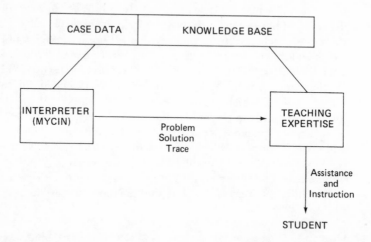

Clancey's work is encouraging in the task of providing computer assisted learning in a domain where the system itself is capable of performing the task that it is expecting the trainee to perform. For example, Barchan, Woodmansee and Yazdani [4] have chosen a domain of application (language teaching) which, to our knowledge, has not yet been the subject of such treatment.

Most language teaching programs rely on a massive store of correct sentences and divisions of them. Despite the large number of legitimate constructs with which they can deal, the programs are really nothing more than a dumb, if effective, pattern matcher, linking unintelligible orders of characters to those pre-stored. As a consequence, the programs cannot recognize or comment upon errors encountered, even if the errors are frequent, unless these have been individually and specifically anticipated by the programmer. Therefore, the standard of accuracy required (coupled with the time for preparation of exercises) seems very high indeed.

Instead, systems such as FROG [12] and FGA [4], which use a general purpose language parser, can cope with an indefinite number of possibilities without being programmed in advance to anticipate all the possibilities.

The use of expert systems in education could be considered as the most promising advance in the 1980s on the earlier CAL systems of the previous three decades. However still more research is necessary before this technology can be considered mature enough.

Most intelligent tutoring systems rely on a good knowledge of the domain where the teaching takes place. For example, Attisha and Yazdani [2] rely on a vast amount of existing data in order to build a full taxonomy of childrens' errors in subtraction. The problem in fact is also suffered by tutoring systems which use production rules or procedural networks which, although more powerful, still rely on a reasonable knowledge of the domain while they are being constructed. Such knowledge is not readily available in cases where we have a more complex domain than arithmetic.

What seems to be obvious (but rather hard yet to contemplate using) is the idea of *machine learning*. The work in this area is already sufficiently advanced [13] for there to be hope that such techniques may be incorporated — so that a computer tutor could, similarly to a human tutor, learn more about the domain in which it is teaching. However, such sophistication requires computational resources well beyond those available to educational establishments.

Instant feedback and individualization have been the twin gods of computer assisted learning [9] for three decades. AI systems seem to provide the possibility of not only instant feedback, but a reasonably rich level of it — good remedial advice for example. However, on the individualisation side, AI does not yet seem to have offered any advances on what CAL had done. GUIDON, for example, suffers from the fact that it is always comparing a trainee doctor's actions with that of MYCIN, while what is needed is a knowledge of what a particular user knows about the topic, his current misconceptions in addition to the terminology with which he is familiar and the forms of explanation which he finds effective.

These needs are shared by most interactive AI systems and a good deal of research is already in progress in what is labelled *user modelling*. My personal view is that these problems can be viewed as extensions of the *machine learning* ones. A human teacher is constantly learning, both about the domain in which he is teaching as well as the pupils being taught.

5   LEARNING ENVIRONMENTS

Intelligent tutoring systems are rather effective for the teaching of narrow domains, but construction of systems based on general competence in areas such as 'problem solving' seems impractical. In their place, Seymour Papert [14] has argued in favour of the development of *learning environments* which provide a student with powerful computing tools. The student thereby engages in an open-ended learning-by-discovery process by programming the computer to carry out interesting tasks. It is argued that the intention is not to learn how to program a computer, but to learn *through* programming a computer.

Artificial Intelligence programming environments are tailored to human beings, minimizing the cognitive load put on a naive user, as opposed to optimising the machine's efficiency. Yazdani [15] presents four such environments based around LOGO, SOLO, PROLOG and POP-11. The practical contribution of such environments is that they make it possible to design computing systems which are educational, fun and which relate to childrens' basic feelings.

Papert has argued that such activity (playing with LOGO for example) has a similar role to that of playing with sand pits in the Piagetian theories of learning. In playing with AI programming environments children build *objects to think with* in place of sand castles. This building process takes place in what is known as a *microworld*: a limited portion of the real world whose characteristics can be easily understood.

AI is fond of using microworlds in all its areas of research, because microworlds can easily be formalized. The most influencial AI work in natural language processing [16] converses with the users about a small world of a table top with a number of coloured boxes inhabiting it. The computer program is capable of not only obeying orders in this world, but also discussing it in detail. Another program will learn new concepts from the old if taught by a human teacher. The obvious hope of researchers has been to generalize principles of representation and manipulation of knowledge in microworlds to the real world, in the same way as a child playing with such blocks would. Unfortunately AI has not yet been able to translate its successful attempts with microworlds to the real world. There seems to be such a level of increase in complexity of the domain when moving away from the microworlds to the real ones, that most lessons need to be relearned.

Papert has argued that such microworlds would constitute a very good complement to the ones usually used by children up to now (such as Meccano sets) and would be as effective, if not more so. The most well-known of these computational microworlds has been turtle graphics. This is a computing package (based around a mechanical device with the same name) which will take commands from children in a way similar to their pet "turtle" if it could understand them. In this way, children succeed in drawing wonderful shapes by giving simple commands to the computer. In addition to this a number of other microworlds have been successfully used, such as one based around a beach [17] and one based around the world of a farmer trying to transport a fox, a chicken and a bag of grain across a river (Sloman,1984). The possibilities in this area seem to be endless.

Lawler has started work on a number of microworlds in which a child communicates with the computer, using an optimal monosyllabic vocabulary in order to program the computer with graphical results corresponding to the meaning of the words. It is conceivable that a successor to such systems would make communication with the computer similar to communication with natives of a foreign land on a foreign visit.

It should be noted that, although such approaches seem to be the most promising, there still remain many unsolved problems.

Using sophisticated AI programming languages, as well as their supplementation with educational microworlds, provides the exciting possibility of using them for learning abstract concepts such as problem solving. However concrete evidence has yet to be given that this process is in fact educationally effective. What is an open question is whether the pupil who learns powerful new ideas while playing with a microworld could, in fact, reapply them in the real world. Lighthill [20] pinpoints the obsession with microworlds in his most effective critique of AI: "Most robots are designed from the outset to operate in a world as like as possible to the conventional child's world as seen by man; they play games, they do puzzles, they build towers of bricks, they recognize pictures in drawing-books ('bear on rug with ball'); although the rich emotional character of the child's world is totally absent".

The major weakness of microworlds and the free-learning idea on which they are based, is exactly what makes them so powerful. They can cope with a large variety of possibilities, limited by the imagination of the user. The user is free to chose his own problems and the route to their solutions. This approach, whilst increasing the pupil's motivation, simultaneously decreases learning efficiency. The pupil is simply not very good at selecting his own learning strategy. However this shortcoming can be alleviated by designing *courseware* within which such activity is fitted. Here a human teacher holds the pupil's hand when necessary and leaves him free to explore when educationally effective. In other words, the shortcoming has so far been in viewing these systems as complete environments: they are in fact elements of a larger human environment where the emotional context is provided by the human teacher.

6   CONCLUSION

The advocates of the use of AI in education seem to be grouped in favour either of Intelligent Tutoring Systems, or the Learning Environments. The first group concern themselves with more powerful teaching systems aiming to be as competent as a good human teacher. The second group intend to build powerful computing tools with which students learn through play. I remember a friend reminding me that education is such an old subject that nothing is new in this field. It is only the terminology which changes every so often. It seems my friend is right, at least as far as AI's contribution to education is concerned. The two approaches indicated above clearly follow the old-fashioned dichotomy of the *teacher-centred* versus *student-centred* view of education.

The tutoring systems concentrate on providing an intelligent teacher. Such ideas would lead to a machine which is capable of rich interaction with the student, would know how to teach and who and what it is teaching. The learning environments, however, ignore such issues, taking as their evidence the fact that learning can happen without any formal instruction. Therefore they concentrate on the motivational aspects, relevance and ease of use of the environments.

I believe that the challenge for the 1990s will be to find a happy medium in which artificial and human teachers as well as students can live together and provide the medium for the highest level of all round education.

References

[1] Yazdani, M. and Narayanan, A. (eds), (1984), *Artificial Intelligence: Human Effects*, Ellis Horwood.

[2] Attisha, M. and Yazdani, M. (1983), "A Microcomputer-based Tutor for Teaching Arithmetic Skills", *Instructional Science* Vol. 12.

[3] Attisha, M. and Yazdani, M. (1984), "An Expert System for Diagnosing Childrens' Multiplication Errors", *Instructional Science* Vol 13.

[4] Barchan, J. Woodmansee, B. and Yazdani, M. (1985), "A Prolog-based tool for French Grammar Analysis", *Instructional Science*, Vol 14.

[5] Sleeman, D. and Brown, J. S. (eds), (1982), *Intelligent Tutoring Systems*, Academic Press.

[6] Skinner, B. F. (1958), 'Teaching Machines', *Science*, 128.

[7] Burton, R. R. (1982), "DEBUGGY: Diagnosis of Errors in Basic Mathematical Skills", in Sleeman and Brown (eds).

[8] Boden, M. A. (1982), "The Educational Implications of Artificial Intelligence", in Maxwell, W. (ed), *Thinking*, Frankline Institute Press.

[9] O'Shea, T. and Self, J. (1983), *Learning and Teaching with Computers*, The Harvester Press.

[10] Shortcliffe, E. H. (1976), *Computer-based medical consultations: MYCIN*, American Elsevier.

[11] Clancey, W. J. (1979), "Tutoring rules for guiding a case method dialogue" *Int J of Man-Machine Studies*

[12] Imlah, W. and du Boulay, B. (1985), *Robust Natural Language Parsing in Computer Assisted Language Instruction*, Cognitive Studies Programme University of Sussex.

[13] Michalski, R. S., Carbonell, J. G. and Mitchel, T. M. (1984), *Machine Learning: An Artificial Intelligence Approach*, Kaufmann Inc/ Springer Verlag.

[14] Papert, S. (1980), *Mindstorms — Children, Computers, and Powerful Ideas*, The Harvester Press / Basic Books.

[15] Yazdani, M. (ed), (1984), *New Horizons in Educational Computing*, Ellis Horwood .

[16] Winograd, T. (1972), *Understanding Natural Language*, Edinbugh University Press.

[17] Lawler, R. (1984), "Designing Computer-Based Microworlds", in [15].

[18] Sloman, A. (1984), 'Beginners Need Powerful Systems' in [15].

[19] Lawler, R. (1986), "Computer Microworlds and Reading: An analysis for their systematic application", *Instruction Science*, Vol. 14.

[20] Lighthill, J. (1972), *Artificial Intelligence : A Report to the Science Research Council*, SRC.

Postword

Steven Dodd, University of Exeter

1 INTRODUCTION

The Exeter conference was interesting by virtue of attracting a very varied collection of contributions, which ran beyond the edges of Computer Assisted Language Learning, to cover a larger area that can only be described as Computer Based Instruction in Languages. There was an offering (Stewart) in the field of Machine Translation, with the suggestion that Machine Aided Translation could be a technique that would find a useful niche in both the traditional translation biased language course and the more recent interpreter training courses. There was a contribution concerning automated dictionary search and grammar analysis (Hartley and Motley). There were papers in the area of Computer Management of Instruction, talking of databases of texts in foreign languages (Gummery and Crompton); there were papers which looked towards the arrival of Artificial Intelligence methods in modern language work (Yazdani), and towards the applications of the "expert system" concept to the provision of aid in composing or checking natural languages (Barchan). Finally, there were many descriptions and demonstrations of currently used CALL materials, mostly dedicated programs, but including some authoring systems.

In a conference of the size and diversity of the one held at Exeter, it is not surprising to find a range of views and aims as well as of techniques. There is truly, as was suggested by the initial keynote welcome, a divergence between what can be done in the short term, the medium term, and the long term with regard to the use of computers in language teaching. In the end, it is clear that unless some major unforeseen occurrence interrupts progress, this field will be dominated by machines having the capacity to process human language in a way that is virtually indistinguishable from that of humans — the Turing test will have been passed with honours.

However, although the more remote future may belong to artificial intelligence, in the present this discipline has serious gaps. In all probability, true natural language processing will have to wait for the advent of entirely new machine architectures, involving parallel processsing. Even with ever increasing rapidity and efficiency, and allowance for tricks such as pipelining, the existing serial architectures do not seem able to deal with the sort of multiple simultaneous interlinked processes which humans apparently perform in making use of language. It may be that the problem is made worse by the fact that much of the work in natural language processing is still barking up the less and less convincing transformational tree, a model never espoused by language teachers or even by many applied linguistics experts. Alternative approaches, such as Systemics and Stratificational Linguistics, look more promising, as also do techniques like the "state and action" table.

In the immediate future, in schools and in higher education as well, if perhaps to a lesser extent, it is unlikely, in any case, that there will be enough funding for equipment to enable the pursuit of many desirable goals. While it is true that 16 bit computers are declining in price quite rapidly, and that random access memory is getting very inexpensive, permitting, for example, the use of the so-called "RAM disk", it is not going to be possible to keep up with the electronic Joneses in all cases. Even if this were not the case, moving to the latest model as soon as it comes out poses a major problem of compatibilities, for almost invariably manufacturers have taken care to avoid easy transfer of software, and the thought of losing all the materials prepared for an earlier machine should give pause for thought. This may change with the growing trend towards equipment compatibility — Centronics and Epson norms in printers, IBM PC as a standard in 16 bit micros, MSX in extensions to BASIC. However, it is a considerable obstacle. In addition, very often the larger size of machine merely allows more space to be wasted. Computer scientists, who, very naturally, are interested in technical developments and, at least in part, have the funds needed to keep up with them, see the world through different eyes from those of a language teacher to whom a computer is, at best, a minor ancillary and often less than that. To decry teachers' unadventurous willingness to stay with the small machines they have at present is fair only if this difficulty is kept clearly in mind. Otherwise it is no fairer than it would have been to criticize a cyclist for using a penny-farthing in 1870 on the grounds that the motor car was about to reach the market: remember, it took fifty years for cars to become reliable, and over a hundred years later it is still always cheaper and sometimes no less efficient to use a bicycle rather than an automobile.

The message that can be seen in a lot of what was demonstrated at the conference is that this restriction to machines which are of quite feeble capacities need not be a wholly negative thing. Many programs shown gave indication of ways in which the possibilities of the 8-bit micro, even when as small as the BBC model B, can be more fully exploited. A number of very exciting ideas have been implemented, many more are still waiting in the wings, for we are far from having exhausted all the capacities of this equipment.

One area that can sometimes be seen as receiving too much attention is the "pretty" screen display, where effort is lavished on graphics and possibly on sound effects as well. It is true that to write hundreds of lines of program which lovingly draws a beautiful picture of a pencil on the screen, and then merely labels it "PENCIL", or perhaps requires the student to type in "PENCIL", but does not recognize or comment on anything other than that single word, puts the cart completely before the horse. Equally, small micros cannot compete with the sophisticated animated graphics or video-disk recordings now routinely used in arcade games, and familiar to a growing proportion of potential users. On the other hand, the distinction between upper case and lower case letters and between letters with and without diacritic marks is vital in numerous foreign languages, and to omit it or distort it is to nullify the paedagogic value of a program in such cases. This is all the more true where a non-Latin script is in use, as in Russian or Greek. We saw a particularly attractive display of Arabic script in one suite of programs (Taylor and Harding). Since computer materials are still largely confined to the written mode, and since the level of acceptable error in spelling, and punctuation is very different from the laxity with which foreign accents are accepted in speech, one might argue that complete spelling accuracy should be given absolute priority. In addition, the use of colour or inverse video to distinguish which part of a screen display is generated by the computer and which by the user is a technique with which it is hard to find fault. A certain amount of graphic display may help enliven and make simpler the use of programs. No programs displayed made use of the "icon" concept, but one suite of programs combined highlighting and limited graphics into an especially attractive whole (Fox).

Another area of interest, much mentioned in the conference, is that of integration with non-computer activities, (see, for example, Benwell) and of moving towards more communicative methods, such as have found increasing favour in the teaching of English as a foreign language and more recently in foreign language teaching. Here there are numerous avenues to explore. They include the connecting of audio reproduction equipment onto the micro, which is difficult for technical reasons at present, but seems likely not to be so for long, and would give access to a colossal bank of materials; and the same connexion for video equipment, already technically easier, but less useful in that there is far less existing material on which to draw. Another line of approach as yet not fully exploited is the use of the micro as an informant, or as a participant in a group work session.

The increasing tendency to link whole suites of programs (see, for example, Richardson) is a welcome one, especially where this leads to a combination of informative "feeder" programs and back-up tests reinforcing them, and is more likely to produce rounded-out courses capable of standing comparison with those employing other media.

The technique of hybridization, where an authoring package is able to be extensively modified by the user, or to accept small user programs as add-ons, or alternatively a dedicated program can be opened up and made more general-purpose, is already finding considerable favour in the USA. One authoring package demonstrated (L'Huillier) was an example of this tendency, as it was dedicated to French verbs, but permitted free input by the user of contexts, questions, responses and other details.

One further interesting concept is the program which is so organized as to contain all of the rules of a particular area of grammar, so that it can make a sensible attempt at responding to a partially correct answer. Of this sort were several items among the Project Pallas software displayed: one program was able to recognize all French personal pronouns and to explain what grammatical details of the student's input pronoun were different from the stored correct answer: another was designed to cope with all the verbal morphology of Spanish, so that a grammatically correct word would always be given a response that indicated it was a valid word, even if not the appropriate one for the context, and would prompt the machine to specify in what ways it differed from this appropriate form. An expansion of this type of program would logically lead to something not far from the more ambitious "expert system" hinted at by another speaker.

In view of all these developments, it is clear that we should soon be leaving behind the isolated program that tests a single area of grammar in a foreign language with no reference to the remainder of the course students are following, and in a structuralist mode which is no further developed than the earliest language laboratory drills of the 1950s.

For these reasons, the call made at the end of the conference for a greater willingness to collaborate is very welcome. Specifically, with an eye to flexibility as new and varied machines gradually arrive, there would be considerable value in a central pool, not of programs, although they also might be so pooled, but rather of algorithms, the formulae explaining how to carry out specific tasks. Mathematicians have had these for many centuries, and logicians for almost as long, but a rigid and detailed account of how a given piece of language should be manipulated to achieve a given result is an extreme rarity still, although computers began to be applied to language and literature over two decades ago, and such formulae are of prime importance in enabling programming. Materials banks are also an area where more collaboration could be of great value. They are quite common in primary and secondary education, but have not yet really reached the tertiary sector. Thus, it is to efforts of this sort that I feel we should be looking in order to advance to the day when CALL is a commonplace.

Index

ROASTING PAN SUPPERS

ROASTING

PAN

SUPPERS

ROSIE SYKES

National Trust

First published in the United Kingdom in 2020 by
National Trust Books
43 Great Ormond Street
London WC1N 3HZ
An imprint of Pavilion Books Company Ltd

ISBN: 9781911657316

A CIP catalogue record for this book is available from the British Library.

25 24 23 22 21 20
10 9 8 7 6 5 4 3 2 1

Reproduction by Rival Colour Ltd, UK
Printed by Toppan Leefung Printing Ltd, China

This book is available at National Trust shops and online
at www.nationaltrustbooks.co.uk, or try the publisher
(www.pavilionbooks.com) or your local bookshop.

NOTES

- Medium, free-range eggs are used unless otherwise specified. Warning:
  recipes containing raw eggs are unsuitable for pregnant women or
  young children.
- Reasonable care has been taken to ensure the accuracy of the recipes and
  instructions in this book. However, any liability for inaccuracies or errors
  relating to the material contained within the book is expressly excluded to
  the fullest extent permitted by law.
- You may not always achieve the desired results. Oven temperatures vary
  between different appliances and different equipment may affect the desired
  outcome. Neither the National Trust, National Trust (Enterprises) Ltd nor
  Pavilion Books Ltd accept any responsibility or liability for the end results
  of the recipes featured in this book.

INTRODUCTION

As a chef of 20-odd years standing, I have spent much time in front of a range, slinging about pans of all shapes and sizes. In the professional kitchen, the oven was really the domain of the pastry section. Yet during the times of day when I was doing my mise en place – i.e. getting ready for the hustle and bustle of service – I sometimes cooked things in the oven when space on the range was at a premium. The all-round heat of the oven is easier to manage than the direct heat of the hob. A roasting pan just requires a shake now and again, whereas a saucepan needs frequent stirring to prevent ingredients from sticking or burning.

As I used the oven more and more, experimenting and learning, I started thinking of various tricks and techniques – for example, thickening up a tomato sauce or making a chutney works really well in the oven. (One of my favourite lessons from writing this book was perfecting the art of the tomato sauce in the oven – the recipe is in the Fish chapter, on page 50.) And so this book was born. I have included flavours from all over the world, to make this an even more interesting culinary journey. I also always aim to cook as sustainably as possible. Nowadays, you can easily pick up affordable, environmentally-friendly alternatives to common kitchenware, such as reusable kitchen towels instead of kitchen paper and beeswax wraps instead of clingfilm.

This kind of cooking is not an exact science: there are just a few basic principles, and it's a great way to build your confidence in the kitchen. Hopefully you'll end up with a repertoire of personal favourites that you make and share again and again.

I've discovered a few things that add value to the experience, chiefly that it is worth having roasting pans in various sizes (especially as a few of the recipes call for more than one roasting pan). Most of the dishes in the book respond very well to being cooked in metal, but ceramic or ovenproof glass baking dishes will work too. The roasting pans I use most – and these are approximate sizes – are:

SMALL: 30 X 20CM
MEDIUM: 35 X 25CM
LARGE: 40 X 30CM

In some recipes I have suggested which size to use, but it may depend on the result you are looking for. Some good pointers are:

• When roasting pieces of meat, and to some extent fish and vegetables, spread them out so that they can cook evenly all over and caramelise a bit – this part of the process contributes rich flavours.

• Select a tray with enough space for the heat to circulate. This will ensure you don't create steam, which is the enemy of crispness. This is important when cooking chicken thighs with their skin on, for example, as you want to get a nice crisp skin.

• As a general rule, a larger surface area will yield a drier result. So if you are trying to thicken a sauce and reduce some juices, go for a bigger pan.

• When braising meat, packing it together in a huddle once it has been browned will help to keep moisture in and make for a more succulent, tender final product.

• When softening vegetables, especially onions, a smaller surface area is preferable. Always add a pinch of salt at the beginning as this helps them break down and release moisture, and in turn steam and soften.

• Most baking works best in a small or medium pan, unless you are going for a whopper cake, in which case you will need to scale up quantities.

I find that many great dishes begin with an onion or something else in that family. Consequently, many of the recipes start with sweating onions in a roasting pan. This works extremely well in the oven and, although it requires patience, it doesn't need constant attention, as it would if cooking in a pan on the hob. The even temperature and steamy environment means they are less likely to stick; a stir now and again is a good idea, but generally if left to their own devices the result will be sweet and rich, which is what a good base flavour relies on.

Most vegetables respond very well to roasting. I occasionally suggest giving them a few minutes in boiling salted water first, otherwise they may dry out too much. Everything else is possible in a roasting pan in the oven.

COOKING MEAT AND FISH

The oven is traditionally home to big pieces of meat, such as hearty roasts and braises, or slow-cooked stews. However, it is also a very efficient way to cook smaller pieces of meat, such as chops and steaks, pieces of chicken, or sausages, especially if your vegetables are cooked in the same pan. You will find plenty of recipes that can be on the table in under an hour from start to finish, along with a few slow cookers, which would be great for weekends when time is not of the essence (see Timing Is Everything, page 10).

Aim always to buy meat with the highest possible welfare standards: eating less meat of higher quality is more environmentally sustainable in the long term. If you have the time, I would encourage you to chat to your local butcher, who may have some interesting pearls of wisdom. When buying fish, look for sustainably sourced fish, which will display the Marine Stewardship Council (MSC) logo (for more information see the Marine Conservation Society website mcsuk.org).

Fish takes less time to cook than meat because its muscle structure is completely different and heat can permeate the flesh much more quickly. Cooking times depend on a variety of factors – the type of fish, the thickness of the pieces used, and whether or not they are on the bone – but it is important not to overcook fish. Perfectly cooked fish becomes opaque and flakes easily. If cooked with its skin, you will know it is ready when the skin peels off with ease.

A number of the recipes in this chapter call for skinless firm white fish. I tend not to specify more than that because it really depends on what is available. If you are lucky enough to have a local fishmonger, take guidance from them and ask them to do all the filleting, skinning and boning – they will have the knives and the skill to do this efficiently.

Having dedicated most of our time to preparing the meat or fish, we often find ourselves turning out the same old thing to have alongside our supper, and side dishes become something of a safe, predictable afterthought. There is nothing wrong with this – I am a big fan of frozen peas, as is my dachshund – but it's good to expand your repertoire with some simple, flavoursome side dishes that you can bung in the oven. Several of these dishes would also group together as a feast in themselves (see Cooking Up a Feast, page 12). I have included quite a few vegan recipes and others are fairly easy to turn vegan with the substitution or omission of dairy.

Britain is truly lucky to have a great array of vegetables available. Look for the Red Tractor logo – the Union Flag in the logo indicates the food has been farmed, processed and packed in the United Kingdom. While it is wonderful to grow our own or visit farmers' markets and farm shops, often there just isn't the time. Some supermarkets have local producers on board, or sell the less-than-perfect veg which, at one time, wouldn't have made it onto their shelves. Choose organic produce whenever possible – look for the Soil Association logo. Organic farming avoids the use of synthetic pesticides, herbicides and fertilisers, so it's better for the environment and better for us. I try and cook seasonally as much as I can and have put together vegetables that generally are picked around the same time of year. That said, frozen vegetables and tinned pulses are a boon for a busy lifestyle.

SWEET

According to current culinary trends, it seems that puddings are increasingly restricted to entertaining rather than the traditional end of an everyday meal. However, a sweet treat now and again is always welcome. Pears, plums, peaches, apricots and figs all respond well to oven-roasting, with the addition of cream, thick Greek-style yoghurt, custard or ice cream and a crisp biscuit. And they may just as easily find their way into a bowl of porridge for breakfast or as the filling for a cake or pie. This chapter includes a range of simple-to-prepare recipes for puddings that work equally well for elevenses or tea.

I am a firm believer that recipes are a framework; once you are in the zone, modification comes easily and then a recipe truly becomes your own. So use this collection as a springboard for your own creativity. Happy roasting pan cooking!

TIMING IS EVERYTHING

Sometimes speed is of the essence: here is an idea of what can be on the table hastily or at a more leisurely pace. The 30-minute column includes a few enticing sides which would be great with some grilled sausages or bacon, or simply cooked fish. The longer recipes don't require you to be hands-on for anywhere near the amount of time stated – the ingredients do their own thing in the oven while you do the same elsewhere!

ABOUT 30 MINUTES

- Lamb steaks in mojo verde with roast potatoes and green pepper
  (see page 47)

- Pork tenderloin and lemon cauliflower
  (see page 31)

- Roast cauliflower and broccoli with toasted almond dressing
  (VEGAN) (see page 125)

- Whole roast mackerel and spring onions with tarragon
  (see page 65)

- Fish wrapped in ham with butter beans and sun-dried tomatoes
  (see page 68)

- Roast asparagus with egg toasts
  (see page 86)

UNDER AN HOUR

- Duck breast with pot-roast chicory and celeriac
  (see page 27)

- Tom's sausages and beans
  (see page 28)

- Pork chops baked with fennel, tomato and potato
  (see page 32)

- Easy moussaka
  (see page 40)

- Yoghurt-baked fish with chilli sweet potato and peanut chutney
  (see page 55)

- Smoked haddock, broccoli and farfalle
  (see page 51)

- Green couscous with prawns
  (see page 61)

- Spiced white fish with noodles and broth
  (see page 62)

- Fancy fish fingers and beans
  (see page 66)

- Cod, orzo, sweet potato and tapenade
  (see page 70)

- Plaice baked with fennel, potatoes and cider
  (see page 67)

- Spinach, walnut and feta in the hole
  (see page 82)

- Pea and artichoke risotto
  (see page 84)

- Vicky's filo pie
  (see page 89)

- Baked angel hair pasta with broccoli and green beans
  (VEGAN) (see page 90)

- Farinata, red pepper and courgette with olive dressing
  (VEGAN) (see page 93)

- Cauliflower kuku
  (see page 94)

- French onion Welsh rarebit
  (see page 96)

- Rice pudding with a difference
  (see page 130)

- Marmalade baked pears (VEGAN)
  (see page 133)

- Baked rhubarb, rose water and pink grapefruit
  (VEGAN) (see page 134)

1 HOUR

- Satay chicken wings and rice noodle salad (see page 20)

- Spice-rubbed steak with sweet red onions and croutons (see page 38)

- Salmon baked with horseradish and hot potato and beetroot salad (see page 58)

- Spiced prawn filo pie (see page 71)

- Lentils, crispy kale and halloumi (see page 92)

- Root vegetable rösti with hazelnut gremolata (see page 98)

- Chestnut, orange and chocolate bread pudding (see page 139)

OVER AN HOUR

- Aromatic chicken with almonds (see page 16)

- Miso aubergine and togarashi chicken skewers (see page 24)

- Ginger and turmeric chicken with potato and chickpea curry (see page 18)

- Beef chilli with cornbread top (see page 36)

- Lamb chops with spiced roots and tahini and roast garlic sauce (see page 44)

- Baked mussels with tomato and fregola (see page 52)

- Tuna and potato baked omelette (see page 57)

- Fish pie with a rösti topping (see page 74)

- Baked beetroot with hazelnut dressing (VEGAN) (see page 113)

- Potato and tomato gratin (see page 120)

- Red cabbage with chestnut and apple (VEGAN) (see page 122)

- Red peppers stuffed with spiced chickpeas and aubergine (VEGAN) (see page 81)

- Minted roast chicken with potatoes, peas and lettuce (see page 17)

- Jerk chicken strips, baked rice and black eye beans (see page 22)

- Baked ham with cider and leeks (see page 33)

- Beef and prune pot pie (see page 34)

- Dawn's slow-cooked shoulder of lamb with Chinese pancakes (see page 42)

- Rhubarb, pistachio and ginger cake (see page 136)

- Apricot and pistachio tart (see page 141)

COOKING UP A FEAST

Most of the roasting pan suppers are a whole meal in themselves, but it is easy to add a side dish and sweet thing when having friends over. We have put together some meal plans to make entertaining a breeze. The book has an array of dishes from around the world, so we have picked flavours that compliment each other. For pudding, a bit of cream, creme fraiche or sorbet never goes amiss.

FEAST WITH FRIENDS

LAIDBACK, WITH TIME TO COOK

- Beef chilli with cornbread top
  (see page 36)

- Roast celeriac with wholegrain
  mustard and rosemary
  (see page 110)

- *A simple green salad*
  to serve

- Baked rhubarb, rose water
  and pink grapefruit
  (see page 134)
  add double cream, Greek
  yoghurt or mascarpone
  with a biscuit

PREPARE IN ADVANCE

- Aromatic chicken
  with almonds
  (see page 16)

- Roasted okra
  (see page 110)

- Baked baby carrots and harissa
  (see page 116)

- *Flatbreads, naan or*
  parathas would go well
  with the above

- Rice pudding with a difference
  (see page 130)
  served with oven-baked fruit
  or a dried fruit compote

A TABLE OF GOODIES

**THESE DISHES WORK WELL
TOGETHER IF YOU ARE PLANNING
A BIG PARTY WITH PEOPLE HELPING
THEMSELVES FROM THE TABLE**

- Miso aubergine and
  togarashi chicken skewers
  (see page 24)

- Dawn's slow-cooked
  shoulder of lamb with
  Chinese pancakes
  (see page 42)

- Charred cabbage with
  chilli and sherry vinegar
  (see page 108)

- Broccoli 'rice', flageolet
  beans and roast vegetables
  (see page 111)

- Marmalade baked pears
  (see page 133)
  served with cream or
  ice cream and some
  simple biscuits

AL FRESCO

- Jerk chicken strips, black rice
  and black eye beans
  (see page 22)

- Baked angel hair pasta with
  broccoli and green beans
  (see page 90)

- Roast cauliflower and broccoli
  with toasted almond dressing
  (see page 125)

- Apricot and pistachio tart
  (see page 141)

QUICK AND MESSY MIDWEEK SUPPER

- Baked mussels with
  tomato and fregola
  (see page 52)

- Roast cauliflower and broccoli
  with toasted almond dressing
  (see page 125)

- *A crunchy cucumber*
  and dill salad to serve

- Chocolate banana
  tahini brownie
  (see page 128)
  crème fraîche or yoghurt ice
  cream will add a nice sharp
  note to the rich pudding

VEGGIE TREATS

LAIDBACK, WITH TIME TO COOK

- Spinach, walnut and feta in the hole (see page 82)

- Baby baked carrots and harissa (see page 116)

- Rhubarb, pistachio and ginger cake (see page 136) *pouring cream or crème fraîche never goes amiss when serving this as pudding*

MIDWEEK SUPPER

- Pea and artichoke risotto (see page 84)

- Charred cabbage with chilli and sherry vinegar (see page 108)

- Raspberry and sour cream squares (see page 138)

QUICK AND EASY

- Roast asparagus with egg toasts (see page 86)

- Oven-baked mushrooms à la grecque (see page 124)

- *Sometimes a pudding just isn't on the cards – some cheese and fresh fruit is just as good*

VEGAN FEAST

RELAXED COOKING TIME

- Baked pearl barley, peas, beans and green sauce (see page 102)

- Baked beetroot with hazelnut dressing (see page 113)

- Baked rhubarb, rose water and pink grapefruit (see page 134)

PREPARE IN ADVANCE

- Red peppers stuffed with spiced chickpeas and aubergine (see page 81)

- Potato and tomato gratin (for a vegan version, substitute the butter for more oil and instead of Parmesan use panko breadcrumbs) (see page 120)

- Walnut, pecan and date squares (for a vegan version, omit the eggs) (see page 140)

QUICK SUPPER

- Broccoli 'rice', flageolet beans and roast vegetables (see page 111)

- Charred cabbage with chilli and sherry vinegar (see page 108)

- Marmalade baked pears (see page 133)

CELEBRATION MEALS

MEAT

- Rice baked with crab, peas and broccoli (see page 56)

- Minted roast chicken with potatoes, peas and lettuce (see page 17)

- Baked roots with Lancashire cheese crumbs (see page 114)

- Walnut, pecan and date squares (see page 140)

FISH

- Cauliflower kuku (see page 94)

- Ana's fish parcels (see page 72)

- Tomato and pepper tian (see page 97)

- Rhubarb, pistachio and ginger cake (see page 136)

VEGGIE

- Baked farinata, red pepper and courgette with olive dressing (see page 93)

- Vicky's filo pie (see page 89)

- Roast celeriac with wholegrain mustard and rosemary (see page 110)

- Marmalade baked pears (see page 133)

MEAT

AROMATIC CHICKEN WITH ALMONDS

This lovely gentle curry comes from my sister – it is a firm favourite in her household. If you plan ahead, you can rub the chicken with lemon and salt and leave it overnight – this has a tenderising effect on the meat.

SERVES 4

8 boneless skinless
  chicken thighs
Juice of ½ lemon
2 teaspoons salt
30g flaked almonds
3 tablespoons sunflower
  or rapeseed oil
3 onions, finely sliced
5 large cloves garlic,
  finely grated or crushed
4cm thumb of ginger,
  peeled and grated
20g butter
1 cinnamon stick
5 black or 10 green
  cardamom pods
8 cloves
3 teaspoons ground
  cumin
3 teaspoons ground
  coriander
2 teaspoons turmeric
1–2 teaspoons cayenne
  pepper
120g ground almonds
300g passata
500g boiling water
Generous handful of
  coriander, chopped

Prick the chicken all over with a fork and rub with the lemon juice and salt. Set aside for at least 30 minutes or overnight.

Preheat the oven to 190°C (170°C fan), gas mark 5. Put the flaked almonds in a roasting pan and put them into the oven to toast gently as the oven heats up. Keep a close eye on the nuts as you want them to be just golden. Once the almonds are toasted, tip them into a bowl and set aside.

Add the oil to the hot roasting pan, then add the onions and a pinch of salt and place in the oven for about 15 minutes until they are light brown, stirring halfway through.

Add the garlic, ginger and butter and cook for 7 minutes, shaking halfway through. Add the whole spices and toast in the oven for a few minutes. Finally add the ground spices and return to the oven for a few minutes. Stir in the ground almonds until you have a smooth thick paste, then add the passata and the boiling water and return to the oven until the mixture is simmering, which should take 5–10 minutes.

Once the sauce is bubbling, add the chicken thighs and cook for about 30 minutes, checking after 20 minutes and adding a little more boiling water if most of the liquid has evaporated.

Once the chicken is cooked through, leave it to sit for a good 15 minutes before serving – you can do this in the cooling oven with the door ajar. Scatter over the chopped coriander and toasted flaked almonds to serve.

I like to serve this with naan breads or paratha and roasted okra (page 110).

MINTED ROAST CHICKEN WITH POTATOES, PEAS AND LETTUCE

Mint sauce is the secret weapon in this dish. If I have any other soft herbs knocking around I will add them to the mint sauce – tarragon and parsley are favourites as they make this into a very simple salsa verde.

SERVES 4

1 whole chicken,
  approx. 1.5kg
2 generous tablespoons
  mint sauce
1 tablespoon sunflower
  or rapeseed oil
320g new potatoes,
  cut in half
30g butter
2 Little Gem lettuce,
  outer leaves removed,
  cut into four or six,
  lengthways
6 spring onions, cut
  into 4cm lengths
400ml boiling chicken
  stock
200g frozen peas,
  defrosted
Sea salt and black pepper

Season the chicken generously all over and rub with the mint sauce – you can do this several hours in advance or even the night before if you like. The chicken needs to be at room temperature before it goes into the oven, so take it out of the fridge and set aside for an hour or two before cooking.

Preheat the oven to 200°C (180°C fan), gas mark 6.

Put the oil into the roasting pan, add the potatoes and stir them about to coat them with the oil. Season the potatoes then sit the chicken on top, dot it all over with the butter and grind over some black pepper. Put the pan into the oven and roast for 20 minutes.

Turn the oven down to 180°C (160°C fan), gas mark 4, and cook for another 15 minutes.

Snuggle the lettuce in among the potatoes and cook for 15 minutes until it starts to soften. Add the spring onions and hot stock and return to the oven for 15 minutes.

To check that the chicken is cooked, pierce the thickest part of the thigh with a skewer: the juices should run clear, with no hint of pink. When the chicken is cooked through, lift it out and leave to rest in a warm place.

Add the peas to the roasting pan and put back in the oven for 15 minutes. If there's a lot of liquid surrounding the vegetables, turn the oven up to 200°C (180°C fan), gas mark 6, to help the liquid reduce while the peas cook.

Cut up the chicken and serve with the vegetables and the lovely juices.

GINGER AND TURMERIC CHICKEN WITH POTATO AND CHICKPEA CURRY

The chicken can be rubbed with the spice paste up to 24 hours in advance to intensify the flavours. This recipe would also work well with a firm fish fillet – simply add the fish nearer the end of the cooking time.

SERVES 4

Small handful of
   coriander, roughly
   chopped, including
   the stalks, plus
   extra to serve
4cm thumb of ginger,
   wiped clean and
   roughly chopped
1 tablespoon turmeric
½ teaspoon sea salt
Grated zest and juice
   of 1 lime
1 tablespoon light
   olive oil
8 chicken thighs, skin on

Put the coriander, ginger, turmeric, salt, lime zest and juice into a food processor or large pestle and mortar. Grind to a smooth paste that will coat the meat, gradually adding the oil to help the process. Rub the chicken with the ginger/turmeric mix and set aside in a dish for as long as you can – ideally up to 24 hours.

Preheat the oven to 190°C (170°C fan), gas mark 5, and put a roasting pan in to heat up.

To make the curry, put the seeds and dry spices into the hot roasting pan, shaking the pan until they start to release their aroma. Put the pan back into the oven for a minute. When you take it out again, add the chickpeas, potatoes, onions, tomatoes, olive oil, tamarind paste and brown sugar, then add the boiling water and mix everything together very thoroughly. Sprinkle with salt and place the chicken thighs on top, skin-side up, spaced apart so that the skin can crisp up all over. Rub or brush the thighs with any marinade that has gathered in the dish. Roast for about 30 minutes and then give everything a good shake and add a little more boiling water if it seems dry.

Return to the oven for another 20–30 minutes.

FOR THE CURRY

½ tablespoon nigella
   seeds

1½ teaspoons smoked
   paprika

1 tablespoon ground
   cumin

¾ tablespoon ground
   coriander

400g tin chickpeas,
   drained and rinsed

8 new potatoes, cut
   in half lengthways

2 red onions, cut in half
   and then into wedges

12 small tomatoes, cut
   in half – I like the
   little plum ones

2 tablespoons light
   olive oil

1 tablespoon
   tamarind paste

1 teaspoon light
   brown sugar

250ml boiling water

Sea salt

After this time the chicken should have crisp, golden skin. Test the potatoes with a thin knife blade or skewer: if they aren't cooked through, cook for another 10 minutes.

If there doesn't seem to be enough curry sauce, use a slotted spoon to transfer the chicken to a warm serving dish, then add some boiling water to the roasting pan with the potato/chickpea mixture and stir vigorously, scraping up any tasty bits. Return the pan to the oven and let the sauce reduce for a few minutes until you have lovely saucy curry to serve with the chicken thighs. Scatter over some chopped coriander to serve.

TIP Although recipes often suggest peeling the ginger, a wise friend of mine suggested it really isn't necessary so long as it has been wiped clean – the skin contains good flavour and if it is being whizzed up in a paste it works perfectly.

SATAY CHICKEN WINGS AND RICE NOODLE SALAD

Satay is a real winner with adults and children alike. This dish is a fun one to have as it requires lots of finger licking and getting down and dirty!

SERVES 4

140g crunchy
   peanut butter
125ml coconut milk
2 red chillies, deseeded
   and chopped
2 tablespoons fish sauce
1 tablespoon soy sauce
Grated zest and juice
   of 1 lime
1.2kg chicken wings, tips
   removed and cut in
   half at the joint
Sea salt and black pepper

FOR THE NOODLE SALAD

80g cashew nuts, roughly
   chopped
200g rice noodles
1 small cucumber
2 carrots
1 bunch of spring
   onions, chopped
1 red chilli, deseeded
   and finely chopped
Small handful of
   coriander, chopped
3 tablespoons sesame oil
2 tablespoons sherry
   vinegar

Put the peanut butter, coconut milk, chillies, fish sauce, soy sauce and lime zest and juice in a food processor and whizz until just combined; don't overdo it if you want some texture from the peanuts. Set aside some of the sauce to use for dipping – about 1 tablespoon per person.

Put the chicken wings in a bowl, add the peanut sauce and toss to coat thoroughly. Set aside for at least 30 minutes or overnight in the fridge. Remember to take the wings out of the fridge 30 minutes before cooking.

Preheat the oven to 220°C (200°C fan), gas mark 7. Put the cashews in a roasting pan and put them in the oven to toast as the oven heats up. Keep a sharp eye on the nuts they can burn very quickly. Tip them into a bowl and set aside.

Put the wings in the hot roasting pan in a single layer, season and bake for 25–30 minutes, turning halfway through. If a lot of liquid is gathering in the pan, tip it out.

While the wings are cooking, make the salad. Cook the rice noodles as directed on the pack and refresh in cold water. Use a vegetable peeler to cut the cucumber and peeled carrot into long strips. Mix the noodles with the cucumber, carrots and the remaining ingredients, including half the toasted cashews. Scatter the remaining cashews over the top.

Serve the wings with any pan juices in a bowl to spoon over, alongside the salad and the peanut sauce for dipping.

JERK CHICKEN STRIPS, BAKED RICE AND BLACK EYE BEANS

This is my version of a Jamaican jerk seasoning. I have suggested using chicken breasts here, but I have also cooked a whole roast chicken in this way.

SERVES 4

3 large skinless chicken
   breasts, sliced into
   3cm strips
1 tablespoon sunflower
   oil

FOR THE JERK MARINADE

3 teaspoons ground
   allspice
1 teaspoon ground
   black pepper
½ teaspoon ground
   cinnamon
½ teaspoon nutmeg
½ tablespoon dried
   thyme
5 spring onions, sliced,
   using as much of the
   green part as possible
2 Scotch bonnet chillies,
   chopped (remove the
   seeds if you don't like
   it too hot)
1 tablespoon soft dark
   brown sugar
2 tablespoons dark
   soy sauce
Juice of 1 lime
1 teaspoon salt

For the jerk marinade, put everything into a food processor and whizz to a smooth paste: it may take a while, but don't be tempted to add water as you want a good thick paste. Taste and add more seasoning if necessary, and an extra chilli if you like it hot. Rub the marinade into the chicken pieces, cover and leave for at least 30 minutes or up to 4 hours.

To prepare the rice, preheat the oven to 200°C (180°C fan), gas mark 6. Put a roasting pan into the oven with the oil. Once hot, add the lardons and onion and a good pinch of salt and cook for 15 minutes, stirring halfway through.

Add the garlic, dried chilli and thyme and return to the oven for a few minutes. Stir in the rice, ensuring it gets well coated. Add the coconut milk, stock and a good pinch of salt, cover the roasting pan with foil and cook for 25 minutes. Check how the rice is doing: if it is nearly tender and there's a lot of liquid, remove the foil – or you may want to keep it covered. Add the beans and return to the oven for 7 minutes.

FOR THE RICE AND BEANS

1 tablespoon
  sunflower oil
100g lardons
1 large onion, sliced
2 cloves garlic, crushed
1 whole dried chilli
Couple of sprigs
  of thyme
300g long grain rice,
  washed until the
  water runs clear
330ml coconut milk
200ml boiling chicken
  or vegetable stock
400g tin black eye beans,
  drained and rinsed
1 tablespoon butter
Small handful of chopped
  coriander
Sea salt and black pepper

About halfway through the rice cooking time, put another roasting pan into the oven for the chicken, adding the oil – if you have a ridged pan this would be excellent. After 5–7 minutes the pan should be good and hot; add the chicken strips and spread out in a single layer. Cook for 10 minutes, shaking the pan halfway through.

When the rice is cooked, take it out of the oven, stir in the butter and try to pick out the thyme stalks and whole chilli. Let it sit for 5 minutes.

Check that the chicken is cooked through and let it rest for a couple of minutes, then serve atop a pile of rice.

MISO AUBERGINE AND TOGARASHI CHICKEN SKEWERS

This recipe draws on a few Japanese influences. The 'yakitori' – little marinated chicken skewers – are marinated with togarashi seasoning, popular in Japan, where it is often added to ramen noodle dishes.

SERVES 2

FOR THE AUBERGINES

2 smallish aubergines
2 teaspoons sunflower oil
5 teaspoons white
 miso paste
1 teaspoon fruity olive oil
3cm thumb of ginger,
 peeled and finely
 grated
1 tablespoon soy sauce
1 teaspoon honey
1 teaspoon Tabasco, or
 less if you are not so
 keen on hot stuff

FOR THE CHICKEN

Juice of 1 orange
1 teaspoon soy sauce
1 clove garlic, finely
 grated or crushed
1 teaspoon sunflower oil
1½ teaspoons togarashi
2 skinless chicken
 breasts, sliced into long
 strips, about 2cm wide
Spring onions, sliced,
 to garnish

Preheat the oven to 190°C (170°C fan), gas mark 5. If you are using wooden skewers, soak them in cold water.

Slice the aubergines in half lengthways, leaving their stalks on. Cut some slashes into the flesh, about halfway through. Rub the aubergines all over with 1 teaspoon of the sunflower oil and set them flesh-side down in a roasting pan. Cover with foil and place in the oven for 20 minutes.

Meanwhile, make the aubergine marinade: in a mixing bowl, whisk together the miso paste, the remaining sunflower oil, olive oil, grated ginger, soy sauce, honey and Tabasco. Take all but a tablespoon of this mixture out of the bowl and set aside.

Make the chicken marinade in the bowl with the tablespoon of miso mixture: add the orange juice, soy sauce, garlic, oil and togarashi. Toss the chicken in the marinade and set aside.

Turn the aubergines over, cover with foil and bake for another 15–20 minutes until soft.

Turn the oven up to its highest setting: 220°C (200°C fan), gas mark 7. Divide the miso mixture between the aubergines and smear it all over the flesh. Return to the oven for a couple of minutes while you thread the marinated chicken onto the skewers, reserving the marinade.

Take the roasting pan with the aubergines out of the oven. Place the chicken skewers next to the aubergines and pour the reserved marinade over the meat. Return to the oven for 5 minutes, then check the chicken. If necessary, turn the skewers over and give it another 5 minutes or so.

Sprinkle over the sliced spring onions and serve with sticky rice.

DUCK BREAST WITH POT-ROAST CHICORY AND CELERIAC

I found cooked chicory to be a revelation the first time I tried it: it becomes soft and loses some of the bitterness. Along with the sweetness of the shallots and apple and the earthiness of the celeriac, it is the perfect foil for duck.

SERVES 4

2 large duck breasts
    or 3 smaller ones,
    trimmed of any
    sinew, fat scored in
    a criss-cross
Splash of sunflower
    or rapeseed oil
6 large banana shallots,
    sliced in half
    lengthways
1 large celeriac, approx
    1.4kg, peeled and cut
    into 2cm wide chips
3 heads of white chicory,
    cut in half lengthways
2 bay leaves
3 tablespoons sherry
    vinegar
100ml boiling vegetable
    or chicken stock
2 apples, cored and each
    cut into eight wedges
Sea salt and black pepper

Preheat the oven to 220°C (200°C fan), gas mark 7, and put a large roasting pan in to heat up.

Rub a good pinch of salt into the scored fat of each duck breast and a little onto the flesh too. Season both sides with a good grinding of pepper.

Once the roasting pan is hot, take it out of the oven, add the oil and the duck breasts, skin-side down. They should sizzle as they go in. Put them into the oven for 10 minutes until the skin becomes crisp and brown and renders out some fat. Halfway through, pour off any fat (reserve this for later). Turn the breasts over and roast for 3 minutes to brown the flesh side. Once browned all over, lift the duck out of the roasting pan and set aside. You need about 2½ tablespoons of fat, so if necessary add a little of the fat you poured off earlier.

Now add the shallots, celeriac, chicory and bay leaves, season generously and stir everything about until well coated with the duck fat. Place in the oven until starting to soften, about 15 minutes.

Throw in the sherry vinegar and return the pan to the oven until it has almost completely evaporated. Then add the stock and apples and give everything a good shake. Sit the duck breasts on top of the vegetables and return to the oven for 5 minutes.

I usually cook the duck breasts until they are pink but not bloody: to test, if you press your chin, then press the flesh side of the duck, that is the consistency you are looking for. Remove the duck and leave to rest.

Give the vegetables 10 minutes more in the oven, until tender and loosely coated with the stock. Slice the duck and serve atop the vegetable mixture. I might serve some watercress and redcurrant jelly alongside.

TOM'S SAUSAGES AND BEANS

Tom is a great friend and an excellent cook. This dish is very simple and the secret here is that the beans shouldn't be in too much liquid by the end – they should have a certain unctuousness about them.

SERVES 2

75g smoked pancetta,
  cut into small cubes
4 best-quality pork
  sausages
2 teaspoons duck fat,
  lard or sunflower oil
  (if needed)
125g banana shallots,
  cut into 2–3cm thick
  rounds
1 carrot, diced
1 celery stick, diced
6 large cloves garlic,
  crushed or grated
400g tin flageolet beans,
  drained and rinsed
200ml boiling chicken
  or vegetable stock
Small handful of parsley,
  chopped
Sea salt and black pepper

Preheat the oven to 200°C (180°C fan), gas mark 6, and put a roasting pan in to heat up.

Once hot, add the pancetta and sausages and place in the oven for about 10 minutes until the sausages brown and the pancetta cubes render down, shaking the pan halfway through. Remove the sausages and set aside.

If the pancetta has not rendered much fat, add a couple of teaspoons of fat or oil. Add the shallots, carrot and celery and stir well to coat with the fat, add a good pinch of salt and return to the oven for 7–10 minutes until everything starts to soften. A little bit of colour is fine but if it is looking too brown, cover with foil.

Add the garlic and beans and stir thoroughly, then pour in the stock and return to the oven for 10–15 minutes so that all the flavours combine.

Add the parsley and give the beans a stir. Taste for seasoning. Pop the sausages on top of the beans and return to the oven for 5–7 minutes to heat through. Serve with lashings of English mustard.

PORK TENDERLOIN AND LEMON CAULIFLOWER

In this recipe I suggest using two roasting pans – the cauliflower is so much nicer when spread out, as it gets lovely caramelised crispy edges. The roasted cauliflower also makes an ideal vegan main course.

SERVES 4

2 teaspoons coriander
  seeds
1½ teaspoons fennel seeds
¾ teaspoon ground ginger
¾ teaspoon smoked
  paprika
½ teaspoon sea salt
1 teaspoon dried thyme
1 sprig each of sage
  and rosemary, leaves
  chopped
2 tablespoons honey
Zest and juice of ½ lemon
Zest of ¼ orange and juice
  of ½ orange
800g pork tenderloin
1 teaspoon sunflower oil

FOR THE CAULIFLOWER
2 tablespoons olive oil
1kg cauliflower (approx.)
1 lemon – juice of ½, the
  other ½ finely chopped
2 red onions, cut in wedges
80g pickled garlic
80g black olives
Small handful of parsley,
  finely chopped
Sea salt and black pepper

Preheat the oven to 200°C (180°C fan), gas mark 6. Put the seeds in a small pan and put them in the oven to toast as the oven heats up. Once they are light golden, remove from the oven. Add the ground spices, salt, thyme, sage and rosemary and grind everything together in a spice grinder or a pestle and mortar.

Gently warm the honey jar and use a hot spoon to measure the honey into a bowl. Add the lemon and orange zest and juice and the herb and spice mix and give it all a good stir.

Trim the pork of any sinew. Rub the pork all over with oil and oil a small roasting pan. Put the tenderloin in the pan and pour over the honey and spice mix. Rub it all over and put it into the oven on the top shelf. At the same time, put your largest roasting pan in to preheat for the cauliflower. The pork will need about 30 minutes in the oven; baste it from time to time.

Take the hot large roasting pan from the oven and add the olive oil, swirl about, then add the cauliflower (leaves and all), lemon pieces, red onions, pickled garlic and plenty of seasoning. Toss to coat everything with oil and return to the oven. The cauliflower will take about 30 minutes, but it's OK if it goes in about 10 minutes after the pork as the meat will benefit from resting in a warm place before serving.

About 5 minutes before the cauliflower is due to come out, add the olives to heat through.

Once the cauliflower is golden and just soft, add the lemon juice and parsley. Serve with slices of pork. It is delicious in a flatbread with some lettuce and chilli sauce.

PORK CHOPS BAKED WITH FENNEL, TOMATO AND POTATO

Pork and fennel are a classic combination, excellent in this all-in-one dish.

SERVES 4

2 tablespoons olive oil
2 heads fennel,
   fronds reserved,
   cut into sixths
320g small potatoes,
   cut into quarters
   lengthways
2 large red onions, each
   cut into eight wedges
4 large tomatoes
   – I favour plum
   tomatoes – cut in
   half lengthways
1 bay leaf
Couple of sprigs of
   thyme – lemon thyme
   is especially good here
1 tablespoon fennel
   seeds, crushed with
   the back of a spoon
½ lemon, a strip of zest
   peeled off, and juice
4 pork chops, approx.
   150–200g each,
   fat scored
Sea salt and black pepper

Preheat the oven to 220°C (200°C fan), gas mark 7. Put a roasting pan into the oven with the oil.

Meanwhile, blanch the fennel in boiling water for 4 minutes, then drain.

Once the oil is hot, add the potato wedges and toss them about to coat with oil, add some salt and pepper and place in the oven. Once the oven has reached temperature, add the remaining vegetables and herbs to the roasting pan, throw in the fennel seeds and strip of lemon zest, season well and mix everything together gently.

Season the chops generously on both sides and put them on top of the vegetables. Put into the oven for 25 minutes until the chops are brown and cooked through and the vegetables are done. Test by piercing a potato with a sharp knife: it should meet no resistance. Lift the chops out and leave to rest in a warm place for 5–7 minutes.

Add the lemon juice to the vegetables, taste for seasoning and leave them to keep warm in the cooling oven. When ready to serve, add any roughly chopped fennel fronds to the roasted vegetables.

BAKED HAM WITH CIDER AND LEEKS

A baked ham is a joyous thing and a lighter alternative to a Christmas glazed ham. I have included pasta in this recipe as the flavours are reminiscent of a carbonara, but leave the pasta out if cooking up a festive feast.

SERVES 6

3 leeks, sliced, using as much of the green part as possible

1.2kg piece boneless gammon

568ml bottle dry cider

250ml boiling water

2 tablespoons Dijon mustard

100ml double cream

227g tub sour cream

480g orecchiette pasta

300g greens, sliced into thick ribbons

Sea salt and black pepper

Preheat the oven to 180°C (160°C fan), gas mark 4, and put a roasting pan in to heat up.

Once hot, fill the pan with the sliced leeks – they may sizzle a little. It will seem like a huge amount, but as they cook slowly in the cider they will break down and become sweet and soft. Sit the gammon on top, add the cider and water and a good grinding of black pepper and place in the oven.

After 30 minutes, give the leeks a stir, turn the oven down to 150°C (130°C fan), gas mark 2, and cook for 1 hour, until the gammon is cooked: you can test its core temperature by inserting a skewer into the centre of the meat and counting to 20; pull it out and test the temperature on the inside of your wrist. Take care as it should be very hot. If it does not feel hot, put the gammon back in for another 20 minutes. Alternatively, if you have a meat thermometer, the core temperature should be around 68–70°C. Remove the ham from the roasting pan and leave to rest in a warm place.

Turn the oven up to 180°C (160°C fan), gas mark 4. Stir the mustard, cream and sour cream into the leeks and return to the oven for 10 minutes.

Meanwhile, cook the orecchiette in salted boiling water for 2 minutes less than suggested on the pack. Drain – reserving the pasta cooking water – and refresh in cold water. Stir the pasta into the leek and cream mixture, adding 100ml of the reserved hot water, and return to the oven for 7 minutes.

Meanwhile, steam the greens for a couple of minutes. Stir the greens into the pasta mixture and return to the oven for 5 minutes.

Check that everything is hot and taste for seasoning (this will depend on the saltiness of the gammon). I sometimes add a squeeze of lemon. Slice the gammon and serve with generous spoonfuls of pasta.

BEEF AND PRUNE POT PIE

Beef and prune is a wonderful traditional mixture. The beef shin needs a long cooking time, but it's all just bubbling away in the oven, so you can go off and then reap the tremendous rewards of unctuously soft beef.

SERVES 4

500ml stout
2 heaped tablespoons
   grain mustard
1kg beef shin off the
   bone, cut into
   2cm cubes
2 tablespoons
   sunflower oil
2 leeks, sliced
2 celery sticks, sliced
3 sprigs of thyme
1 bay leaf
900ml boiling beef
   or vegetable stock
100g no-soak pitted
   prunes
1 heaped tablespoon
   cornflour
2 onions, finely sliced
Handful of parsley,
   roughly chopped
3–4 pickled walnuts,
   roughly chopped
   (optional)
Sea salt and black pepper

If you have time, mix the stout and mustard with several grindings of black pepper and pour over the beef the day before you want to make the pie. If you're in a hurry, half an hour will help.

To make the pastry, put the suet and flour in a bowl, strip the thyme leaves and scatter in along with some salt and pepper. Mix the flour and suet together, make a well in the centre and slowly add about 100ml of cold water – adding just enough to bind the dough together. Tip the dough onto a floured surface and knead briefly until smooth. Flatten into a disk and leave to rest in the fridge while you make the filling.

Preheat the oven to 200°C (180°C fan), gas mark 6. Put a large roasting pan in to heat up with the oil.

Lift the beef out of the stout and set aside. Put the stout into a large saucepan with the leeks, celery, thyme, bay leaf, stock and prunes and bring back to the boil, then turn the heat right down so it is just bubbling gently.

Dry the meat and then toss in the cornflour with a good pinch of salt and little pepper.

Once the roasting pan is hot, add the meat and onions in an even layer, then place in the oven for about 18 minutes, shaking halfway through, until the meat is well browned. Pour the hot liquid over the meat, stir thoroughly and cover with foil. Turn the oven down to 180°C (160°C fan), gas mark 4, and return the pan to the oven for about 1–1¼ hours until the meat is meltingly soft.

FOR THE SUET PASTRY

200g suet

400g plain flour, plus
  extra for dusting

2 sprigs of thyme

1 egg, beaten, to glaze

While the meat is braising, roll out the pastry and measure against your smallest roasting pan or a pie dish; leave the rolled-out pastry to rest for 5–10 minutes, as it sometimes shrinks a little. Cut out a pastry lid and some long strips to put around the rim of the pan or pie dish.

Once the filling is ready, turn the oven up to 200°C (180°C fan), gas mark 6. Stir the parsley into the pie filling and lift out the bay leaves and thyme stalks. You could also add a few roughly chopped pickled walnuts and a couple of tablespoons of the liquid from their jar. Spoon the filling into the small roasting pan or pie dish.

Put a pie funnel in the middle or, if you don't have one, use an upturned egg cup or some scrunched-up foil to support the centre of the pastry. Brush the rim of the pan or dish with egg and line with strips of pastry, then brush the pastry strips with egg and put the pastry lid on top and press down well. I usually go round again, pressing with the tines of a fork. If you have some excess pastry, cut out some decorations for the top of the pie. Cut a cross in the middle for the funnel to stick out.

Brush well with egg and bake for 20–30 minutes until the pastry is golden brown and crisp. Serve hot, with roasted root vegetables, or the roast celeriac with wholegrain mustard and rosemary (page 110).

BEEF CHILLI WITH CORNBREAD TOP

*One of the great joys of cornbread is that you can keep it simple or make little additions,
such as a few spring onions, some chopped chilli or even some sweetcorn.*

SERVES 6

2 tablespoons
    sunflower oil
400g minced beef
3 onions, sliced
1 tablespoon chilli
    powder
2 teaspoons ground
    cumin
1 tablespoon cocoa
    powder
2 celery sticks, sliced
2 red peppers, deseeded
    and sliced
4 cloves garlic, crushed
2 teaspoons dried thyme
    or a few sprigs of fresh
340g tin sweetcorn
400g tin kidney beans,
    drained and rinsed
400g tin chopped
    tomatoes
Sea salt and black pepper

Preheat the oven to 220°C (200°C fan), gas mark 7. Put a roasting pan in to heat up, with 1 tablespoon of the oil.

Put the beef and onions in a bowl with the chilli, cumin, cocoa powder and salt and pepper and mix thoroughly. Once the oil is hot, put the beef mixture into the roasting pan, spreading it out so it covers the pan in a thin layer. Cook for 7 minutes until lightly browned, then stir well and give it another 7 minutes.

Meanwhile, for the cornbread, sift the flour, baking powder and bicarbonate of soda together into a bowl, then stir in the polenta, sugar, paprika, some salt and all but a small handful of the cheese. In another bowl, whisk together the eggs, milk or yoghurt, butter and oil, adding the spring onions, if using.

Once the beef has some colour, tip it into a bowl. Pour a small cup of boiling water into the pan and stir it about to lift off any tasty bits lurking on the pan, then pour this liquid in with the beef. Wipe the roasting pan dry, add the remaining tablespoon of oil, the celery and red peppers and cook for 10 minutes, shaking the pan after 5 minutes to make sure everything is cooking evenly.

Add the garlic, thyme, sweetcorn and beans and give everything a good stir. Return to the oven for about 7 minutes, then mix in the tomatoes and the beef, taste for seasoning and return to the oven for 10 minutes while you prepare the top.

FOR THE CORNBREAD

80g plain flour

2½ teaspoons baking
    powder

1 teaspoon bicarbonate
    of soda

300g fine polenta

1 heaped tablespoon
    soft light brown sugar

1 generous teaspoon
    smoked paprika

100g mature Cheddar,
    grated

4 eggs

240ml milk or
    plain yoghurt

30g butter, melted

90ml sunflower oil

4 spring onions, finely
    sliced (optional)

To finish the cornbread, add the wet ingredients to the dry and stir until just combined, taking care not to overmix. Pour the batter over the beef chilli and scatter the remaining cheese on top. Cook for 25–35 minutes or until a thin knife blade or skewer inserted into the centre comes out clean. Serve with sour cream if you like, and perhaps a green salad.

TIP You can use this recipe to make a loaf of cornbread, which is a great accompaniment to a pan of roasted vegetables. Half the quantities would make a 450g loaf and you would need to use approximately 60ml more milk or plain yoghurt. Since it has a low flour content you can make it gluten free pretty easily by using gluten-free plain flour.

SPICE-RUBBED STEAK WITH SWEET RED ONIONS AND CROUTONS

This recipe works well with any kind of steak, the rub has a tenderising effect even if you cook the meat straight away. Leave the rub overnight or just for the time it takes to cook the onions and preheat the grill.

SERVES 4

1 tablespoon light
   brown sugar
2 teaspoons salt
1 teaspoon ground
   allspice
1 generous teaspoon
   ground coriander
1½ teaspoons
   mustard powder
4 steaks
2½ tablespoons olive oil
4 red onions, peeled
   and finely sliced
Few sprigs of thyme
200ml cider or apple
   juice
1 tablespoon cider
   vinegar
225g rustic bread,
   brown or white, cut
   into 1cm chunks and
   tossed in 1 tablespoon
   olive oil
1 tablespoon extra
   virgin olive oil
60g rocket

Make a dry rub by mixing together the sugar, salt, allspice, coriander and mustard powder. Rub it thoroughly into the beef and set aside.

Preheat the oven to 190°C (170°C fan), gas mark 5. Preheat a roasting pan with 2 tablespoons of the olive oil. Once the oil in the roasting pan is hot, add the red onions, thyme cider and cider vinegar, stir everything about thoroughly, cover with foil and return to the oven for 15 minutes for them to steam and become soft.

Once the onions are in the oven, preheat the grill to its highest setting and give it 10 minutes to be red hot.

When the onions have softened, turn the oven up to 220°C (200°C fan), gas mark 7, and remove the foil. Lift out the onions and all but a tablespoon of the liquid in the roasting pan. Add the chunks of bread to the roasting pan and toss everything together well. Return to the hotter oven to let any remaining cooking liquor evaporate and the bread become golden and crisp, this will take about 8–10 minutes and it is worth shaking everything about after a few minutes. Once they look ready, take out and set aside.

Once you have returned the croutons to the hotter oven. Oil a roasting pan which will fit under the grill and place the steaks on it, turn them over a couple of times so both sides get oiled. Place the steaks under the grill for about 4 minutes on each side for rare or add on a couple more minutes per side for more cooked steak. Set the meat aside to rest in a warm place for 5 minutes.

Toss the croutons, warm red onions and their cooking liquor with the rocket, extra virgin olive oil and a dose of seasoning. Top with the sliced steak.

EASY MOUSSAKA

Moussaka has such fabulous flavours, but it can be quite a process. You will need two pans for this simple version, which has a quick and easy topping of Greek yoghurt, feta, mint and eggs.

SERVES 4

3 tablespoons
   sunflower oil
500g minced lamb
2 onions, finely sliced
2 teaspoons ground
   cinnamon
2 teaspoons paprika
2 small aubergines,
   sliced 1–2cm thick
2 large cloves garlic,
   crushed or finely
   grated
1 bay leaf
2 generous sprigs
   of dill, chopped
400g tin chopped
   tomatoes
250ml boiling lamb
   or vegetable stock
Sea salt and black pepper

Preheat the oven to 220°C (200°C fan), gas mark 7. Put a roasting pan in to heat up with 1½ tablespoons of the oil.

Mix the lamb and onions with the spices and plenty of salt and pepper. Place in the hot roasting pan and brown in the oven for 15 minutes, stirring occasionally to break up the meat, until the onions are starting to soften.

Meanwhile, toss the aubergine slices with the remaining oil and a generous pinch of salt. Place the slices in one layer in a second roasting pan and put in the oven to soften and brown – this should take about 10–15 minutes – turning the slices over halfway through. Set the aubergines aside.

Turn the oven down to 200°C (180°C fan), gas mark 6, and add the garlic, bay leaf, dill, tomatoes and hot stock to the lamb mix, stir thoroughly and return to the oven for 15 minutes, stirring from time to time. If the mixture is looking dry add a cup of boiling water.

FOR THE TOPPING

2 eggs

400g Greek yoghurt

200g feta, crumbled

Small handful of
    coriander

Couple of sprigs of mint,
    thick stalks removed

25g pine nuts

While the lamb is cooking, make the topping. In a food processor or using a stick blender, blend together all the ingredients except for the pine nuts. Season to taste.

Taste the lamb mixture for seasoning then lay the aubergine slices over the lamb. Pour the topping over and scatter over the pine nuts. Return to the oven for 20 minutes until the topping is set and golden brown. Serve with a green salad.

DAWN'S SLOW-COOKED SHOULDER OF LAMB WITH CHINESE PANCAKES

This comes from my friend's mum and is an absolute winner. It is super simple and all you need is time while it cooks – time when you can be doing other things. It's a great hands-on meal to enjoy with friends.

SERVES 6

1kg piece lamb
    shoulder, boned
6cm thumb of ginger,
    wiped clean and
    finely grated
4 heaped teaspoons
    five spice powder
3 tablespoons rice
    wine vinegar
3 tablespoons soy sauce
3 tablespoons honey
Sea salt and black pepper

TO SERVE

24 Chinese pancakes
    or soft flatbreads
200g jar hoisin sauce
1 cucumber, sliced into
    long thin sticks
8 spring onions,
    cut in half and
    sliced lengthways
    into quarters

Preheat the oven to 220°C (200°C fan), gas mark 7.

To cook the lamb, mix together all the ingredients except 1 tablespoon of honey. Season the lamb with salt and rub the mixture all over. Wrap in two layers of foil, place in a roasting pan and cook for 20 minutes.

Turn the oven down to 180°C (160°C fan), gas mark 4, and cook for 3 hours, by which time the meat should be meltingly soft.

Open up the foil, drizzle over the last spoonful of honey and return to the oven with the foil open. Leave for about 10–15 minutes for the honey glaze to crisp up the skin. Remove from the oven and leave to rest in a warm place for 15 minutes.

Meanwhile, assemble all the accompaniments and wrap the pancakes in foil.

When the lamb has rested, lift it out of the roasting pan and pour any juices that are sitting in the foil into the pan and return it to the oven to heat through. Put the pancakes in the oven at the same time.

Break the lamb up into bite-sized pieces: it will naturally shred, having been cooked for so long. Put it into a serving dish and pour over the cooking juices from the oven.

Everyone has their own way of eating this, but I go for a good smear of hoisin sauce on the pancake, followed by cucumber, spring onions and meat before rolling up the pancake.

LAMB CHOPS WITH SPICED ROOTS AND TAHINI AND ROAST GARLIC SAUCE

Ras el hanout is a spice blend found in North Africa. The name in Arabic means 'head of the shop' and implies a mixture of the best spices the seller has to offer. These days it's readily available from supermarkets.

SERVES 4

8 lamb chops
4 potatoes, scrubbed,
   not peeled, cut into
   3cm chunks
4 large carrots, cut
   into 3cm lengths
1 small swede,
   peeled and cut
   into 2cm chunks
2 small red onions, cut
   in half and half again
4 spring onions
8 fat cloves garlic, any
   loose skin removed
1–2 tablespoons
   sunflower oil
   (optional)

Preheat the oven to 180°C (160°C fan), gas mark 4.

Preheat the grill to its highest setting and give it 10 minutes to get really hot. Put a roasting pan under the grill to heat up. Season the lamb chops well on both sides and pop them on the hot roasting pan: they should sizzle. Grill for a couple of minutes, as close to the heat as possible, until they are browned and have rendered some fat. The underside should have browned when it hit the hot pan but if not, turn over and grill for 1–2 minutes on the other side. Remove the chops from the roasting pan and set aside.

Put the potatoes, carrots, swede, both types of onion and the garlic into the roasting pan with the lamb fat, stir to coat everything with the fat and, if there isn't enough fat, add 1–2 tablespoons of sunflower oil. Now add the ras el hanout and a good pinch of salt, stir well and place in the oven for 20 minutes.

Add the sweet potato and give everything a good stir. Return to the oven for 15 minutes.

1 generous tablespoon
  ras el hanout
1 sweet potato,
  peeled, cut in half
  lengthways and cut
  into 2cm chunks
200g cavolo nero or
  other greens, washed,
  thick stalks removed,
  thoroughly dried
1 tablespoon olive oil
Sea salt and black pepper

FOR THE SAUCE
Small handful of parsley
Few sprigs of mint, thick
  stalks removed
2 tablespoons tahini
1 tablespoon sesame
  seeds
75ml hot water

Meanwhile, make the sauce: put all the ingredients in a food processor or blender and whizz until smooth and the consistency of double cream. Add more hot water if necessary. Leave the sauce in the machine.

Put the cavolo nero in a bowl with the olive oil and some salt and toss together while roughly tearing up the leaves.

Check on the roots in the oven: they should be crisp around the edges and nearly cooked. Add the cavolo nero and cook for 10 minutes more. Remove the roasting pan from the oven, fish out the garlic cloves and set aside: it sounds like a needle in a haystack task, but it isn't that difficult. Put the lamb chops on top of the vegetables and return to the oven for 7 minutes to heat the chops through.

Now squeeze the garlic cloves out of their skins, add to the tahini sauce and whizz again. Season with salt to taste.

Once the chops are hot, leave them to rest in a warm place for 5 minutes. Leave the vegetables in the cooling oven and put in some plates to warm. Serve the chops on a pile of the spiced roots with a spoonful of sauce over the top.

LAMB STEAKS IN MOJO VERDE WITH ROAST POTATOES AND GREEN PEPPER

Mojo verde is an excellent sauce from the Canary Islands, its main components being fresh coriander, cumin, garlic and chilli – but not enough chilli to make it fiery. You will need two pans.

SERVES 2

2 large potatoes,
    scrubbed, not peeled,
    sliced to the thickness
    of a pound coin
1 large green pepper,
    deseeded and cut into
    2cm wide strips
1 onion, sliced into
    1cm circles
2 tablespoons olive oil
2 lamb leg steaks
Sea salt and black pepper

FOR THE MOJO VERDE

1 large clove garlic, sliced
3 tablespoons sherry
    vinegar
Large handful of
    coriander, chopped,
    including the stalks
1 green chilli, deseeded
    if you prefer, sliced
1½ teaspoons ground
    cumin, toasted
1 teaspoon sea salt
10 tablespoons extra
    virgin olive oil

Preheat the oven to 200°C (180°C fan), gas mark 6.

Toss the potatoes, pepper and onion with the olive oil and a good pinch of salt and pepper in a roasting pan. Bake for 30 minutes until everything is golden and soft, shaking the pan halfway through to make sure that nothing is sticking.

Meanwhile, season the leg steaks well with salt and make the mojo. Put the garlic, sherry vinegar, coriander, chilli, cumin and salt in a food processor and whizz to a paste. Slowly add the olive oil with the motor running until you have a smooth sauce. Spoon a generous amount of the sauce over the lamb steaks. Set the rest of the mojo aside.

Once the vegetables are soft, turn the oven right down and leave them in to keep warm.

Preheat the grill to its highest setting and give it 5–7 minutes to heat up. Grill the lamb, close to the heat, for about 4 minutes until brown. Turn over and cook for 4 minutes on the other side. Leave to rest for 5 minutes.

Serve the lamb with a pile of the potatoes and extra mojo sauce.

TIP Mojo verde keeps well in a jar in the fridge and has so many uses – it can be stirred through rice or pasta, rubbed onto fish or even spread over toast.

FISH

FISH BAKED WITH TOMATO SAUCE AND GNOCCHI

Making tomato sauce in the oven is a revelation – it becomes such a simple task and is much less likely to stick. I keep a supply in my freezer to use with pasta or on a pizza base.

SERVES 4

1–2 tablespoons olive oil
500g gnocchi
4 x 130g firm white
   fish fillets
Sea salt and black pepper
½ lemon, cut into
   wedges, to serve

FOR THE TOMATO SAUCE

2 tablespoons olive oil
30g butter
3 red onions, finely sliced
4 cloves garlic, sliced
1 large red chilli,
   deseeded and chopped
1 tablespoon sherry
   vinegar
400g tin chopped
   tomatoes
250ml boiling water or
   fish or vegetable stock
1 bay leaf
2 sprigs of thyme
½–1 teaspoon sugar
1 tablespoon capers
Small bunch of basil,
   chopped (optional)

Preheat the oven to 180°C (160°C fan), gas mark 4. Start by making the tomato sauce. Put a roasting pan in to heat up with the olive oil and the butter. When the butter has melted, add the onions, stir and add a good pinch of salt. Return to the oven for 15 minutes, stirring every now and then, until soft and sweet and very lightly golden brown. Add the garlic and chilli and return to the oven for a couple of minutes.

Turn the oven up to 200°C (180°C fan), gas mark 6. Splash in the sherry vinegar and return the pan to the oven for a minute or two, for the vinegar to evaporate. Add the tomatoes, hot water or stock, bay leaf, thyme, ½ teaspoon salt and the sugar, and bake for 30 minutes, stirring halfway through, until the sauce has reduced slightly.

Fish out the bay leaf and thyme, tip the sauce into a food processor and blend until smooth, adding a little more hot water if the sauce seems very thick. Stir in the capers and basil, if using.

Rinse and dry the roasting pan, then oil the base of the pan. Scatter over the gnocchi in an even layer, then cover with the tomato sauce. Bake for about 10 minutes to start the gnocchi heating through.

Season the fish fillets well on both sides. Place them on top of the gnocchi, skin-side up, and drizzle over the remaining olive oil. Bake for about 10–15 minutes until the fish is cooked: the skin should be crisp and will lift off easily when the fish is ready. Serve with small lemon wedges to squeeze over.

TIP Once accustomed to the tomato sauce in the oven method, you can add and subtract ingredients at will. Jarred peppers or olives to chase away winter blues or fresh herbs to complement whatever else you are cooking.

SMOKED HADDOCK, BROCCOLI AND FARFALLE

With this recipe I had in mind an interpretation of macaroni and/or cauliflower cheese.
The result is a lot lighter, with the added bonus of smoked fish.

SERVES 4

2 tablespoons olive oil
200g farfalle
250g broccoli, broken
   into small florets
2 cloves garlic, crushed
   or finely grated
Generous pinch of
   chilli flakes
320g undyed smoked
   haddock, skinned
Juice of ½ lemon
40g Parmesan, grated

Preheat the oven to 180°C (160°C fan), gas mark 4. Put a roasting pan in to heat up with the olive oil.

Meanwhile, cook the farfalle in boiling salted water for 10 minutes and steam the broccoli until very tender – I steam the broccoli over the pasta.

Once the oil is hot, add the garlic and chilli flakes and stir for a couple of minutes, then add the smoked haddock. When the pasta is ready, drain it, reserving the water. Pour 400ml of pasta water over the fish and place in the oven for 10 minutes until it is just cooked. Using a slotted spoon, lift out the fish and set aside.

Add the broccoli to the roasting pan and start to break it up with a spoon, then place in the oven for about 15 minutes, stirring halfway through, until it is really soft.

When the haddock has cooled slightly, flake it into nice big pieces, add to the pasta and toss with the lemon juice.

When the broccoli has broken down and the liquid reduced, add the pasta and fish and the Parmesan. Return to the oven for 5 minutes to heat through. Serve immediately, with extra Parmesan or lemon if you like.

A little tomato salad would go really nicely with this.

BAKED MUSSELS WITH TOMATO AND FREGOLA

This is a wonderfully messy dish that requires hands-on eating! It's great fun, but make sure you provide lots of napkins and a bowl for the shells, and bread for mopping up the sauce. You will need two pans.

SERVES 4

3 tablespoons olive oil
6 banana shallots, cut
    in half lengthways
    and sliced
20g butter
1 large leek, cut in half
    lengthways and sliced
1 large head fennel, cut
    into quarters and sliced
    (fronds reserved)
3 cloves garlic, crushed
    or finely grated
1–2 teaspoons chilli
    flakes (to taste)
1 teaspoon fennel seeds,
    crushed or chopped
250g fregola or giant
    couscous
125ml white wine or
    cider (optional)
400ml boiling fish or
    vegetable stock
300g passata
1kg mussels, scrubbed,
    beards removed, rinsed
3 sprigs of mint, leaves
    chopped
Juice of 1 lemon
Sea salt

Preheat the oven to 180°C (160°C fan), gas mark 4. Put the smaller of your two roasting pans in to heat up, with 2 tablespoons of the olive oil.

Once the oven is hot, add the shallots, butter and a generous pinch of salt to the roasting pan and place in the oven for 10 minutes.

Stir in the leek and fennel and return to the oven for 10 minutes until the vegetables are starting to soften. Add the garlic, chilli and fennel seeds and cook for another 5 minutes.

Add the fregola and stir well. Now add the wine or cider, if using (if not, add an extra 125ml stock or water), the stock and passata and return to the oven for 10 minutes.

Turn the oven up to 220°C (200°C fan), gas mark 7. Give everything a good stir and if the fregola mix is looking very thick you can add more hot water – about 150ml. Return this roasting pan to the oven and place a larger roasting pan, with the remaining tablespoon of olive oil, in to get good and hot. Have your mussels ready in a colander.

When the oven is hot, take out the large roasting pan and throw in the mussels, they should sizzle a little. Add the tomato mixture and give everything a good stir, adding some more hot water or stock if it seems thick. Return to the oven until the mussels open – this will take about 10–15 minutes. When all the mussels are open, stir in the mint and lemon juice, garnish with the reserved fennel leaves, and serve immediately.

YOGHURT-BAKED FISH WITH CHILLI SWEET POTATO AND PEANUT CHUTNEY

*Harissa is a North African spice paste made with cumin, chilli and oil
– when mixed with yoghurt it will give the fish a bit of spice without being too fiery.*

SERVES 2

2 x 130g skinless firm
   white fish fillets
100g natural yoghurt
1 tablespoon harissa
Sea salt

FOR THE SWEET POTATO

1 large sweet potato,
   unpeeled, cut into
   wedges lengthways
1½ tablespoons olive oil
1 teaspoon chilli powder
1 teaspoon cumin seeds
1 large clove garlic,
   crushed or finely grated

FOR THE PEANUT CHUTNEY

40g raw peanuts
2 teaspoons garam masala
Small handful coriander
Juice of 1 lime
1 tablespoon dark
   brown sugar
1 green chilli, deseeded
   and roughly chopped
1 small red onion,
   chopped

Preheat the oven 200°C (180°C fan), gas mark 6. For the peanut chutney, put the peanuts in a roasting pan with 1 teaspoon of salt and garam masala and put them in the oven to toast as the oven heats up. When lightly browned, set aside.

Place the fish in a dish. Mix the yoghurt, harissa and a generous pinch of salt together – taste and add more harissa if you like it spicy. Pour the yoghurt mixture over the fish, gently rubbing it in, and leave to marinate while you prepare the sweet potato.

Put the sweet potato wedges in the roasting pan, add the olive oil and toss together very well. Add the remaining ingredients, season with salt, mix thoroughly and bake for 15 minutes.

Give the sweet potatoes a good shake and add the fish to the roasting pan: either push the potatoes to the sides of the pan and put the fish in the middle, or put the fish on top of the potatoes. Return to the oven for 15 minutes until the fish is cooked.

Meanwhile, make the chutney. Put the spiced peanuts into a food processor (reserve some to garnish at the end) with the coriander, lime juice, sugar, chilli and onion and whizz everything together to a smooth paste.

When the fish is done, sprinkle with the reserved roasted peanuts and serve hot with a dollop of peanut chutney. This is nice served with naan bread or rice.

RICE BAKED WITH CRAB, PEAS AND BROCCOLI

I am a big fan of purple and white sprouting broccoli and, when they are in season in early spring, I use them instead of regular broccoli – in April/May I will use asparagus. If you can't get crab, brown shrimps are also lovely.

SERVES 4

50g butter

3 tablespoons olive oil

5 banana shallots, finely sliced

360g arborio or other short grain rice

100ml white wine or cider (optional)

900ml boiling vegetable or fish stock

120g frozen peas, defrosted

100g broccoli, broken into bite-sized florets

150g crab meat (brown, white or a mixture)

Small handful of dill, finely chopped

3 sprigs of tarragon, leaves finely chopped

Small handful of parsley, finely chopped

Grated zest and juice of 1 lemon

Sea salt

Preheat the oven to 180°C (160°C fan), gas mark 4, and put a roasting pan in to heat up.

Once hot, add the butter, olive oil, shallots and a good pinch of salt and return to the oven for 5 minutes. Give the shallots a stir and cook for another 5 minutes until softened: if they are looking a bit brown, cover with foil.

Once the shallots are soft, stir in the rice to coat well with the buttery mixture. If you like, add the wine or cider and return the pan to the oven for 5 minutes until the wine is absorbed. Add the hot stock (adding an extra 100ml if you didn't use wine or cider), stir, then cook for 20 minutes.

Add the peas and broccoli, stir well, and return to the oven for 5 minutes.

Stir in the crab and cook for another 5 minutes. By this time the stock will have been absorbed and the rice should be cooked through but the dish shouldn't be entirely dry.

Mix the herbs with the lemon zest. Set aside a tablespoon of the mixture.

Stir the herb mixture and lemon juice into the rice, cover the roasting pan with a clean tea towel and leave to settle for a few minutes. I usually put the plates in the cooling oven to warm up.

Serve the rice with a little of the reserved herb mixture scattered over the top.

TUNA AND POTATO
BAKED OMELETTE

This thick Spanish-style omelette is quick and easy to make. It is also really good cold. The Spanish often eat a slice of tortilla in a soft roll with a smear of mayo and some salad for a delicious picnic lunch.

SERVES 4

2 large potatoes, cut
    into 2cm chunks
1 large red onion, sliced
4½ tablespoons olive oil
5 eggs
160g tuna in spring
    water, drained and
    flaked
80g frozen peas,
    defrosted
Small handful of
    parsley, chopped
Sea salt and black pepper

Preheat the oven to 180°C (160°C fan), gas mark 4.

Put the potato chunks and onion in a roasting pan with 3 tablespoons of the olive oil and a good pinch of salt. Place in the oven for 15–20 minutes until soft and a little brown at the edges.

Break the eggs into a jug or bowl, season well, add a dash of olive oil and whisk thoroughly. Add the tuna, peas and parsley and more seasoning.

Tip the potato and onion mixture into a bowl.

Rinse out the roasting pan and dry well. Add the remaining tablespoon of olive oil to the pan and place in the oven for 5 minutes to heat the oil.

Take the roasting pan out of the oven and add the egg mixture and then spoon the potatoes evenly throughout the egg. Shake the pan gently then return to the oven until set, which will take about 25 minutes. The middle sets last, so check that it's done.

Remove from the oven and let the omelette sit for a few minutes. Run a knife around the edge and turn it out onto a board – or serve it straight from the pan. Serve with aïoli or herby mayonnaise and a salad; in the summer I would always go with a tomato salad.

SALMON BAKED WITH HORSERADISH AND HOT POTATO AND BEETROOT SALAD

This dish has vibrant colours and well-matched flavours. The idea is to cook two pieces of salmon with a horseradish mixture sandwiched between them. You need two roasting pans: one for the fish and one for potatoes.

SERVES 4

2 x 300g pieces of salmon
   fillet, skinned
2 tablespoons grated
   horseradish
60g crème fraîche
Grated zest and juice
   of ½ lemon
Small bunch of chives,
   snipped
Generous drizzle of
   sunflower oil
Sea salt and black pepper

**FOR THE POTATO AND
BEETROOT SALAD**

300g new potatoes,
   cut into quarters
2 tablespoons olive oil
200g cooked beetroot,
   cut into 3cm chunks
Small bunch of dill,
   chopped
3 spring onions, sliced
1 tablespoon balsamic
   vinegar
20g salad leaves
   or pea shoots

Preheat the oven 180°C (160°C fan), gas mark 4. Put the potatoes in a large roasting pan and drizzle over a generous tablespoon of olive oil and plenty of seasoning. Roast for 20 minutes.

Meanwhile, for the salmon, mix together the horseradish, crème fraîche, lemon zest, chives and plenty of seasoning. Place a piece of foil large enough to wrap the salmon in a roasting pan. Oil the foil with the sunflower oil and place one fillet on it, skinned-side down. Season the fish and spread over the horseradish filling. Season the other piece of fish and place on top of the filling with the skinned side facing up. Season, then squeeze over the lemon and add about 4 tablespoons of water. Bring the foil together to seal the parcel. Place in the oven for about 20 minutes.

While the oven is open, shake the pan of potatoes; they will need another 20 minutes. Add the beetroot after 10 minutes.

After 20 minutes, check the salmon. Take the pan out of the oven and very carefully open the foil. Insert a knife blade into the centre of the fish: the flesh should look opaque, and will be falling into flakes. If it is a little on the translucent side, that is fine, as it will continue to cook in its warm parcel while you finish the potato and beetroot salad. If you are at all concerned, return the salmon to the oven for another 5 minutes.

When the potatoes are cooked, take them out of the oven and add the dill and spring onions and taste for seasoning. Toss in the remaining olive oil and the balsamic. Once mixed, gently fold the salad leaves through.

Lift the salmon from its parcel and cut into four slices. Pour over any pan juices and serve immediately with the hot potato and beetroot salad.

GREEN COUSCOUS WITH PRAWNS

A brilliant green colour and easily adaptable. Make a vegetarian version of this dish by replacing the prawns with crumbled feta, and use vegetarian stuffed olives.

SERVES 4

300g couscous
500ml boiling vegetable
  or fish stock
200g frozen peas,
  defrosted
150g frozen spinach,
  defrosted
40g butter
300g North Atlantic
  peeled prawns
4 spring onions,
  thickly sliced
90g green olives stuffed
  with anchovies,
  roughly chopped
30g preserved lemon,
  shredded small, or
  grated zest of 1 lemon
Juice of 1 lemon
Small handful of parsley,
  roughly chopped
Sea salt and black pepper

Put the couscous in a bowl and pour over 350ml of the hot stock, cover and leave to expand for a good 10 minutes.

Preheat the oven to 180°C (160°C fan), gas mark 4.

Put the peas, spinach and butter into a blender or food processor with the rest of the hot stock and whizz to a coarse purée.

Once the couscous has absorbed all the stock, stir it well with a fork or rub between finger and thumb to get rid of any clumps. Stir in the vibrant green purée and tip the couscous into a roasting pan with the prawns, spring onions, olives, preserved lemon or lemon zest and plenty of seasoning. Place in the oven to heat through for 15–20 minutes.

Once the couscous is hot, stir in the lemon juice, taste for seasoning and add the parsley. Serve in warmed bowls.

SPICED WHITE FISH WITH NOODLES AND BROTH

Making noodle soup in the oven is just as easy as doing it on the hob. You will need two roasting pans, one for the broth and one for the fish. You can coat the fish in the spice mix several hours in advance if you like.

SERVES 2

2 x 130g skinless firm
   white fish steaks, such
   as monkfish
1 teaspoon soft light
   brown sugar
1 teaspoon sea salt
1 teaspoon ground ginger
1 teaspoon ground
   coriander
½ teaspoon cayenne
   pepper
Grated zest and juice
   of ½ lime
1 tablespoon sunflower oil
300ml boiling fish stock
3cm thumb of ginger,
   peeled and grated
2 cloves garlic, crushed
   or finely grated
2 spring onions, sliced
   diagonally into long
   thin pieces
1 large carrot, cut
   into matchsticks
1 celery stick, sliced
100g fresh thick
   udon noodles
Handful of coriander,
   roughly chopped

Place the fish in a dish. Mix the sugar, salt, spices and lime zest together in a small bowl. Brush the fish with oil on both sides then rub the spice mixture all over. Set aside in the fridge for up to 5 hours if you have the time, but even 15 minutes while the oven is heating will be beneficial.

Preheat the oven to 200°C (180°C fan), gas mark 6.

Pour the hot fish stock into a deep roasting pan, add the ginger and garlic and put into the oven for 5 minutes.

Lightly oil a small roasting pan, add the fish and put into the oven – it should take about 10 minutes to cook.

At the same time, add the spring onions, carrot and celery to the broth in the oven.

Cook the noodles as directed on the pack, then add to the fish broth. Taste and add salt if needed.

When the fish is ready, squeeze the lime juice over it.

Add the coriander to the broth. Ladle the noodles and broth into serving bowls and put a piece of fish on top. Pour over any juices from the fish roasting pan and serve immediately with some coriander leaves to garnish.

ROAST MACKEREL AND SPRING ONIONS WITH TARRAGON

*Roasting small whole fish is a super simple quick supper.
The herby sauce has enough acidity to cut the richness of the mackerel.*

SERVES 2

2 whole mackerel, gutted
1 lemon – ½ thinly
   sliced, the other ½ cut
   in half to serve
Small handful of herbs
   (parsley, tarragon, etc)
2 tablespoons olive oil
6 spring onions, trimmed
   and left whole
Sea salt and black pepper

FOR THE SAUCE

100g stale bread
2 tablespoons white
   wine vinegar
Small handful of flat-leaf
   parsley, chopped
5 sprigs of tarragon,
   leaves removed – use
   the stalks to go in the
   fish cavities
1 egg, hard-boiled –
   white finely chopped,
   yolk crumbled
6 tablespoons extra
   virgin olive oil
1 banana shallot, diced
1 heaped tablespoon
   capers

Start by making the sauce. Soak the bread in water until it is soft but not disintegrating. Lift it out of the water and give it a good squeeze, then put the bread, vinegar, herbs and boiled egg yolk in a food processor and whizz to a smooth paste, gradually adding the oil: you don't want the bread whizzing round for too long or it might go gluey. Once all the oil is incorporated, turn the sauce into a bowl and add the egg white, shallot and capers. Taste for seasoning.

Preheat the oven to 200°C (180°C fan), gas mark 6.

Cut a couple of slashes on each side of the fish and stuff the cavities with lemon slices, herbs and seasoning. Season the outsides too.

Oil a roasting pan and add the spring onions in a row, season, drizzle with more oil and place the fish on top. Drizzle the remaining oil over the fish.

When the oven is hot, roast the mackerel for 12–15 minutes until they are cooked through: the skin will peel off easily if the fish is done. Serve the fish and spring onions with a good dollop of the sauce and a wedge of lemon.

FANCY FISH FINGERS AND BEANS

Fish fingers are universally popular. A polenta coating gives them an extra crispness, but dried breadcrumbs such as panko work just as well. You can use any white fish, but if using flat fish fillets they will need a shorter cooking time than suggested here. The beans are cooked separately and make a good vegan side dish or light supper.

SERVES 4

1 egg
100g fine polenta
4 x 120g skinless white
    fish fillets, cut into
    3cm wide pieces
4 tablespoons olive oil
Sea salt and black pepper
½ lemon, cut into wedges
    to serve

FOR THE BEANS

3 tablespoons olive oil
1 red onion, thinly sliced
2 celery sticks, finely
    sliced
2 cloves garlic, crushed
    or finely grated
1 tablespoon sherry
    vinegar
400g tin borlotti beans,
    drained and rinsed
400g tin cherry tomatoes
400ml boiling vegetable
    stock
Few sprigs of dill,
    chopped (optional)

Preheat the oven to 180°C (160°C fan), gas mark 4. Put a small roasting pan in to heat up with 2 tablespoons of the olive oil for the beans.

Once hot, add the onion and a good pinch of salt and place in the oven to soften for about 7 minutes. Add the remaining tablespoon of oil and the celery, mix thoroughly and return to the oven for another 7 minutes until it has all started to soften and get some gentle golden colour. Add the garlic and vinegar to the onions and celery, give it all a good stir and pop back in the oven for a couple of minutes.

Turn the oven up to 200°C (180°C fan), gas mark 6. Add the beans, cherry tomatoes and vegetable stock to the roasting pan, stir and return to the oven for 20 minutes until the liquid has reduced down to a sauce.

While the beans are cooking, make the fish fingers. In a shallow dish, whisk the egg with 2–3 tablespoons of water and some salt and pepper. Put the polenta in another shallow dish. Line a pan with a reusable silicone baking mat or foil. Dip the fish pieces into the polenta and then into the egg; once coated with egg, let any excess drip off before putting them back into the polenta. Ensure each piece is evenly coated with polenta before placing in a single layer on the baking mat or foil.

Preheat a large roasting pan, adding the 4 tablespoons of olive oil. Once this oil is smoking hot, add the fish fingers in a single layer and cook for about 5 minutes until crisp and golden, then turn over and cook for another 5 minutes – if you have used flat fish fillets they will need much less time. Lift the fish onto FSC kitchen paper to absorb any excess oil.

By the time the fish is cooked the beans should be ready too. Taste and adjust the seasoning and add the dill. Serve immediately, with lemon wedges to squeeze over the fish.

PLAICE BAKED WITH FENNEL, POTATOES AND CIDER

Flat fish are really quick to cook and convenient if you can get them ready filleted.
Plaice vary in size, but the important thing is that the fish should be really fresh.

SERVES 2

2 tablespoons olive oil
6 new potatoes, scrubbed
    and cut in half
    lengthways
1 large head fennel,
    trimmed and
    finely sliced
2 red onions, sliced
1 red apple, skin on,
    cored and cut into
    eight wedges
120ml cider
Few sprigs of parsley,
    chopped
2–4 skinless plaice fillets,
    about 300g total weight
20g butter
Sea salt and black pepper

Preheat the oven to 200°C (180°C fan), gas mark 6. Put a roasting pan in to heat up with 1½ tablespoons of the olive oil.

Once hot, add the potatoes and cook for 15 minutes.

Meanwhile, mix the fennel, onions and apple together with a good pinch of salt and set aside.

Add the cider to the roasting pan and return to the oven for 5 minutes.

Now add the fennel mixture and stir well. Test the potatoes with the point of a sharp knife: it should meet no resistance, but if necessary cook for a little longer.

Stir in the parsley and sit the fish fillets on top, skinned-side down. Season the fish and dot with the butter. Bake for 7 minutes or until the fish is opaque. Serve immediately.

FISH WRAPPED IN HAM, WITH BUTTER BEANS AND SUN-DRIED TOMATOES

This is inspired by saltimbocca, an Italian dish of veal wrapped in Parma ham. The salty ham works well with firm white fish. You will need a second roasting pan for the butter bean mixture.

SERVES 4

1 tablespoon olive oil
1 red onion, finely sliced
Grated zest and juice of
   1 lemon
2 x 400g tins butter
   beans, drained and
   rinsed
4 x 130g skinless firm
   white fish fillets
4 sage leaves, rolled up
   together and sliced
   into thin ribbons
4 slices of Parma ham
100g semi-dried or
   sun-dried tomatoes
   in oil, drained and
   chopped, plus
   2 tablespoons of
   their oil
120g baby spinach
125ml boiling water
Sea salt and black pepper
½ lemon, cut into wedges
   to serve (optional)

Preheat the oven to 200°C (180°C fan), gas mark 6. Put a large roasting pan brushed with a little of the olive oil into the oven to heat up.

Mix the red onion with the lemon juice and a good pinch of salt and leave to macerate while you prepare the fish.

Put the butter beans into a pan or bowl of boiling water to heat through.

Line up the fish fillets in a row, season well with salt and pepper, scatter over the sage and lemon zest and drizzle over the remaining olive oil, then wrap each piece of fish in a slice of ham – don't worry if it's not entirely enveloped. Put the seam of the ham on the underside of the fish. Once the roasting pan is hot, lift the fish fillets into the hot pan, seam-side down, and put in the oven.

Drain the beans and place in a smaller roasting pan. Add the tomatoes and their oil, the spinach, plenty of seasoning and the boiling water, and place in the oven at the same time as the fish.

By the time the fish is cooked – about 10 minutes – the beans should be hot and the spinach wilted. Add the pink lemony onions and all their juice to the beans. Serve the fish on top of the beans with a small lemon wedge to squeeze over if you like.

COD, ORZO, SWEET POTATO AND TAPENADE

The southern French olive paste known as tapenade is great with fish: the salty umami flavours bring all the elements of this dish together. You can get different types of tapenade, but for this dish I favour a green one.

SERVES 4

2 tablespoons olive oil
1 large sweet potato,
    peeled and cut into
    3cm chunks
2 banana shallots,
    quartered lengthways
320g orzo
650ml boiling vegetable
    or fish stock
4 x 130g skinless
    cod fillets
2 tablespoons green
    tapenade
Small handful of basil
Sea salt and black pepper
½ lemon, cut into wedges
    to serve

Preheat the oven to 200°C (180°C fan), gas mark 6. Put a roasting pan in to heat up with the olive oil.

Once the oil is hot, add the sweet potato and shallots and roast for 15 minutes until the vegetables have started to soften.

Add the orzo and stir until it is well mixed with the vegetables. Add the boiling stock and return to the oven for 15 minutes.

Meanwhile, season the fish with salt and pepper and divide the tapenade between the four fillets, smoothing it over the top of each one.

By now the orzo will have absorbed most of the stock. Tear the basil into the pasta and give everything a good stir, taste and adjust the seasoning and sit the fish fillets on top. Bake for 12 minutes until the fish is opaque and readily breaks into flakes. Serve immediately, with small lemon wedges to squeeze over.

SPICED PRAWN FILO PIE

The flavours in this pie are based on those in a Moroccan pastilla – a filo pastry pie filled with pigeon, apricots and spices. This version has prawns, spinach and red peppers, which marry well with the spicing.

SERVES 4

1 tablespoon olive oil

3 red onions, sliced

2 red peppers,
  deseeded and cut
  into 2cm wide strips

1 tablespoon ground
  cumin

1 heaped teaspoon
  ground cinnamon

2 teaspoons paprika

250g frozen large
  cold-water prawns,
  defrosted

2 fat cloves garlic,
  crushed or finely grated

250g cooked brown rice

200g frozen spinach,
  defrosted and
  squeezed dry

Grated zest and juice
  of ½ lemon

Small handful of
  coriander, chopped

80g butter, melted

250g filo pastry

2 tablespoons
  sesame seeds

Sea salt

Preheat the oven to 200°C (180°C fan), gas mark 6. Put a roasting pan in to heat up with the olive oil.

Once hot, add the onions, peppers, spices and a generous pinch of salt and return to the oven for 15 minutes.

Meanwhile, mix together the prawns, garlic, rice, spinach, lemon zest and juice and coriander. Once the peppers and onions are soft, add the prawn mixture, taste and adjust the seasoning.

Butter a small (approx. 30 x 20cm) roasting pan and line with two overlapping sheets of filo pastry, leaving plenty hanging over the edge; brush the pastry with melted butter and scatter over a quarter of the sesame seeds. Repeat the process twice more, using a total of six sheets of filo, but not scattering sesame seeds over the final layer.

Add the prawn mixture and then fold all the overhanging filo over the filling – it should completely cover the filling. Brush the top with butter, scrunch up the ends and scatter over the remaining sesame seeds. Bake for 25 minutes until the pastry is crisp and golden and the filling is piping hot.

ANA'S FISH PARCELS

Ana, a great friend of mine from Spain, taught me a lot about cooking and encouraged me to experiment. This is one of her recipes. You will need two roasting pans – and string if using baking parchment for the parcels.

SERVES 2

1½ tablespoons olive oil
3 cloves garlic,
   finely sliced
1 teaspoon sweet
   smoked paprika
1 leek, finely sliced
1 potato, diced into
   small pieces
2 skinless cod loins,
   approx. 200g each
Sea salt and black pepper

FOR THE BAKED VEGETABLES

1 courgette, cut into
   long thin strips using
   a peeler
1 aubergine, cut into
   long thin strips
1½ tablespoons olive oil
1 clove black garlic (or
   regular garlic), crushed
1½ tablespoons extra
   virgin olive oil
2 teaspoons balsamic
   vinegar
Couple of sprigs of
   fresh oregano, basil or
   thyme, leaves stripped
   from stalks

Preheat the oven to 180°C (160°C fan), gas mark 4. Put a large roasting pan and a small roasting pan with the olive oil into the oven to heat up.

When the oil is hot in the small pan, throw in the garlic and return to the oven until it turns light golden and crisp – don't let it burn or it will become bitter. Remove from the oven, strain off any oil into a bowl and drain the garlic on FSC kitchen paper, then toss with the paprika. Set aside: this is the garnish for the cod parcels.

Mix the leek and potato together with the garlic oil and season generously.

Cut two large rectangles of baking parchment or foil and make a bed of the leek and potato mixture in the centre of each. Season the fish and place it on the vegetables. Bring the parchment or foil up around the fish to form a parcel, leaving space for the steam to circulate. If using parchment, tie with string so it is like a spacious but well sealed bag. If using foil, fold over and crimp the top to create a nice tight seam.

Place the parcels on the hot large roasting pan and cook for about 15–20 minutes until the parcels are puffed up and full of steam.

While the fish is cooking, put the courgette and aubergine ribbons in the small roasting pan with a splash of the olive oil and season with salt and pepper. Cook for 10–15 minutes until soft and golden.

To make a dressing for the aubergine and courgette, using a stick blender, whizz together the garlic, extra virgin olive oil, balsamic and herbs until smooth. Once the vegetables are ready, toss them in the dressing.

Serve the fish in its little parcel topped with the garlic slices. Serve the courgettes and aubergines separately, to go on top of the fish once the parcel has been opened.

FISH PIE WITH A RÖSTI TOPPING

*Fish pie is a firm family favourite – this one cuts out a lot of the work,
such as making a white sauce and mashed potato.*

SERVES 4

500g firm white
　fish fillets
1 leek, finely sliced,
　using as much of the
　green part as possible
300ml hot milk
100g cream cheese
　with herbs and garlic
100g baby spinach
Small handful of
　parsley, chopped
Few sprigs of tarragon
　(optional), leaves
　chopped
80g smoked mackerel,
　flaked
1 tub (approx. 55g)
　potted shrimps
Grated zest and juice
　of ½ lemon
700g large red-skinned
　potatoes, peeled
2 tablespoons capers
60g butter, melted
Sea salt and black pepper

Preheat the oven to 220°C (200°C fan), gas mark 7.

Put the fish, leek and milk into a small roasting pan, season well and
cover with foil. Bake for 15 minutes until the fish is cooked and the
leek has softened.

Strain off the milk into a food processor and add the cream cheese,
spinach and herbs. Whizz to make a smooth, thickish sauce.

Separate the fish from the leeks, remove the skin if there is any, and flake
the fish. Mix together the poached fish, mackerel and leeks. Break up
the potted shrimps as best you can and add them, too. Add the lemon
juice and zest and stir in the herby sauce. Taste and adjust the seasoning.
Spread this mixture evenly in the roasting pan.

Coarsely grate the potatoes and toss with the capers, melted butter
and plenty of seasoning. Spread the potato mix evenly over the fish.

Bake for 35 minutes until the topping is golden and crisp on top and
fluffy underneath. Test by piercing the potato topping with a sharp knife:
it should slide through easily. Leave to stand for 5 minutes before serving.
I like to have fish pie with peas.

GRILLED MUSTARD SMOKED HADDOCK AND LENTILS

I use this mustard marinade with rabbit, chicken or pork, as well as smoked fish. It's great if you can do it the night before, but is equally good if the fish only marinates for a short time before being grilled.

SERVES 4

2 spring onions, sliced
2 cloves garlic, chopped
2 tablespoons Dijon
   mustard
1 tablespoon wholegrain
   mustard
1 tablespoon cider
   vinegar
Small handful of parsley,
   roughly chopped
3 tablespoons olive oil
4 x 130g pieces of
   undyed smoked
   haddock or other
   smoked white
   fish, skinned
2 x 400g tins lentils,
   drained and rinsed
150ml boiling water
30g rocket, roughly torn
Small bunch of chives,
   snipped
Sea salt and black pepper
½ lemon, cut into wedges
   to serve (optional)

Put the spring onions, garlic, mustard, vinegar and parsley in a food processor and whizz to a smooth paste. Add 2 tablespoons of the olive oil, salt and pepper and whizz for a bit longer. Pour into a dish, add the fish and coat all over with the marinade. Cover and leave for at least 30 minutes or overnight.

If you have left it overnight, take the fish out of the fridge. Preheat the grill to its highest setting and give it 5–7 minutes to get really hot. At the same time drop the lentils into a pan of boiling water to heat them through, then drain.

Put the remaining olive oil into a roasting pan that will fit under your grill; add the lentils and some salt and pepper and stir to get them well coated with oil.

Lift the fish out of the marinade, wiping off excess marinade, and set aside on a plate.

Add the boiling water to the marinade, pour over the lentils and stir well. Place the fish on top of the lentils. Grill for about 5 minutes; if the pieces of fish are very thick, turn and grill for a few minutes on the other side until the fish is cooked and readily breaks into flakes.

Lift the fish off and set aside on a warmed plate. Stir the rocket and chives into the lentils and taste for seasoning. Spoon the lentils onto serving plates and place the fish on top. If you like, add a small lemon wedge to squeeze over.

If you want something extra, try the charred cabbage (see page 108). Or on warmer days, a bitter leaf and orange salad.

VEG

MUSHROOMS STUFFED WITH RICE, SPINACH AND PINE NUTS

What an easy supper. A recent revelation has been ready-cooked rice and other grains in pouches
– they make all-in-one meals in the oven an absolute breeze. I have used a basmati and wild rice mix.

SERVES 2

30g pine nuts
2 tablespoons olive oil
250g flat mushrooms,
   stalks removed –
   this should be four
   nice-sized mushrooms
250g pouch cooked
   basmati and wild rice
200g frozen spinach,
   defrosted
3 spring onions,
   finely sliced
1 large clove garlic,
   crushed or finely
   chopped
40g butter, melted
25g Parmesan-style
   vegetarian cheese,
   finely grated
15g breadcrumbs –
   fresh or panko
Sea salt and black pepper

Preheat the oven to 160°C (140°C fan), gas mark 3. Put the pine nuts in a roasting pan and put them in the oven to toast gently as the oven heats up. Their high fat content means they catch very quickly – in commercial kitchens chefs are renowned for setting three alarms and still managing to burn the pine nuts! – so watch them carefully. Once the pine nuts are golden, tip them into a bowl and set aside.

Drizzle 1 tablespoon of the olive oil into the roasting pan and add the mushrooms, white cap-side down. Drizzle the remaining oil over the mushrooms and season generously. Cook for about 15 minutes until soft.

Meanwhile, make the filling. Put the cooked rice, spinach, spring onions, garlic, butter and 20g of the cheese into the bowl with the pine nuts and stir well. Taste and adjust the seasoning.

After 15 minutes the mushrooms should be soft. Spoon the spinach mixture onto the mushrooms, then scatter over the breadcrumbs and the remaining Parmesan. Return to the oven for about 20 minutes until the stuffing is piping hot. Serve immediately.

TIP For a vegan version, replace the butter with another 3 tablespoons of olive oil and omit the cheese.

SQUASH, TOMATO AND GOATS' CHEESE STRATA

A delicious September dish, when all the wonderful squashes are appearing and the tomatoes are having their swansong – it works well with green tomatoes, too, and out of season there are tinned cherry tomatoes.

SERVES 6

2 tablespoons olive oil
500g squash, peeled, deseeded and cut into 2cm thick slices
3 red onions, cut in half and each half cut into four wedges
1 small sprig of rosemary, leaves roughly chopped
250g cherry tomatoes
125g soft goats' cheese
1–2 tablespoons chilli jam or sauce (optional)
300g sliced bread, approx. 10 medium thick slices – I like to use a white sourdough
5 eggs
200ml milk
250g crème fraîche
30g Parmesan-style vegetarian cheese, grated
Sea salt and black pepper

Preheat the oven to 180°C (160°C fan), gas mark 4. Put a roasting pan in to heat up with the olive oil.

When hot, add the squash and onions, the rosemary and plenty of seasoning. Shake everything about and place in the oven for about 15 minutes. Shake or stir well, add the cherry tomatoes and return to the oven for about 10 minutes.

Meanwhile, mix the goats' cheese with the chilli jam and spread over the bread. Cut in half diagonally to make triangles. To make the custard, whisk the eggs with the milk, crème fraîche and half of the cheese. Season well.

Once the squash has started to soften, tip the vegetables into a bowl. Using half of the bread triangles, arrange them in a layer in the roasting pan, cheese-side up, overlapping them if need be. Add the squash mixture, seasoning to taste. Then add the final layer of bread, cheese-side down.

Pour over the custard and leave to stand for at least 20 minutes or overnight in the fridge. Be sure to take it out of the fridge a good 25 minutes before you plan to cook it.

Turn the oven down to 160°C (140°C fan), gas mark 3. Scatter over the remaining Parmesan-style cheese and bake for 25–30 minutes until just set. Leave to stand for 5–7 minutes before serving. I like to serve this with a green salad.

RED PEPPERS STUFFED WITH SPICED CHICKPEAS AND AUBERGINE

When peppers and tomatoes are abundant in summer this is a great dish to serve as a vegan main course or alongside barbecued meat or fish or as part of a mezze. It's good at room temperature or straight from the oven.

SERVES 4

VEGAN

1 large aubergine, cut
    into 2cm cubes
2 red onions, roughly
    sliced
3 tablespoons olive oil
2 teaspoons ground
    coriander
1 teaspoon ground cumin
1 teaspoon turmeric
Pinch of chilli flakes
400g tin chickpeas,
    drained
4 red peppers, cut in half
    lengthways, deseeded
    and white pith
    removed
6 ripe tomatoes
3 cloves garlic, crushed
    or finely grated
3cm thumb of ginger,
    peeled and finely grated
Juice of ½ lemon
Generous handful of
    coriander, roughly
    chopped
Sea salt and black pepper
Coconut yoghurt,
    to serve

Preheat the oven to 190°C (170°C fan), gas mark 5, and put a roasting pan in to heat up.

Toss the aubergine and onions together with 1½ tablespoons of olive oil and plenty of seasoning. Once the oven is hot, add a splash of oil to the pan and swirl around. Add the aubergine and onions and shake to distribute them evenly. Roast for 15 minutes until the aubergine is golden and the onion has softened.

Sprinkle over the dry spices and return to the oven for a minute to let them toast. Add the chickpeas and then tip the mixture into a bowl, scraping with a spatula to ensure all the toasted spices come too, and set aside.

Turn the oven down to 180°C (160°C fan), gas mark 4. Place the peppers cavity-side down in the roasting pan, drizzle with olive oil and season well. Put in the oven for 10–20 minutes until softened but not cooked through.

Meanwhile, prepare the tomato sauce. Put the tomatoes, garlic and ginger in a blender and whizz until smooth.

Once the peppers have softened, remove them from the pan and set aside. Pour the tomato sauce into the hot pan. Turn the oven up to 220°C (200°C fan), gas mark 7. Return the pan to the oven to heat the sauce for about 5 minutes. Add the aubergine and chickpea mixture and cook for about 20 minutes until the sauce reduces down slightly. Once you are happy with the consistency, add a squeeze of lemon and three-quarters of the coriander and taste for seasoning. Set aside in a bowl while you rinse and dry the pan.

Add a splash of oil to the clean pan and put the peppers back in. Spoon the chickpea mixture into the peppers and bake until the peppers are soft, about 15–20 minutes. Serve with flatbreads and coconut yoghurt.

SPINACH, WALNUT AND FETA IN THE HOLE

A vegetarian version of toad in the hole without using a vegetarian sausage. Cooked spinach is mixed with walnuts and feta to form patties – and the batter works equally well with sausages of course.

SERVES 4

500g large leaf spinach,
    thick stalks discarded,
    or 200g frozen
    chopped spinach,
    defrosted
3 spring onions, finely
    chopped, using as
    much of the green
    part as possible
1 clove garlic, crushed
    or finely grated
150g feta, crumbled
1 tablespoon olive oil
45g walnuts, toasted
    and chopped
30g panko or other dried
    breadcrumbs (optional)

FOR THE BATTER

3 eggs
150g plain flour
190ml milk
1 heaped tablespoon
    wholegrain mustard,
    dissolved in 65ml
    warm water
1 tablespoon sunflower
    or rapeseed oil
Sea salt and black pepper

Start by making the batter, as it benefits from a 15-minute rest before cooking. In a bowl, whisk the eggs until thick and voluminous – use an electric whisk if you have one; otherwise consider it a small cardio workout. Now beat in a third of the flour, followed by a third of the milk, and repeat the process twice more until you have used all the flour and milk. Fold in the mustard and water and season generously.

Preheat the oven to 200°C (180°C fan), gas mark 6. Put a roasting pan, which you have oiled with the sunflower oil, in to heat up.

If using fresh spinach, steam until it wilts, run it under cold water to cool it quickly, then roughly chop. Squeeze the spinach to remove as much water as possible, then place the nice dry spinach in a bowl. Add the spring onions, garlic, feta, olive oil and walnuts and mix thoroughly. Try squeezing some of the mixture together and see if it will form a clump: if it is too wet – this will depend on the type of spinach you have – add the breadcrumbs gradually until it forms a cohesive mass. Divide this into eight equal clumps, shape into balls and flatten with the palm of your hand.

Take the roasting pan out of the oven and turn the oven down to 180°C (160°C fan), gas mark 4. Give the oil a quick swirl to coat the whole pan and add the patties, evenly spaced apart. Now pour in the batter and return the pan to the oven immediately so that the batter can start puffing up straight away.

Bake for 20–25 minutes until set, well risen and golden. Serve immediately. Traditionalists would suggest gravy alongside; alternatively some grilled or roasted tomatoes would be nice.

POTATO, LEEK, SWISS CHARD AND BLUE CHEESE GRATIN

This is a simple vegetarian main course that takes minutes to assemble. I would choose a blue cheese such as bleu d'Auvergne for this – something soft and creamy. A soft goats' cheese would work well, too.

SERVES 4

3 leeks, sliced, using as much of the green part as possible

600g Swiss chard, stalks sliced, leaves torn

200g soft blue cheese, crumbled

1 tablespoon sunflower oil

600g waxy potatoes, cut into ½cm thick slices

Sea salt and black pepper

Preheat the oven to 200°C (180°C fan), gas mark 6.

Bring a large pan of salted water to the boil. Throw in the leeks and chard stalks and blanch for 2 minutes. Add the chard leaves and blanch for another minute. Drain and place in a bowl; don't worry if there is some water clinging to the vegetables. Add two-thirds of the cheese to the hot leek mixture and stir so that it pretty much melts. Season to taste: blue cheese can be salty so you may not need much salt, but a good grinding of black pepper is in order to cut through the richness.

Drizzle the roasting pan with the oil and add half of the potatoes, spread out in a layer and season with salt and pepper. Cover with half of the leek/ blue cheese mixture. Now cover with the remaining potatoes, seasoning, and the remaining leeks with any liquid in the bowl. Dot the top with the remaining blue cheese, cover with foil and place in the oven for 35 minutes. Remove the foil and cook for another 10 minutes.

Check it is ready by inserting a sharp knife: it should slide through the potatoes with no resistance. Leave to stand for 5 minutes before serving.

A peppery watercress and almond salad would be a nice accompaniment.

TIP For a vegan version, substitute some chopped toasted almonds and hazelnuts for the cheese and add a good glug of nut oil or olive oil.

PEA AND ARTICHOKE RISOTTO

Cooking rice in the oven like this is not risotto in the strictest sense – although in the north-west coastal strip of Italy, home of pesto, they do cook rice in this way.

SERVES 2

45g butter
2 tablespoons olive oil
2 shallots, finely sliced
Small sprig of rosemary,
    leaves finely chopped
200g arborio rice
100ml white wine or
    cider (optional)
600ml boiling
    vegetable stock
120g frozen peas,
    defrosted
2 generous tablespoons
    artichoke purée or
    50g artichokes in oil,
    drained and chopped
30g Parmesan-style
    vegetarian cheese,
    grated
Sea salt and black pepper

Preheat the oven to 180°C (160°C fan), gas mark 4, and put a roasting pan in to heat up.

Once the oven is hot, put 30g of the butter, the olive oil, shallots and rosemary into the roasting pan, add a good pinch of salt and place in the oven. After 5 minutes, give the shallots a stir and cook for another 3–5 minutes. They may take on a little bit of colour but cover with foil if they are looking too brown.

Once the shallots are soft, add the rice and stir to coat well with the buttery mixture. If you like, you can add a small glass of white wine or cider and return the pan to the oven for 5 minutes until the wine is absorbed. Add the hot stock, give everything a good stir and bake for 20 minutes.

Add the peas and artichokes and stir well. Return to the oven for 12 minutes. By now the stock will have been absorbed, but the risotto shouldn't be entirely dry.

Stir in the remaining 15g of butter and the cheese, cover with a clean tea towel and leave to settle for 4 minutes. I usually put the plates in the cooling oven to warm up. Serve this comforting supper with a green salad if you wish.

TIP I like using peas and artichokes in this simple recipe because they require very little preparation, but you can use other vegetables. Jerusalem artichokes and some soaked dried wild mushrooms are a winter favourite: you need to slice the artichokes into half moons (I don't bother peeling them as long as they are good and clean) and add them at the same time as the shallots to ensure they are cooked through – I would suggest the same for any root veg. Leafy vegetables could go in later after a couple of minutes in boiling water.

ROAST ASPARAGUS
WITH EGG TOASTS

Asparagus is definitely one of my top five vegetables. During its British season it's at its very best and a real treat. The season traditionally starts on St George's Day in April and runs for a good six to eight weeks.

SERVES 4

2 brioche rolls
1 red onion, finely sliced
1½ tablespoons white
   balsamic vinegar, or
   cider vinegar and a
   drizzle of honey
1½ tablespoons olive oil
500g asparagus, trimmed
40g cream cheese with
   herbs and garlic
4 eggs
200g frozen peas,
   defrosted
20g Parmesan-style
   vegetarian cheese,
   coarsely grated
Sea salt and black pepper

Preheat the oven to 200°C (180°C fan), gas mark 6.

Cut the rolls in half, also cutting off the crown of the top half, to make a stable base. Using a glass or small cup, make an indent in each half roll and remove a little of the crumb to make a hollow to cradle the egg that you will be breaking into it later in the recipe. Place the rolls in the roasting pan and pop them in the oven for about 5 minutes so they dry out a bit and become crisp. Meanwhile, mix the onion with the vinegar and some salt and leave to soften and turn bright pink.

Remove the brioche toasts from the oven and set aside. Add the olive oil and the asparagus to the roasting pan, season generously and shake until the asparagus is well coated with oil. Roast for 8 minutes until the spears are just beginning to yield to the touch, but not too soft. While the asparagus is cooking, spread the cream cheese on the toasts – I use a spoon to do this and encourage the central indent a little more.

Pour some boiling water over the peas to heat them up. Push the asparagus to the sides of the roasting pan, add the toasts and put the pan back in the oven for a few minutes to warm the bread.

With the roasting pan still in the oven, pull it out on its shelf and crack an egg onto each toast, aiming to get the yolk into the central dip, but don't worry – it will be delicious even if the egg is everywhere! Return to the oven for a couple of minutes until the eggs have begun to set. When they have set enough that they are not going to move about, scatter the peas into the pan and season generously. Give the whole lot another 4 minutes or until the egg whites are completely set but the yolks are still runny.

Serve an egg-filled toast on each plate, with some asparagus and peas. Scatter over the red onions and Parmesan-style cheese. Serve immediately.

VICKY'S FILO PIE

I have a great friend called Vicky who gave me this pie for supper recently and I absolutely loved it.
It's a moveable feast in that you can use various vegetables, depending on what you have.

SERVES 4

250g mushrooms, sliced
3½ tablespoons olive oil
2 leeks, sliced, using as
   much of the green part
   as possible
450g spinach
150g Greek yoghurt
180g feta, crumbled
1 teaspoon wholegrain
   mustard
3 sprigs of mint,
   leaves chopped
250g filo pastry
4 eggs
10g Parmesan-style
   vegetarian cheese,
   grated (optional)
Sea salt and black pepper

Preheat the oven to 200°C (180°C fan), gas mark 6.

Put the mushrooms in a roasting pan with 1 tablespoon of the olive oil and a good pinch of salt. Put in the oven for about 10 minutes until soft.

Bring a large pan of salted water to the boil. Throw in the leeks and blanch for 2 minutes. Add the spinach leaves, then immediately drain and refresh in cold water. Drain very thoroughly. I usually leave the vegetables in the colander and press down on them with a small plate or place a small bowl filled with water on top and leave to drain for several minutes.

While the mushrooms are roasting and the leeks and spinach are draining, mix the yoghurt and feta together in a bowl, add the mustard and mint and a good grinding of black pepper. Taste and add salt if necessary.

Once the leek mixture is thoroughly drained, add the mushrooms and the yoghurt mixture, mix thoroughly and taste for seasoning.

Rinse and dry the roasting pan. Brush the pan with oil and line with filo pastry; it can hang over the sides of the pan, but trim if there is a lot of excess pastry. Brush the pastry with oil and add another layer of filo. Repeat until you have used four sheets of filo.

Add the vegetable mixture and make four hollows, evenly spaced in the pie, one towards each corner. Crack an egg into each hollow.

Cover with another sheet of filo pastry, fold in any overhang and brush with the remaining oil. Score the top in a diamond pattern and scatter with the Parmesan-style cheese, if using. Cook for 30 minutes until golden and crisp. Serve hot.

BAKED ANGEL HAIR PASTA WITH BROCCOLI AND GREEN BEANS

This is based on the Catalan dish fideuà: essentially it's a paella made with thin noodles instead of rice. You will need a second roasting pan to roast the broccoli and green beans.

SERVES 4

VEGAN

3 tablespoons extra
   virgin olive oil
2 small onions,
   finely sliced
4 cloves garlic – 3 finely
   sliced, 1 finely grated
1½ teaspoons cayenne
   pepper
1½ teaspoons smoked
   paprika
1 teaspoon fennel
   seeds, ground
1 bay leaf
A few sprigs of thyme
500g angel hair pasta
   (capelli d'angelo)

Preheat the oven to 220°C (200°C fan), gas mark 7. Put a roasting pan in to heat up with 1½ tablespoons of the olive oil.

Once hot, add the onions and a pinch of salt and cook for 5 minutes. Add the sliced garlic, cayenne, paprika, fennel seeds, bay leaf and thyme and cook for a further 2 minutes.

Meanwhile, break up the angel hair a bit. When the onion is softened and lightly golden, add the pasta to the roasting pan and cook for 7 minutes, shaking the pan halfway through.

Put another roasting pan with the remaining olive oil into the oven.

Add the peppers to the pasta along with the butter beans, tomato juice and 300ml of the hot stock. Ensure that the pasta is immersed in the liquid and return to the oven for a few minutes. Once the stock is bubbling, add the saffron strands and water, if using. Give everything a stir and ensure that the pasta is covered with liquid with a couple of centimetres to spare, adding more hot stock if necessary.

¼ x 450g jar roasted
  peppers
400g tin butter beans,
  drained and rinsed
300ml tomato juice
500ml boiling vegetable
  stock
Pinch of saffron soaked
  in 100ml warm water
  (optional)
1 head broccoli, broken
  into small florets
100g green beans
Grated zest and juice
  of ½ lemon
Generous handful of
  parsley, finely chopped
Sea salt

While the pasta is cooking, throw the broccoli and green beans into the second roasting pan, toss well to coat with oil and add a good pinch of salt. Roast for 15 minutes.

Check the pasta after 7 minutes: it may need another 5–7 minutes until perfectly al dente with just a little liquid remaining. Season to taste.

Remove from the oven and leave to stand while the broccoli and beans finish cooking. When the vegetables are done, squeeze the lemon juice over them and scatter over the parsley, grated garlic and lemon zest; toss it through thoroughly. To serve, spoon out the fideuà and top with some of the broccoli and beans.

LENTILS, CRISPY KALE
AND HALLOUMI

Tinned lentils are a brilliant cupboard staple. There is nothing more nourishing than a bowl of lentils with plenty of vegetables. Finish with kale and halloumi – cooked in a second roasting pan – for a bit of texture.

SERVES 4

5 tablespoons olive oil
2 onions, sliced
2 leeks, finely sliced, using as much as of the green part as possible
3 celery sticks, finely sliced
3 carrots, cut in half lengthways and sliced into fine half moons
3 cloves garlic, sliced
1 heaped teaspoon chilli flakes
2 tablespoons sherry vinegar
400g tin green lentils, drained and rinsed
400g tin cherry tomatoes
400ml boiling vegetable stock
200g kale, thick stalks removed, washed and thoroughly dried
2 x 250g blocks halloumi, cut into cubes
Sea salt and black pepper

Preheat the oven to 190°C (170°C fan), gas mark 5. Put a roasting pan in to heat up with 2 tablespoons of the olive oil.

Once hot, add the onions and a good pinch of salt and cook for about 10 minutes until softened and lightly golden. Add another tablespoon of oil, the leeks, celery and carrots and mix thoroughly, then return to the oven for another 10 minutes so that the vegetables start to get some golden brown edges.

Add the garlic, chilli and sherry vinegar, give everything a good stir and return to the oven for 5 minutes. Next add the lentils, cherry tomatoes and hot stock, stir and return to the oven for 30 minutes.

Meanwhile, place the kale in a bowl with 1 tablespoon of the remaining olive oil and some salt and pepper and rub the oil thoroughly into the kale while breaking it up into bite-sized pieces. Place the kale in a single layer in a large roasting pan. Put the halloumi into the same bowl with the final 1 tablespoon of olive oil and toss it about to ensure it is well coated, then scatter among the kale.

After the lentils have been in the oven for about 10 minutes, place the roasting pan of kale on the top shelf of the oven and cook for 20 minutes until the kale is crisp and the halloumi golden.

Taste the lentils for seasoning, bearing in mind that halloumi can be quite salty. Serve the lentils with the cheese and kale crisps on top.

TIP For a vegan version, omit the halloumi – you could add some pumpkin seeds to the kale for extra protein and texture.

BAKED FARINATA, RED PEPPER AND COURGETTE WITH OLIVE DRESSING

Farinata is a sort of pancake made with chickpea flour, originating in Genoa in north-west Italy. For a non-vegan version, you could serve it with some soft goats' cheese underneath the olive dressing.

SERVES 4

VEGAN

3 tablespoons olive oil
3 courgettes, sliced into 3cm thick circles
2 red peppers, cut in half lengthways, then each half into 4 long pieces
2 red onions, sliced into 2cm thick circles
1 large sprig of rosemary, leaves roughly chopped
150g chickpea flour
½ teaspoon baking powder
400g tin chickpeas, drained, reserving the liquid, and rinsed
Sea salt and black pepper

FOR THE OLIVE DRESSING

120g pimento-stuffed olives
Small handful of basil, roughly torn
1 clove garlic, crushed
1 small red chilli, deseeded and chopped
Grated zest of ½ lemon, juice of 1 lemon
1 tablespoon olive oil

Preheat the oven to 200°C (220°C fan), gas mark 6. Put a roasting pan in to heat up with 2 tablespoons of the olive oil.

When the oil is hot, add the courgettes, peppers and onions, the rosemary and plenty of seasoning. Shake to coat all the vegetables in the oil and roast for about 25 minutes until they are soft and lightly golden.

Meanwhile, make the batter: put the flour, baking powder and 1 teaspoon of salt into a bowl, make a well in the centre and add the liquid from the chickpeas made up to 300ml with warm water, whisking until smooth. Set aside.

When the vegetables are soft, take the pan out of the oven and turn the oven up to 220°C (200°C fan), gas mark 7. Add the chickpeas to the pan with the remaining olive oil, stir everything together and then pour in the batter. Return the pan to the oven until the batter is set and crisp and golden brown around the edges – this will take about 20 minutes, but check after 15 minutes and cover with foil if it is browning too much and not setting.

While the farinata is cooking, make the dressing. Put the olives, basil, garlic, chilli and lemon zest into a food processor and whizz to a rough paste. Add the olive oil and lemon juice and season to taste.

When the farinata is set, take it out of the oven and let it stand for 5 minutes, then turn out onto a board and cut into squares. Serve with some of the olive dressing on top. This would be delicious with a tomato salad.

CAULIFLOWER KUKU

Kuku is the name for a Persian-style omelette. There are many versions, I am particularly keen on this one, with cauliflower, spices and raisins. It's great served cold for a picnic or warm as a nibble with drinks.

SERVES 4

1 small cauliflower,
  broken into small
  florets
4 spring onions,
  finely sliced
2 tablespoons olive oil
1 tablespoon ground
  rice or cornflour
5 eggs
½ teaspoon baking
  powder
1½ teaspoons turmeric
1 teaspoon ground cumin
1 teaspoon smoked
  paprika
Few sprigs of dill,
  finely chopped
Small handful of
  coriander, chopped
20g butter
2 cloves garlic, crushed
  or finely grated
40g raisins
Sea salt and black pepper

Preheat the oven to 200°C (180°C fan), gas mark 6.

In a roasting pan, toss the cauliflower, spring onions and olive oil together with plenty of salt and pepper and roast for 15 minutes.

Meanwhile, mix the ground rice or cornflour with some boiling water to make a pourable paste. Whisk the eggs in a bowl, then whisk in the rice or cornflour paste, the baking powder, spices, herbs, 100ml water, salt and pepper.

Add the butter, garlic and raisins to the roasting pan and toss together with the cauliflower. Return to the oven for a few minutes, then add the egg mixture. Turn the oven down to 180°C (160°C fan), gas mark 4, and cook the omelette for about 20 minutes or until set. Serve with flatbreads and maybe a simple carrot salad.

FRENCH ONION WELSH RAREBIT

This recipe is a mixture of French onion soup, which is such a comforting dish, with the added goodness of cabbage among the slow-cooked onions, and a Welsh rarebit topping. What a combo!

SERVES 6

6 onions, cut in half and then into wedges
4 cloves garlic, sliced
3 sprigs of thyme
1½ tablespoons balsamic vinegar
2 tablespoons sunflower oil
1 small pointed (sweetheart or hispi) cabbage, cut in half lengthways and then into 2cm wide ribbons
20g butter
100ml white wine or cider (optional)
100ml vegetable stock
Sea salt and black pepper

FOR THE TOPPING
6 slices of white bread or 18 slices of baguette, about 2–3cm thick
100g mature Cheddar, grated
50g Gruyère, grated
1½ tablespoons Worcestershire sauce
1 teaspoon English mustard
½ teaspoon cayenne pepper
1 egg, beaten
3 tablespoons crème fraîche

Preheat the oven to 180°C (160°C fan), gas mark 4. Put the bread slices in to toast while the oven is heating up: you want them to be crisp but still yielding. Set aside.

In a roasting pan, toss the onions, garlic and thyme with the balsamic vinegar, oil, and a generous pinch of salt. Cover with foil and cook for about 25 minutes until the onions are soft and sweet; after 10 minutes, stir and add a cup of boiling water.

When the onions are soft, take the pan out of the oven and turn the oven up to 200°C (180°C fan), gas mark 6. Remove the foil, add the cabbage, butter, a good grinding of black pepper and a little more salt and give everything a good stir. Return to the oven for 7 minutes until the onions absorb their cooking liquid and brown a little.

Add the wine or cider, if using, and stock (adding an extra 100ml of stock if you didn't use wine) and return to the oven for a few minutes to heat the liquid.

While the onions are cooking, prepare the topping: mix the cheeses with the Worcestershire sauce, mustard, cayenne, egg and crème fraîche. Spread this mixture onto the toasts.

Take the roasting pan out of the oven and pick out any thyme stalks you can see. Pop the toasts on top and return to the oven until the cheese melts and the top is golden and bubbling.

Spoon into warm soup plates and serve immediately.

TIP For a vegetarian version, omit the Gruyère cheese and Worcestershire sauce, or use vegetarian substitutes.

TOMATO AND PEPPER TIAN

My friends the Russell family are keen tian makers. They have several variations, usually based on green vegetables, and all are delicious. This is my red version.

SERVES 4

2 large red peppers,
   deseeded and cut
   into 3cm chunks
2 banana shallots,
   cut into quarters
   lengthways
2 sprigs of thyme –
   lemon thyme if you
   can get it
2 tablespoons olive oil
500g cherry tomatoes
200ml boiling vegetable
   stock
2 eggs, beaten
40g Parmesan-style
   vegetarian cheese,
   grated
180g cooked rice
20g fresh or dried
   breadcrumbs
Sea salt and black pepper

Preheat the oven to 200°C (180°C fan), gas mark 6.

Toss the peppers, shallots and thyme together in a roasting pan with the olive oil, season well and place in the oven for 15 minutes, shaking the pan halfway through the cooking time.

Add the tomatoes and cook for another 15 minutes.

Crush the tomatoes with the back of a spoon, add the hot stock and cook for another 10 minutes.

Meanwhile, fold the eggs and all but a tablespoon of the cheese into the rice.

By now the peppers and shallots will be soft and there should be plenty of liquid in the roasting pan. Stir in the rice mixture, scatter over the breadcrumbs and the remaining Parmesan-style cheese and bake for 10–15 minutes until golden. Serve hot or at room temperature, with a green salad.

ROOT VEGETABLE RÖSTI WITH HAZELNUT GREMOLATA

A lovely winter warmer of a dish. Sometimes I might put a poached egg with it, but it's great as is. It also works well as a side dish with sausages or chops.

SERVES 4

200g floury potatoes, scrubbed, not peeled, coarsely grated

150g each of parsnips, sweet potatoes and carrots, peeled and coarsely grated

1 large onion, grated

1 sprig of rosemary, leaves finely chopped

1 tablespoon plain four

40g butter, melted

1½ tablespoons sunflower oil

Sea salt and black pepper

FOR THE GREMOLATA

30g hazelnuts, chopped

1 clove garlic, grated

Small handful of parsley, finely chopped

Small sprig of sage, leaves finely chopped

Grated zest of ½ lemon

10g Parmesan-style vegetarian cheese, finely grated

Preheat the oven to 190°C (170°C fan), gas mark 5. Put the hazelnuts in a roasting pan and put them in the oven to toast gently as the oven heats up. Keep a close eye on them as they can burn very quickly. Once they are golden, remove from the roasting pan and set aside.

Mix together all the root vegetables with the onion, rosemary, flour and plenty of seasoning. Fold in the melted butter and stir to ensure all the roots are well coated.

Wipe the roasting pan with FSC kitchen paper, then return it to the oven with the oil for 5–7 minutes until it is nice and hot. Swirl the pan to coat it thoroughly with the oil and tip in the root vegetables. Shake to level them out and return to the oven for 35–45 minutes until the vegetables are cooked through and crisp on top. Check from time to time: if they are getting too brown you can cover the pan with foil.

Meanwhile, mix together the ingredients for the gremolata topping.

To test the rösti, insert the point of a sharp knife, which should meet no resistance. Remove from the oven and leave to rest for a few minutes. Scatter the top with the gremolata and serve straight from the roasting pan. I often accompany this with charred cabbage (page 108).

TIP For a vegan version, use a nut or olive oil instead of butter and omit the cheese.

BUTTER BEANS, LEEKS AND RICOTTA WITH A CRISPY KALE TOP

When I first thought about this dish I was imagining a sort of lasagne, but I have become so addicted to crispy kale that I thought it would make a great topping for a baked dish – much lighter and quicker!

SERVES 2

2½ tablespoons olive oil

2 leeks, sliced, using as much of the green part as possible

400g tin butter beans, drained and rinsed

2 tablespoons cider vinegar

150ml boiling vegetable stock

200g kale, thick stalks removed, washed, thoroughly dried

200g ricotta

3 generous tablespoons vegetarian pesto

20g pine nuts

20g Parmesan-style vegetarian cheese, grated

Sea salt and black pepper

Preheat the oven to 190°C (170°C fan), gas mark 5. Put a roasting pan in to heat up with 1½ tablespoons of the olive oil.

When hot, add the leeks and plenty of seasoning, and place in the oven for 7 minutes. At the same time, put the butter beans into some boiling water so they start to heat up. Splash the vinegar in with the leeks and place in the oven to evaporate for a couple of minutes. Now drain the butter beans and add them to the roasting pan, along with the stock. Return to the oven for 10 minutes.

Meanwhile, place the kale in a bowl with the remaining olive oil and some salt and pepper and rub the oil thoroughly into the kale while breaking it up into bite-sized pieces. Put the ricotta in a bowl and season it well.

Stir the pesto into the leek and bean mixture. Blob the ricotta all over the mixture and scatter over the kale. Return to the oven for about 15–20 minutes until the kale is starting to crisp up. Add the pine nuts and cheese and cook for a further 5 minutes. Serve hot.

TIP For a vegan version, omit the ricotta and use a vegan pesto.

BAKED PEARL BARLEY, PEAS, BEANS AND GREEN SAUCE

Pearl barley is quite an old-fashioned ingredient, often used in stews – it has a delicious nutty flavour and it bakes well.

SERVES 4

VEGAN

2 tablespoons olive oil
1 large onion, sliced
1 leek, sliced, using as much of the green part as possible
200g pearl barley
850ml boiling vegetable stock
120g frozen peas, defrosted
120g frozen edamame beans, defrosted
100g baby spinach
Sea salt and black pepper

FOR THE GREEN SAUCE
Generous handful of parsley, chopped
6 sprigs of mint, leaves chopped
2 cloves garlic, crushed
1 tablespoon Dijon mustard
1 tablespoon red wine vinegar
6 tablespoons extra virgin olive oil
2 tablespoons capers

Preheat the oven to 200°C (180°C fan), gas mark 6. Put a roasting pan in to heat up with the olive oil.

When hot, add the onion and leek and plenty of seasoning and place in the oven to soften for 15 minutes, stirring a couple of times.

Add the barley and cook for about 4 minutes, then add the boiling stock and cook for 25 minutes.

Meanwhile, make the green sauce. If you would like a very smooth sauce, put everything except the olive oil and capers into a blender or food processor and whizz to a paste – you may need to add some of the oil to help the process on its way. Add the remaining oil with the motor running. Finally fold in the capers, either on pulse or by hand. For a more rustic version, whisk everything together by hand.

After 25 minutes, add the peas and edamame beans to the barley and return to the oven for 10 minutes. The barley should be quite moist – if necessary add some boiling water.

When the barley is soft and nutty-tasting, fold in the spinach and a couple of tablespoons of the green sauce. Leave to stand for 5 minutes before serving with the remaining green sauce in a bowl.

ROAST SQUASH, CHESTNUTS AND MUSHROOMS WITH GNOCCHI

A lovely autumnal combination for a warming quick supper.

SERVES 2

2 tablespoons olive oil
300g squash, peeled,
    deseeded and cut
    into 2cm chunks
1 red onion, cut into
    six wedges
Couple of sprigs of
    sage, leaves chopped
200g mushrooms – I like
    to use a mixture of
    oyster, chestnut
    and button
200g fresh gnocchi
50g peeled cooked
    chestnuts, roughly
    chopped
2 tablespoons balsamic
    vinegar
20g Parmesan-style
    vegetarian cheese,
    grated
Sea salt and black pepper
Sage leaves, to garnish

Preheat the oven to 200°C (180°C fan), gas mark 6. Put a roasting pan in to heat up with the olive oil.

Toss the squash, onion and sage together with plenty of seasoning and throw into the hot roasting pan. Stir until everything is coated with oil and roast for 15 minutes.

Add the mushrooms and cook for another 15 minutes.

Meanwhile, drop the gnocchi into boiling water for a minute to heat through. Drain, mix with the chestnuts and add to the roasting pan. Toss everything together well and add the balsamic vinegar. Return to the oven for 7 minutes.

Stir in the cheese. Taste for seasoning, garnish with a couple of sage leaves and serve immediately.

TIP For a vegan version, omit the cheese and take care to check the ingredients list of the gnocchi as some brands use egg.

SIDES

CHARRED CABBAGE WITH CHILLI AND SHERRY VINEGAR

Unbelievably simple, this dish is addictive! It's great with sausages, pork chops or gammon steaks. A generous grating of cheese on top and a buttery baked potato served alongside makes a good vegetarian supper.

SERVES 2–3

VEGAN

1 pointed (sweetheart or hispi) cabbage, about 500g
3 tablespoons olive oil
1 tablespoon sherry vinegar
Generous pinch of chilli flakes
Sea salt

Preheat the oven to 200°C (180°C fan), gas mark 6, with a large roasting pan in it.

Cut the cabbage lengthways into six wedges, discarding any unwanted core. Give it a little dunk in water, then shake off the excess.

Oil the hot roasting pan with 1 tablespoon of the olive oil, add the cabbage and the other 2 tablespoons of olive oil and a good pinch of salt. Pop into the oven for 15 minutes.

After this time the cabbage will be soft, with wonderful caramelised outer leaves. As soon as you take the very hot pan out of the oven, splash in the vinegar – it will almost completely evaporate. Scatter over the chilli flakes and give the whole pan a good shake. Serve immediately.

ROASTED OKRA

*Okra makes an unusual and very easy side dish, good with any grilled
fish or meat. I use urfa chilli for this, but any chilli flakes will do.*

SERVES 4

VEGAN

2 tablespoons olive oil
600g okra, tops removed
1 bunch of spring onions
1 teaspoon onion seeds
½ teaspoon chilli flakes
Small handful of
  coriander, chopped
Juice of ½ lime

Preheat the oven to 200°C (180°C fan), gas mark 6. Put a roasting pan
in to heat up with the olive oil.

When the oil is hot, slice the okra and spring onions in half lengthways,
throw in the roasting pan with the onion seeds and chilli and toss
everything about until well mixed. Return to the oven, ensuring the
okra is in a single layer as much as possible, and roast for 25 minutes
until crisp and golden.

Scatter over the coriander and lime juice and serve.

ROAST CELERIAC WITH WHOLEGRAIN MUSTARD AND ROSEMARY

*Celeriac has an earthy sweet flavour that goes brilliantly with mustard. Celeriac remoulade is a classic
French salad of shredded celeriac with a mustardy dressing, and this is my variation on that theme.*

SERVES 4

VEGAN

2 tablespoons olive oil
1 large celeriac
1 large sprig of rosemary,
  leaves finely chopped
2 large tablespoons
  wholegrain mustard
2 cloves garlic, sliced
Sea salt and black pepper

Preheat the oven to 190°C (170°C fan), gas mark 5. Put a roasting pan
in to heat up with the olive oil. Peel the celariac and cut into 2cm cubes.

When the oven is hot, pop the celeriac and rosemary into the pan, season
generously and stir well; the celeriac should be in a single layer. Roast for
10 minutes until the celeriac is starting to colour. Give it a good stir and
then cover the pan with foil. Roast for another 20 minutes, shaking the
pan halfway through, until the celeriac is soft.

Remove the foil, stir in the mustard and garlic and return to the oven for
another 10 minutes. Taste for seasoning and serve hot.

BROCCOLI 'RICE', FLAGEOLET BEANS AND ROAST VEGETABLES

You can use any vegetables you like in this recipe, but bear in mind that some will need more roasting than others. They should all be soft and golden brown before you add the beans and broccoli.

SERVES 4

VEGAN

30g pine nuts

350g broccoli, broken into florets, stem reserved

4 tablespoons olive oil

1 head fennel, fronds reserved, cut in half lengthways, thick core removed, cut into 3mm-thick slices

4 spring onions, cut into 3cm lengths, using as much of the green part as possible

2 courgettes, cut in half lengthways then cut into 3cm lengths

Small handful of parsley, finely chopped

Grated zest of ½ lemon, juice of 1 lemon

1 large clove garlic, finely grated

400g tin flageolet beans, drained and rinsed

150ml boiling water or vegetable stock

Sea salt and black pepper

Preheat the oven to 190°C (170°C fan), gas mark 5. Put the pine nuts in a roasting pan and put them in the oven to toast gently as the oven heats up. Watch them like a hawk as they can burn very quickly. Once the pine nuts are golden, remove from the roasting pan and set aside.

Put the broccoli florets in a food processor and whizz to small confetti-sized pieces; set aside. Trim the broccoli stem of any stringy or hard outer skin; the inside is tender and delicious, so cut the stem into slices the thickness of a pound coin.

Add 2 tablespoons of the olive oil to the roasting pan along with the broccoli stem, fennel, spring onions and courgettes. Add 3 tablespoons of hot water (this will evaporate, and ensures the fennel doesn't get wrinkly), season generously and roast for about 15 minutes, shaking halfway through.

Meanwhile, chop the fennel fronds and mix with the parsley, lemon zest, garlic and cooled pine nuts.

After 15 minutes the vegetables should be soft and golden brown – if not, return to the oven for a few minutes. Add the flageolet beans, broccoli 'rice' and the remaining olive oil, then add the hot water or stock and stir to ensure everything is well coated with oil. Return to the oven for 15 minutes.

Squeeze over the lemon juice, scatter with the pine nut mixture and serve.

BAKED BEETROOT WITH HAZELNUT DRESSING

New-season beetroot are perfectly complemented by this herby hazelnut dressing, which also goes well with goats' cheese.

SERVES 4

VEGAN

650g raw beetroot
2 tablespoons olive oil
Sea salt and black pepper

FOR THE HAZELNUT DRESSING
150ml olive oil
100ml verjuice, or
    60ml cider vinegar
    plus 40ml apple juice
1 clove garlic, crushed
125g hazelnuts, skinless,
    toasted and roughly
    chopped
125g whole blanched
    almonds, toasted and
    roughly chopped
Generous handful of
    flat-leaf parsley,
    chopped
5 sprigs of basil, leaves
    chopped

Preheat the oven to 180°C (160°C fan), gas mark 4.

Wash the beetroot thoroughly, leaving the skins on – beetroot is easier to peel once cooked. Place in a roasting pan – they should fit snugly – and toss with the olive oil and plenty of salt and pepper. Pour in some water to cover the base of the pan by about 1cm. Cover with foil and roast for 45–60 minutes, or until a knife can slide easily into the largest beetroot.

While the beetroot bake, make the dressing. Whisk the olive oil, verjuice and garlic together until thoroughly mixed. Stir in the nuts and herbs and season to taste with salt and pepper.

Once the beetroot is done, leave it until cool enough to handle, then peel: the skins should slip off easily. Cut the beetroot into bite-sized chunks and toss with enough dressing to coat generously. Serve warm or at room temperature.

Any leftover dressing will keep well in the fridge for several days; the herbs may discolour a little, but you can add a few fresh herbs, if you wish.

TIP Verjuice is a gentle acidulant, usually made from unripe grapes. It is fruitier and sweeter than vinegar, so if you can't get hold of it, I suggest substituting a mixture of apple juice and vinegar.

BAKED ROOTS WITH LANCASHIRE CHEESE CRUMBS

Lancashire cheese is a good foil to the robust, slightly sharp flavours of swede and turnip. The carrots and parsnips bring sweetness to this wonderful autumn/winter warmer.

SERVES 4

2 tablespoons sunflower
  or rapeseed oil
1 small swede,
  peeled and cut
  into 3cm chunks
3 parsnips, peeled and
  cut into 3cm pieces
2 carrots, peeled and
  cut into 3cm pieces
2 turnips, peeled and
  cut into 3cm chunks
2 banana shallots, peeled
  and cut into sixths
  lengthways
40g panko or other
  dried breadcrumbs
30g Lancashire cheese,
  crumbled
3 sprigs of sage, leaves
  finely chopped
1 tablespoon sherry
  vinegar
Sea salt and black pepper

Preheat the oven to 190°C (170°C fan), gas mark 5. Put a large roasting pan in to heat up with the oil.

Once the pan is hot, add the vegetables, season generously and toss to ensure everything is well coated with oil. Bake for 35–40 minutes until the vegetables are soft and have golden edges here and there.

Meanwhile, mix together the breadcrumbs, cheese and sage.

Once the vegetables are done, splash in the sherry vinegar and scatter over the crumbs, then return to the oven for 5 minutes until the crumbs are brown and melty. Serve hot.

BAKED BABY CARROTS
AND HARISSA

Harissa is a North African chilli paste that goes really well with carrots (I like the rose version). This dish would be good on a table of salads and is great for vegans: try it in a flatbread with some pickles and toasted nuts.

SERVES 4

VEGAN

2 tablespoons olive oil
500g baby carrots
1 tablespoon harissa
Juice of 1 lime
Small handful of
   coriander, chopped
Sea salt and black pepper

Preheat the oven to 180°C (160°C fan), gas mark 4. Put a roasting pan in to heat up with the olive oil. Once hot, add the carrots, season well and give everything a good stir.

Roast for about 25 minutes, until the carrots are just tender, but not too soft; give them a stir halfway through, which is a good opportunity to test them and adjust timings. Once the carrots are done, add the harissa, lime juice and coriander and mix together thoroughly. Serve hot.

OVEN-BRAISED BEANS WITH SMOKED PAPRIKA AND THYME

This works well with any beans, so you can decide which will go best with whatever else you plan to serve. I've used butter beans, which are great with sausages.

SERVES 4

2 tablespoons olive oil

20g butter

125g banana shallots, sliced

4 sprigs of thyme

1 bay leaf

2 generous teaspoons smoked paprika

1 leek, sliced, using as much of the green part as possible

1 carrot, sliced

1 celery stick, sliced

1 tablespoon red wine vinegar

4 large cloves garlic, crushed or grated

400g tin butter beans, drained and rinsed

200ml boiling vegetable stock

Sea salt and black pepper

Preheat the oven to 180°C (160°C fan), gas mark 4. Put a roasting pan in to heat up with the oil and butter.

Once hot, add the shallots, thyme, bay leaf, paprika and a generous pinch of salt and place in the oven until they soften – this will take about 15 minutes – shaking the pan halfway through.

Add the leek, carrot and celery and stir well to coat with the fat, add another good pinch of salt and return to the oven for 12 minutes until everything has softened. A little bit of colour is fine, but if the vegetables are looking too brown, cover the pan with foil.

Add the vinegar and then the garlic and beans and stir thoroughly, pour in the stock and return to the oven for 5–7 minutes. Give the beans a stir and taste for seasoning.

POTATO AND TOMATO GRATIN

This is a summer version of a gratin dauphinoise, with tomatoes and lemon thyme instead of cream.
It goes really well with a barbecue and is equally good hot or at room temperature.

SERVES 4–6

3–4 tablespoons olive oil
20g butter
500g plum tomatoes,
 sliced
2 red onions, finely sliced
3 cloves garlic, crushed
 or grated
3 sprigs of lemon thyme
 or regular thyme
600g potatoes,
 thinly sliced
50g Parmesan or
 Parmesan-style
 vegetarian cheese,
 grated
400g boiling vegetable
 stock
30g fresh or dried
 breadcrumbs
Sea salt and black pepper

Preheat the oven to 180°C (160°C fan), gas mark 4. Put a roasting pan into the oven with 1 tablespoon of the olive oil and half the butter.

In a bowl, mix the tomatoes with the onions, garlic, thyme and plenty of salt and pepper.

Once the butter has melted, remove the roasting pan from the oven and brush the butter all over the pan. Put a third of the potatoes into the pan in an even layer and season well. Scatter over half the tomato mixture, including half of the liquid which will have accumulated in the bowl and 1 tablespoon of olive oil, then scatter over a third of the Parmesan. Next add another third of the potatoes and seasoning, then the remaining tomato mixture and juice with another tablespoon of oil, then another third of the Parmesan. Add the potatoes and season well, then pour in the hot stock.

Scatter the breadcrumbs and the remaining Parmesan over the top and dot with the remaining butter and a drizzle of olive oil. Cover with foil and place in the oven for 35 minutes, by which time the potatoes should be starting to give when pierced with a sharp knife. Remove the foil and return to the oven for 10–15 minutes until the potatoes are tender. Leave to stand for 5–10 minutes before serving.

TIP For a vegan version, substitute the butter for more oil and instead of Parmesan use Panko breadcrumbs through each of the layers.

RED CABBAGE WITH CHESTNUT AND APPLE

Red cabbage is such a comforting winter dish and it goes wonderfully with everything from baked potatoes to roast pheasant. This just goes in the oven and does its thing while you do yours.

SERVES 4–6

VEGAN

1 red cabbage, cut in half, cored and sliced

3 onions, finely sliced

2 tablespoons sunflower or rapeseed oil

3 tablespoons nut or olive oil

2 apples – I like red-skinned ones – quartered, cored and sliced

100g peeled cooked chestnuts, chopped

3 tablespoons cider vinegar

1 cinnamon stick

1 tablespoon dark brown sugar

Sea salt and black pepper

Put the cabbage and onions in a large bowl, sprinkle with plenty of salt and leave them to soften for at least 20 minutes or longer if you have time.

Preheat the oven to 180°C (160°C fan), gas mark 4. Put a roasting pan in to heat up with the two types of oil.

Mix the cabbage, onions, apples and all the remaining ingredients together. Add to the hot roasting pan and stir to ensure everything is well coated with the fat. Press down to an even layer, cover with foil and place in the oven for about an hour, shaking everything about from time to time. If there is a lot of liquid, remove the foil for the last 20 minutes or so. The end result should be soft and sweet with not too much liquid. Taste for seasoning before serving.

OVEN-BAKED MUSHROOMS À LA GRECQUE

À la grecque is a proper old French treatment of vegetables, served cold as a first course. This is a simple oven version. It does improve if left overnight, but is delicious eaten straight away with bread to mop up the tasty sauce.

SERVES 4

2 teaspoons
   coriander seeds
3 tablespoons olive oil
500g chestnut
   mushrooms, wiped
   clean and halved
4 spring onions, chopped
   into 4cm lengths
1 small head fennel,
   trimmed and thinly
   sliced
1 bay leaf
2 cloves garlic,
   crushed or grated
3 tablespoons white
   wine (optional)
1 teaspoon honey
1 tablespoon tomato
   purée
120ml boiling vegetable
   stock
2 tablespoons white
   wine vinegar
Few sprigs of tarragon
   or parsley, leaves
   finely chopped
Sea salt and black pepper

Preheat the oven to 180°C (160°C fan), gas mark 4. Put the coriander seeds in a roasting pan and put them in the oven to toast gently as the oven heats up. Once toasted, tip them onto a board and roughly crush the seeds while still warm.

Now put 2 tablespoons of the olive oil in the roasting pan and add the mushrooms, spring onions, fennel and bay leaf, mix thoroughly and put in the oven for 15 minutes to soften. The mushrooms usually exude quite a lot of liquid at this stage.

While they are cooking, mix the coriander seeds, the remaining olive oil, garlic, white wine (if using), honey, tomato purée and stock together and keep hot. If you are not using wine, add another 3 tablespoons of hot stock.

After 15 minutes, turn the oven up to 200°C (180°C fan), gas mark 6. Add the vinegar to the mushrooms and stir well. Return to the oven for about 10 minutes until the juices are reabsorbed into the mushrooms.

Add the hot stock mixture and cook for a further 15 minutes. By this time the liquid should have reduced down to make a nice rich sauce over the mushrooms. Fish out the bay leaf, stir in the tarragon or parsley, taste for seasoning and serve.

ROAST CAULIFLOWER AND BROCCOLI WITH TOASTED ALMOND DRESSING

Roasting broccoli and cauliflower is a dream, giving golden crisp edges and tender insides. The almond dressing works so well with the broccoli and cauliflower and is also good as a dip for crudités.

SERVES 4

VEGAN

1 head broccoli,
    broken into florets
1 small cauliflower,
    broken into florets
2 tablespoons olive oil
Sea salt and black pepper

FOR THE ALMOND
DRESSING

150g skin-on almonds,
    or a mixture of skin
    on and blanched
1 tablespoon olive oil,
    for drizzling
1 large clove garlic,
    peeled
2 tablespoons
    sherry vinegar
75ml extra virgin
    olive oil

Preheat the oven to 200°C (180°C fan), gas mark 6. Put the almonds in a large roasting pan with a drizzle of olive oil and a scattering of salt and put them in the oven to toast gently as the oven heats. Keep an eye on them as they can burn very quickly. You want them to be golden inside and you can crush one to check; they will carry on colouring as they cool. Remove from the roasting pan and set aside.

Once the almonds are done and the oven is hot, put the broccoli and cauliflower into the roasting pan with the olive oil and plenty of salt and pepper; toss to coat them with the oil. Roast for 15–20 minutes until the vegetables are just tender, with some nice golden brown edges.

Meanwhile, while the almonds are still warm, put them in a food processor and whizz until the oil is starting to come out of them. Add the garlic and a couple of tablespoons of boiling water to help the process along, and keep going until you have an almost smooth purée. Add the sherry vinegar and gradually add the extra virgin olive oil, a little at a time. Taste and adjust the seasoning and whizz once again. If very thick, add some more boiling water: you are looking for a coating or dipping consistency.

Once the vegetables are ready, spoon over the dressing and serve immediately.

SWEET

CHOCOLATE BANANA TAHINI BROWNIE

Imagine this warm with some cream or ice cream on top! The tahini gives the brownie a distinctive flavour and the banana keeps it wonderfully moist.

SERVES 8–10

300g dark chocolate
75g butter
100g tahini, plus a
   generous tablespoon
   to finish
3 eggs
200g soft light
   brown sugar
2 ripe bananas, mashed
80g rye flour
1 teaspoon sesame seeds
Sea salt

Preheat the oven to 180°C (160°C fan), gas mark 4. Line a small roasting pan or baking tin (approx. 30 x 20cm) with a reusable silicone baking sheet.

Melt the chocolate, butter and tahini in a heatproof bowl over a pan of barely simmering water.

Meanwhile, whisk the eggs, sugar and a pinch of salt together until light and fluffy. Fold in the mashed bananas, then the melted chocolate mix. You will notice that the mixture starts to thicken a little. When everything is thoroughly mixed, carefully fold in the flour until fully incorporated.

Turn into the prepared tin and drizzle the remaining tablespoon of tahini all over the top. Then sprinkle over the sesame seeds.

Bake for 25–30 minutes until the brownie is just set – it should still feel soft and moist. Leave the tin on a wire rack to cool for an hour or so.

TIP These brownies could be made gluten-free by substituting the rye flour for a gluten-free flour.

RICE PUDDING WITH A DIFFERENCE

I have been making this rice pudding for years using almond milk, but oat milk is equally good. Maple syrup and lemon zest give a delicious caramelised flavour. For a vegan version, omit the butter or use almond butter instead.

SERVES 4

150g short grain rice
1 litre almond or oat milk
4 tablespoons maple
    syrup
1 long peeled strip
    of lemon zest
20g butter
1 tablespoon coconut
    sugar or dark brown
    sugar
Sea salt

Preheat the oven to 150°C (130°C fan), gas mark 2, and put a roasting pan in to heat up.

Put the rice, milk, maple syrup, lemon zest and a pinch of salt into a saucepan and bring to a simmer, then leave to bubble very gently for a good 20 minutes.

Pour the mixture into the hot roasting pan, dot with butter and sprinkle over the sugar. Place in the oven for 20–30 minutes until the pudding has a golden brown top and is thick and creamy.

I would urge you to let the pudding sit for at least 15 minutes before serving. Add a spoonful of your favourite jam – gooseberry or apricot are especially good to complement the maple syrup and lemon. It is also delicious with the marmalade baked pears (page 133).

TIP If you have all the time in the world you can put the rice, milk, maple syrup and lemon into a roasting pan in the preheated oven without simmering it first. You may think it will never thicken up: it will, but it can take up to 2½ hours, or longer if you use brown rice. After about 2 hours, when the rice has started to absorb the milk, dot on the butter and sprinkle over the sugar.

LUMBERJACK FLAPJACK

I came across lumberjack cake in New Zealand and thought it would make a great hybrid with flapjack, with an oaty fruity base and a coconutty top. I usually make this with gluten-free oats and flour.

SERVES 6–8

4 eating apples, skin on –
  2 coarsely grated;
  2 quartered, cored and
  sliced into half moons
360g oats
100g soft light
  brown sugar
60g plain flour
200g butter, melted
Sea salt

**FOR THE LUMBERJACK
  TOPPING**
150g soft dark brown
  sugar or coconut sugar,
  or a mixture of both
150g butter, melted
130g flaked unsweetened
  coconut
375ml boiling milk

Preheat the oven to 180°C (160°C fan), gas mark 4. Line a small roasting pan (approx. 30 x 20cm) with a reusable silicone baking sheet.

Mix the grated apple, oats, sugar, flour and a pinch of salt together in a bowl. Pour in the melted butter and stir until the mixture comes together. Press into the lined pan and bake until golden, about 20 minutes.

While the base is baking, make the lumberjack topping by mixing all the ingredients together.

Scatter the sliced apples over the flapjack and then pour over the lumberjack mixture. Bake for another 15–20 minutes until the top is golden and set.

Serve hot as a pudding or leave to cool to enjoy with coffee, in a lunchbox or at teatime.

MARMALADE BAKED PEARS

These pears are so easy to do and are lovely as a pudding with some cream or custard and a ginger biscuit, or to go on top of porridge. They will keep for several days in the fridge, so are well worth doing.

SERVES 4

VEGAN

3 tablespoons marmalade
2 teaspoons ground ginger
300ml boiling water
4 pears, peeled and cut in half, no need to core

Preheat the oven to 150°C (130°C fan), gas mark 2.

Mix the marmalade and ginger together and stir into the boiling water. Put the pears, core-side down, into a roasting pan. Pour in the hot liquid, cover with foil and cook for 30–40 minutes until the pears are soft. Remove the foil for the last 15 minutes to thicken the sauce a little.

If you want more of a glaze than a sauce, you can lift out the pears, turn the oven up to 200°C (180°C fan), gas mark 2, and let the sauce reduce slightly, stirring regularly. Serve hot or leave to cool before storing in the fridge.

BAKED RHUBARB, ROSE WATER AND PINK GRAPEFRUIT

Baked rhubarb is wonderful with rice pudding or porridge, or as a fool made with cream and yoghurt. I also use it in the rhubarb, pistachio and ginger cake on page 136.

SERVES 4–6

VEGAN

1 pink grapefruit
1kg rhubarb, cut into
    5cm lengths
200g unrefined
    caster sugar
1 teaspoon rose water

Preheat the oven to 150°C (130°C fan), gas mark 2.

Using a vegetable peeler, peel off a couple of strips of zest from the pink grapefruit and set aside. Cut the grapefruit in half and squeeze the juice into a bowl, adding some of the pulpy flesh.

Toss the rhubarb with the sugar, grapefruit and rose water. Put everything into a roasting pan and cover with foil. Place in the oven and cook for 20 minutes, stir and continue to cook until the rhubarb is very tender but still has its shape – this will probably take another 20 minutes. Outdoor-grown rhubarb often collapses more, but don't worry, it will be delicious anyway.

TIP This is a lovely way of cooking rhubarb, especially early in the season when you can buy forced rhubarb – it will end up with the most glorious pink colour. As the season goes on you'll find outdoor-grown rhubarb, which is slightly more tart and not so vibrant in colour. The amount of sugar I have suggested is for outdoor rhubarb, so you may want to cut it back if you are lucky enough to get early forced rhubarb.

RHUBARB, PISTACHIO AND GINGER CAKE

This recipe is inspired by one from my favourite cookbook, Margaret Costa's Four Seasons Cookery Book. She calls it orange snow cake and says it doesn't need icing as it is lovely and moist and keeps very well.

SERVES 6

175g butter, softened, plus extra for greasing
150g unrefined caster sugar
2 eggs, separated
280g self-raising flour
2 heaped tablespoons baked rhubarb (page 134), or rhubarb jam or honey
55g crystallised ginger, chopped into small confetti-sized pieces
85g pistachios, finely chopped
5 tablespoons rhubarb juice reserved from cooking the rhubarb, or water
Sea salt

Preheat the oven to 180°C (160°C fan), gas mark 4. Butter a small (30 x 20cm) roasting pan.

Gradually beat the sugar into the butter until light and fluffy. Beat in the egg yolks, one at a time, adding a little flour to keep the mixture stable.

Stir in the rhubarb, ginger, pistachios and rhubarb juice or water and mix thoroughly.

Beat the egg whites with a pinch of salt until stiff. Gently fold the flour into the cake mixture and then fold in one-third of the egg whites and combine very well. Carefully fold in the remaining egg whites, ensuring everything is very well mixed and taking care to keep it as light as possible. Turn the mixture into the roasting pan and bake for 45 minutes.

Test by inserting a thin skewer or a piece of spaghetti into the centre of the cake. It should come out easily and perfectly clean. Leave to cool before turning out on a plate.

RASPBERRY AND SOUR CREAM SQUARES

This recipe works well with many other fruits, such as blueberries, sliced peaches, apricots or plums, quartered figs and – in winter – prunes, but is especially delicious with raspberries and very hard to resist.

SERVES 6–8

FOR THE BASE
250g plain flour
70g icing sugar
225g butter, melted
Sea salt

FOR THE TOPPING
3 eggs
100g unrefined caster
 sugar
3 tablespoons cornflour
Seeds scraped from ½ a
 vanilla pod
225g sour cream
300g raspberries

Preheat the oven to 180°C (160°C fan), gas mark 4. Line a small roasting pan (approx. 30 x 20cm) with a reusable silicone baking sheet.

Mix the flour, icing sugar, butter and salt together and press into the base of the pan in an even layer. Bake for about 15 minutes until golden.

While the base is cooking, prepare the topping. Whisk the eggs, sugar, cornflour and vanilla together until completely smooth. Gradually stir in the sour cream until fully combined.

Turn the oven down to 150°C (130°C fan), gas mark 2.

Pour the egg mixture over the hot base and scatter over the raspberries. Return to the oven for about 30 minutes until the top is set – you may want to turn the pan once during cooking to ensure it cooks evenly.

Leave on a wire rack to cool before cutting into squares. The first one may be tricky to remove but that's the cooks reward!

CHESTNUT, ORANGE AND CHOCOLATE BREAD PUDDING

*Bread pudding is traditional English fare – but this is an updated version,
with chestnut purée, fresh orange and cocoa and some dark chocolate melted on top.*

SERVES 4–6

50g butter, coarsely
grated, plus extra
for greasing

250g bread – use any
type you like

3 oranges

200g chestnut purée

65g dark brown sugar

1 egg

1 teaspoon vanilla extract

1 tablespoon cocoa
powder

20g dark chocolate,
roughly grated or
chopped

1–2 teaspoons demerara
sugar

Preheat the oven to 180°C (160°C fan), gas mark 4. Butter a roasting pan
(approx. 35 x 25cm).

Soak the bread in water until it is soft and disintegrating.

Meanwhile, grate the zest of one orange and set aside. Using a sharp
knife, cut off the peel and pith from all three oranges, then separate the
segments, catching any juice.

Lift the bread out of the water and give it a good squeeze. Put it in a bowl
with the butter, chestnut purée, brown sugar, egg, vanilla, cocoa, orange
zest and any juice. Mix everything thoroughly with a wooden spoon until
you have a silky mass. Fold in the orange segments then tip the mixture
into the roasting pan and level it out.

Sprinkle over the dark chocolate and the demerara sugar and bake for
45 minutes until just set. It will seem slightly wobbly when hot, but it will
become firmer as it cools. I like to serve it warm with double cream or
crème fraîche – or custard for comfort!

WALNUT, PECAN AND DATE SQUARES

This is my take on pecan pie. The dates make a lovely rich top: I added the eggs to make it a little lighter, but you can omit them to make an excellent vegan pud. It is also gluten free.

SERVES 8–10

75g ground almonds
75g walnuts, finely
  chopped
50g ground rice
100g cornflour
70g icing sugar
100g almond butter
50ml boiling water
Sea salt

FOR THE TOPPING
250g dates
150ml coffee
1 teaspoon vanilla extract
80g walnuts
2 eggs
125g pecans

Preheat the oven to 180°C (160°C fan), gas mark 4. Line a small roasting pan (approx. 30 x 20cm) with a reusable silicone baking sheet.

Mix the almonds, walnuts, ground rice and a pinch of salt together and sift in the cornflour and the icing sugar. In a jug, mix the almond butter with the hot water. Make a well in the centre of the dry ingredients and pour in the hot liquid. Gradually mix in the dry ingredients until it comes together like a slightly wet dough. Put it into the roasting pan and press it out to the corners, using your slightly dampened hands or the back of a spoon to level out the dough. Bake for 15 minutes until light brown and set.

Meanwhile, put the dates in a saucepan with the coffee and simmer until they are very soft and the coffee has reduced slightly. Leave to cool, then put into a food processor with the vanilla and walnuts and whizz to a paste. Add the eggs, one by one, with the motor running. Tip the date mixture over the base and scatter the pecans over. Bake for 20 minutes until the top is set. Serve warm or leave on a wire rack to cool to make it easier to cut into squares.

APRICOT AND PISTACHIO TART

*Fresh apricots are a delicious treat in early summer. They look beautiful in this tart,
with its fragrant filling based on a Turkish milk pudding.*

SERVES 6

Approx 500g ready-made
  sweet shortcrust pastry
500ml whole milk
50g ground pistachios,
  plus an extra
    15g pistachios, roughly
    chopped, to serve
30g ground almonds
35g ground rice
100ml single cream
50g golden caster sugar
Few drops of rose water
12 apricots, halved
  and stoned
5 tablespoons vanilla
  sugar
Small nut of butter
2 tablespoons apple juice,
  cider or rosé wine
Sea salt

Preheat the oven to 200°C (180°C fan), gas mark 6. On a lightly floured
surface, roll out the pastry to about 3mm thick, then use it to line a
small roasting pan (approx. 30 x 20cm). Trim off any excess, then line
the pastry with a reusable silicone baking sheet. Fill with baking beans
or rice, then blind bake the pastry case for 20 minutes. Carefully remove
the parchment and beans and bake for another 5 minutes until the
pastry is cooked through.

Scald 150ml of the milk and pour it into a food processor with the
ground nuts. Whizz for 20 seconds.

Mix together the ground rice, cream and a pinch of salt. Heat the
remaining milk in a saucepan and bring to a simmer, then add the
ground rice mixture and cook, stirring, for a couple of minutes until
thickened. Now add the ground nut mix and the sugar and continue
to simmer until the mixture thickens.

Remove from the heat and beat in the rose water. Pour into the
cooked pastry case and gently spread out in an even layer. It will
solidify as it cools.

Turn the oven up to 220°C (200°C fan), gas mark 7. Place the apricots
in a roasting pan, cut-side up, sprinkle over the vanilla sugar and dot
over the butter. Sprinkle the juice, cider or wine around the fruit. Bake
for 20–25 minutes until the apricots are just soft, with some syrupy
juices. Arrange the fruit on top of the tart filling and brush with the
juices to glaze. Scatter over the chopped pistachios.

INDEX

ACKNOWLEDGEMENTS

A recipe book always requires plenty of collaboration and this one is no exception. So here is my roll call of gratitude and recognition.

Many thanks Helen Lewis, excellent creative director at Pavilion and Gemma Doyle, design manager, and the fantastic photo team: Dan Jones image-capturer extraordinaire and his assistant, India Whiley-Morton. The incredible cooks and stylists Rosie Ramsden (fellow sausage dog owner – extra kudos there) and Rosie French, along with Davina Perkins and her gorgeous props. Also thank you to those foresighted people at Pavilion: Polly Powell for your initial interest and Peter Taylor and the National Trust thereafter. Thanks Kristy Richardson for your support and Maggie Ramsay for making sense of my recipes. And of course eternal gratitude to my agent Victoria Hobbs who is endlessly encouraging.

Thanks to the friends who inspire me in the world of food: Laura Jackson for her amazing Towpath kitchen, where I always feel excited and inspired to cook with her marvellous team – with Lori de Mori a big part of that joy. Leila McAlister, whose shop and general wonderfulness constantly hearten. Joyce Molyneux, Shaun Hill and Juliet Peston my most eminent head chefs, still behind me when I cook. Tim Dillon, Karl Goward, Kevin Mcfadden, Steve Williams, Adam Sellar, James Ferguson, Jack Van Praag, Lucas Hollweg all stellar chefs with whom I have worked, learnt and laughed. Pauline Griffiths whose wonderful sense of style has helped me hone my craft and William Griffiths and Emily Heath, always nearby. I am fortunate to have a tiptoe in the food writer fraternity – a source of ongoing inspiration – my very favourites whom I call friends too: Rachel Roddy, Claire Thomson, Sarit Packer, Itamar Srulovich, Jenny Linford along with Patricia Niven – amazing photographer – and my surrogate brother and pensmith Bob Granleese. Heidi White, a powerhouse of the Cambridge food scene. Duncan Catchpole, a visionary food pioneer, Tyler Cotton a brilliant grower and Kenneth Mackay who is helping me set up my own veg patch. Finally Barny Haughton, founder and force behind the Square Food Foundation, a deeply inspiring individual who, among many other things, has helped me to see a future in the food world and beyond.

So to the nearest and dearest who test, taste, correct and encourage: My sisters Annabel and Camilla and their families. Polly Russell a dear, dear friend and most excellent cook – she and her family are super guinea pigs thanks Steve, Milly, Trixie and godson George. My co-pilot, great friend and very good cook Thomas Blythe (see Tom's Sausages and Beans, page 28). Claire Roberson, always there with wise words and laughter. Eric Ssewagudde, top buddy and appreciative taster. George Perry, dear friend with generous reading and writing wisdom. Countless more to mention including: Sam Walker, George Sinclair, Lucie Reeder, Jacq Burns, Ana Garcia, Kate Brewin, Aunty Mary and my lovely neighbours Andrea, Alan and Amy.

I have had two untimely losses in the past years who are always with me – great cooks themselves, we spent a lot of our times together talking about food, preparing it, cooking it and eating it. Thank you Dad and my brother Chris – you are both still part of what I create in the kitchen.

My life has two constants, to whom I would like to dedicate this book: one is my very, very dearest and closest friend Imogen who is so clever and full of ideas and helps and supports me endlessly – I would be lost without you. The same goes for the sausage dog (she lives with me but I hesitate to claim ownership she is very much her own dog!) Florence Salome, she is the most heartwarming creature one could hope for with so much pluck and spirit – a steadfast companion.